TEXTUAL PRACTICE

MW01516235

VOLUME 4

NUMBER 2

SUMMER 1990

PLEASURE/POLITICS?

The 4th Annual Lesbian, Bisexual and Gay Studies Conference
Harvard University
October 26th–28th 1990

CONTACT:

Vernon Rosario
Lesbian, Bisexual, Gay Studies
Harvard University
University Hall, Room B-5
Cambridge, MA 02138

Telephone:

Arthur Lipkin
(617) 547–2197

Contents

A Special Issue
Lesbian and Gay Cultures: theories and texts

Guest editor: Joseph Bristow

Articles

Reviews

Carnival of Repetition

Gaddis's *The Recognitions* and Postmodern Theory

John Johnston

Although published over thirty years ago, William Gaddis's *The Recognitions* is only now beginning to receive the critical attention it deserves. *Carnival of Repetition*, the first full-length study of the novel, is a sophisticated analysis that places it in a new literary and cultural context. Johnston uses the theories of Bakhtin and Deleuze (and others, such as Julia Kristeva) to map out a context for this most unusual and difficult work. From Bakhtin, he appropriates the concepts of "carnivalesque" fiction and dialogism. From Deleuze, he borrows the idea of the simulacrum. With these instruments, Johnston analyzes the labyrinth of copy and counterfeit that Gaddis constructs in his novel. 184 pages, £24.65 cloth

A new volune in the Penn Studies in Contemporary American Fiction.

University of Pennsylvania Press

1 Gower Street London WC1E 6HA

THE GREAT SOCIAL EVIL.

TIME :—Midnight. A Sketch not a Hundred Miles from the Haymarket.

Bella. "AH ! FANNY ! HOW LONG HAVE YOU BEEN *GAY !* "

Introduction: texts, contexts

The year is 1857. And the journal is *Punch*, with its regular diet of satire and parody, all poking fun at the social and political affairs of the day. There are, for example, amusing pictures displaying the impractical sweep of the crinoline. Elsewhere, patriotic portraits exhibit a victorious Britannia trampling hundreds of sepoy rebels. And in the corner of one page, there is a cartoon – which has been reproduced here – casually remarking on the increasing numbers of prostitutes working the London streets. Each item, of course, if seemingly random, in fact relates to the other. A restrictive women's fashion; the suppression of an emergent Indian nationalism; and the proliferation of women turning to prostitution: all these phenomena brought together contradictory images of woman – as ideal lady; as valiant monarch (Victoria as Britannia); and as social evil. Since these types of femininity were so closely and dangerously connected in Victorian Britain, the dominant culture went to strenuous lengths to divide them.

The illustration reprinted from *Punch* bears out this point. It shows – no matter how unintentionally – how the much-maligned prostitute could defy the slanders set against her, and so become precisely what the dominant did not want her to be. Two women, presumably old acquaintances, accidentally meet outside a doorway to a West End theatre where, appropriately enough, Verdi's *La Traviata* ('the wandering one') is playing. One is poorly dressed, the other richly attired. The poor friend asks the woman who is plying for trade: 'How long have you been *gay*?' The joke, of course, lies in the adjective. To be 'gay' is to be involved in 'vice' of this kind. But there is something more to this piece of word-play. To be 'gay' here signals how London prostitutes resisted moral definitions of their supposedly evil actions. They, their friends, and their clients could together redefine this ill-famed profession as work that was cheerfully happy – 'gay'. If prostitution was degrading in one sense, it was 'gay' in another. And if the prostitute was a common woman at home, she could be a 'lady' at work.

This illustration belongs to a significant piece of history that, in all its brutal judgements meted out against sexual desire, persists just as demonizingly to the present day. Frequently known as a 'gay lady', the prostitute represented both the pleasure she brought her customers and the financial rewards she reaped from them. Gratifying male lust, she subversively took the income of men who, in all other spheres of life, controlled the market economy. But she was neither 'gay' nor a 'lady' in the eyes of the law. And it was the law that would put more and more constraints on the prostitute to control her multiple deviances: her 'immoral earnings' (that flouted the patriarchy); her threat to family life (that led to a tightening of the family unit); and, finally, her public expression of female sexuality (that encouraged some doctors to speculate on the apparent overactivity of her reproductive system). In countless ways, she disrupted notions of production and reproduction. Officially an object of contempt, the prostitute was, unofficially, the bearer of the sexual subtext of Victorian Britain. An outlaw, she would continue, defiantly, to be 'gay', even if it meant risking imprisonment. It is from Victorian 'gay lady' that modern definitions of gayness, in part, discover their origins. And in 1990, to be 'gay', in a different but connected sense, means facing up to a world in which a proudly declared sexual identity remains, in its deviancy, a challenge to the moral order. Times, dispiritingly, seem not to have changed that much.

Victorian Britain devised the most severe means to clear the streets of prostitutes. The controversial imposition of the Contagious Diseases Acts of the 1860s and the subsequent battles by feminists over the age of consent in the 1880s have been well charted,[1] and there is no need to recount them here. But if one point needs to be stressed in this Introduction, it is the dynamics of the struggle that took place at that time between the law and sexual deviants over the representation of sexual desire. This is a form of contestation between dominant cultures and subcultures that historically links the gay ladies of the 1850s to today's lesbians and gay men. In the late twentieth century, the world is still full, as Foucault says, of the 'other Victorians' – even if modern and/or postmodern people may care to designate the Victorians as our 'others'.[2] Long after Victoria's reign, prevailing ideas of sex and sexuality still circulate in the popular imaginary in insistently nineteenth-century terms, and the law, to reiterate, is largely responsible for preserving conservative attitudes. Every year, to take just one example, men over 21 are sentenced for having intercourse with male 'minors' where both parties consented to sexual acts. (Male homosexuality is still outlawed in the armed services.)

It is worth, for a moment, to fill in a few more details about this particular piece of sexual history which attributes 'the great social evil' to those sexual beings whose desires refuse to comply with prevailing morals. Among other controversies concerning gender that caught the public's attention in the panic-stricken year of 1857 (such as the much-debated Divorce and Matrimonial Causes Bill) was the Obscene Publications Act. For well over a century, this law has done an untold amount of damage to sexual radicals. And court cases about obscenity, particularly in relation to literary writings, retain a distinctly old-fashioned mind-set that cannot conceive of sexual representation other than in terms of the morally degrading effects of obscene works upon those who read them. (Feminist theories have, thankfully, established an altogether different ground for debate. They point out that pornography routinely misrepresents the – usually female – *object* portrayed in this material rather than ruins the moral fibre of the – habitually male – *subject* consuming it.) In the early 1980s, this frequently abused law concerning obscenity was put into motion against Gay's the Word bookshop, London. (Hundreds of books were confiscated, including works by – of all people – Jean-Paul Sartre, along with publications containing vital information about AIDS.) In fact, the first to suffer at the hands of legal definitions of obscenity were not male pornographers but campaigners for birth-control. The most famous case was brought against Annie Besant and Charles Bradlaugh in the late 1870s. Both were thought to be interfering with the natural ordering of sexual relations. They were doing what Gay's the Word had also rightly done: supplying publications that would enable people to take control of their sexual lives, and, in many respects, to continue living.

Finally, one other piece of legislation needs mentioning in this context. This is the 1885 Criminal Law Amendment Act. This highly punitive act, concerning the age of consent and the protection of young women from prostitution, introduced into its eleventh and final clause a ban on 'gross indecency' between males (even in private). (This clause is often seen as the founding moment of the modern conception of the 'homosexual'.) It would take nearly a century for the prohibition of 'gross indecency' to be lifted from the statute books. In 1921, during a reading of the Criminal Law Amendment Bill, it was suggested that lesbianism should also be outlawed. At that time, the Queen Victoria principle ('No woman would ever do that') won the day. But in 1988, a new clause was instituted (Section 28), which infamously prohibited local authorities from 'promoting' male and female homosexual relations, notably in the guise of 'pretend families'. More visible and more liberated than ever before, the lesbian now became a prime object of conservative moralizing.

The Thatcherite belief that we should all subscribe to Victorian values (family life, thrift, self-help, and so on) is far from an illusion in contemporary Britain. In an era driven forward by distinctly Victorian notions of 'progress' (alias 'enterprise'), the lesbian, the gay man, and the prostitute remain icons of long-standing forms of fear, loathing, and hate. In the 1980s, particularly with the emergence of AIDS, the association of sex, disease, and death appeared like the restaging of nineteenth-century reactions to the monstrosities of prostitution. As I write, in late 1989, a Tory MP, Anne Winterton, is submitting an Early Day Motion to outlaw the Pregnancy Advisory Service from assisting lesbians who require artificial insemination by donor. The motion is unlikely to be successful (although it might have been by the time you read this article), but it points, once again, to how the law remains a powerful tool to decide whether we should or should not desire what we desire. Decades after Freud, Winterton can draw on plenty of popular support for her view that lesbianism and motherhood are incompatible. A woman's sexuality is still seen to be at odds with her right to choose – whether to have an abortion, to inseminate herself, or make love to another woman.

Yet also as I write, there is much to celebrate. To take one current example, a three-part adaptation of Jeannette Winterson's novel *Oranges are Not the Only Fruit* (1985) is about to be broadcast on BBC Television (on BBC 2 with its more specialized – namely, middle-class – audience). In such a popularly homophobic climate, this is quite an achievement. That this lesbian-feminist novel (an 'alternative bestseller') has been given so much pre-view publicity indicates, to some degree, how far limits in specific areas of the media have shifted around left-liberal attitudes towards both lesbianism and feminism. Admittedly, the BBC has, in part, a tradition of commitment to tackling controversial issues in its drama scheduling, and the decision to produce *Oranges* acknowledges the cultural standing of feminist writers and, just as important, the demands of feminist viewers. Although the producers of this adaptation are aware that the series will cause offence (whether the scenes of two girls in bed together or the attack on pentecostal evangelism will prove the most sensitive remains to be seen), the fact that Winterson's novel has gone into production at all shows how a 1960s radicalism in television has not been driven entirely underground. Similarly, Channel 4 was established in the early 1980s with an obligation written in to its charter to meet the requirements of viewers with minority interests. Even if the radical edge of that commitment was quickly blunted, the Channel's 1989 season brought the first lesbian and gay weekly programme, *Out on Tuesday*, on to our screens. (Once again, clauses in the current Broadcasting Bill may threaten lesbian and gay representation of this kind, and this in turn will produce the need, once more, to organize against conservative forms of censorship.)

British television, in many ways, tends to lag behind literary writing in its support for lesbian and gay lives, as the example of the adaptation of Winterson's successful novel demonstrates. It is, instead, in fiction, poetry, and drama where some of the most avant-garde representations of same-sex desire have been able to thrive, if under all sorts of pressures (the law, again), and for specific reasons (often the privileges of upper-class, elite culture). The histories of lesbian and gay writing, and the critical analysis of the strategies undertaken to dramatize our desires, have only recently been revealed. One work, in particular, stands out here, and that is Lillian Faderman's *Surpassing the Love of Men* (1981), which traces, across a vast range of materials, differing formations of desire between women. It is a book whose hypothesis of 'romantic friendship' in shaping the history of lesbian desire has been highly influential. Yet it should be added that Faderman's work has also been argued against by other lesbian writers, who point out that *Surpassing*, if comprehensive, is not the definitive historical account of women's love for women. Some lesbian historians have questioned Faderman's belief in the sexual unknowingness of female partners who enjoyed romantic love before the twentieth century. Others have wondered whether the issue of genital contact should be taken as the defining ground of lesbianism.[3] Certainly, a gathering body of work has been steadily growing around this touchstone text. (It has to be said there is no comparable work of scholarship on literary representations of male homosexuality to match *Surpassing the Love of Men*.)

For perhaps ten years in Britain (somewhat longer in North America), there has been the development of 'out' and increasingly visible lesbian and gay studies, although these fields of inquiry are hardly prominent (as yet) in humanities degrees. And there are networks of literary, social, and cultural historians adding to our knowledge of the lesbian and gay past and present. This current collection of essays grew out of one such group of largely informal contacts, and the fact that *Textual Practice* is prepared to publish these papers, as a special issue, marks something of a new turn in literary studies in Britain. This move, however, is not so extraordinary when we consider the notorious conservatism of 'Literature', and the journals that circulate around it, especially in what remains of British 'university English'. It is worth reminding ourselves that lesbian and gay reading and writing has been educationally successful not on lecture syllabuses but in publishers' lists and so in bookshops. And the serious discussion of different traditions of lesbian and gay writing is much more likely to be taking place in readers' homes than in seminar rooms. Similar points could be raised about feminist reading and writing in the 1970s. In order to find out more about ourselves, and to work through our sense of lesbian and gay identity, we have frequently turned to literature. It has been in the spaces rendered available by literary genres that our desires – no matter how obliquely – have been celebrated. 'English' has so often failed to see what we have been looking for – and found.

It goes without saying that the polemic against orthodox 'English' raged in Britain since the advent of critical theory and poststructuralism. The hauteur guiding the civilizing mission of traditional literary study was exposed, largely because it could no longer convert the uncultured. The old heavyweight canon has been gradually collapsing, as new so-called 'minority' canons – with perhaps greater flexibility than before – have come to take its place. And so different bodies of theory have emerged with diverse groups of texts, which in themselves often not only demand the interrogation of inherited critical practices but also need to be handled through a more democratic pedagogy. There is not space here to explicate how and why 'English', with its aesthetico-moral preoccupations, is barely capable of articulating much that is valuable for understanding lesbian and gay fiction, drama, and poetry – largely because received notions of literary value are inapposite to the histories, forms, and styles to be found in these works. However, since much lesbian and gay writing came into its own in a cultural climate where notions of 'Englishness' and 'good culture' had full rein, the aesthetic and moral propositions that guided 'English' frequently saturate narratives representing same-sex desire. Moreover, it needs to be recognized that such 'great' (or canonical) writing was produced by homosexual men and women who worked within the highest echelons of the literary world. Examples are fairly obvious (members of Bloomsbury, for instance). The point is, these highly 'English' writings often reveal the ideological parameters that delimit 'Englishness'.

No novel could raise this issue more clearly than Radclyffe Hall's *The Well of Loneliness* (1928), a book abundant in a love of the English landscape, the life of the landed classes, and the culture of a spiritually ennobling life. Based in the realist tradition, with an upper middle-class audience in mind, the novel presented itself as an appeal for tolerance towards female homosexuality. 'English' would not find much to applaud here, not exactly because of the subject-matter. (Liberal humanism would seek a way of admitting to the 'reality', but perhaps not the 'universality', of lesbian desire.) Rather, the novel would be (and, indeed, has been) dismissed as a 'minor' work, with some very 'bad' patches, like the strained melodrama that fills out its every other scene. But for all its clumsiness, *The Well* was, and remains, the most important fiction *for lesbians* that has ever been written. It is testimony to the prejudice and pain those of us who desire own sex have experienced since the moment we knew we were lesbian or gay. *The Well* can provide a useful starting-point to consider how lesbian and gay representation might be theorized.

INVERSIONS, PERVERSIONS

The Well is essentially a classic realist narrative. It has all the period charm of a Galsworthy novel. In almost every respect, it tells a tale commonly told in English fiction. A young woman from the landed classes, who morally deserves all that the world can offer her, is tragically alienated from the home she dearly loves. She becomes an outcast and an exile in search of true spiritual passion, and, after many an emotional struggle, eventually finds what she desires, only to have to sacrifice it for noble reasons. The plot, therefore, is relatively conventional. Hall's novel contains nothing remotely pornographic. It does not celebrate crime of any sort. Hall rightly claimed that her work had no 'unnecessary coarseness'. But, as Hall also told her publisher, 'nothing of the kind had ever been attempted before in fiction'.[4] Few novels had until that time created such controversy.

Shortly after its publication, *The Well* was deemed obscene by the courts. During the course of the trial, where many of Hall's supporters expressed reservations about the quality of her writing, people endlessly petitioned public libraries for copies (one London library received 600 requests alone). Although for many years unavailable in Britain (editions had to be imported from America and Europe), *The Well* has sold well ever since it was first banned. And it has recounted a story that, if familiar in its tale of ultimately unrequited love, is also familiar to the sexological history of homosexuality itself.

In the speech she drafted, but never gave, at her trial, Hall stated:

I claim emphatically that the true invert is born and not made. I have opinion behind me in this claim, the weight of most of the finest psychological opinion. This is precisely one of the things that I wished to bring home to the thinking public. Only when this fact is fully grasped can we hope for the exercise of that charitable help and compassion that will assist inverts to give of their best and thus contribute to the good of the whole.[5]

Hall's belief in the invert arose from the writings of Havelock Ellis who furnished a preface for her novel and Richard von Krafft-Ebing (who is mentioned in *The Well* itself).[6] Inversion meant the congenital entrapment of a man in a woman's body, or vice versa. Theorists of inversion were led to hypothesize about the Darwinian emergence of a 'third sex' (such as to be found in Edward Carpenter's writings). Hall offered up this sexological type as pure, authentic, and unassailable.

In *The Well*, Hall presents her born invert superior in both emotional and physical strength. Her heroine is named – by a rather awkward ruse – Stephen Gordon. She is given a boy's name since her father had wanted a son. Stephen develops a love of boyish pleasures and a mannish lifestyle. But already the novel betrays the shaky foundations of its firm commitment to Stephen's congenital inversion. Although her father's desire for a son is introduced to make certain aspects of Stephen's childhood seem plausible, the desire for her to be a boy is as pronounced as her inborn desire to be an invert. So which is it? Are inverts born or made? Almost in spite of itself, *The Well* produces competing definitions of homosexuality. Clearly, Stephen's privileged background enables her to make the most of building an athletic body: 'Stephen did not learn to lift pianos with her stomach, but as time went on she did become quite an expert gymnast and fencer'.[7] And never does she have to worry about financing her unusual life and manner of dressing (like a man) in the worlds she moves in – rural England, London, and Paris. (She buys one of her lovers a unique pearl ring from a jeweller in Bond Street.) Indeed, if high-minded in its intentions, and extremely predictable in its plotting, this very solemn novel gives extraordinary licence to a heroine who represents, as Hall stated, something never to be found before in fiction. Stephen is a woman who has the power (either inborn or socialized; it is a telling equivocation) to live, not as the world wants her to, but as she wants to: as a woman-loving woman. Mannish she may be in both name and costume, but Stephen Gordon is not a man. She is, in a word never used in the novel, a lesbian. And her lesbianism is the one thing that, even if the courts tried to prohibit it, would not censor itself. Even if Stephen is ostensibly represented within the negative and limiting terms of sexology, her sexual identity is securely and positively founded in its resistance to a world intent on punishing her desires. Inversion, then, if part of dominant sexual ideology, is soon marked out as the main term in what may be called a reverse-discourse.

The key point about *The Well* is that inversion is at the very centre of

Stephen's identity, more than class, gender, or national affiliations. As the novel reaches its close, this sexual identity becomes a political one as well:

> And what of the women who had worked in [the First World] war – those quiet, gaunt women she had seen about London? England had called them and they had come; for once, unabashed, they had faced the daylight. And now because they were not prepared to slink back and hide in holes and corners, the very public whom they had served was the first to turn round and spit upon them; to cry: 'Away with this canker in our midst, this nest of unrighteousness and corruption!' That was the gratitude they had received for the work they had done out of love for England![8]

Here, then, is a voice opposing the dictates of the British establishment which has shaped Stephen's life. This fine nation has taught her chivalry, self-sacrifice, and heroism – all displayed by her courageous deeds as an ambulance worker during the war. And yet Britain cannot tolerate this genuinely conservative woman who subscribes to its reactionary nationalistic values. Her transgression threatens to bring chaos to an order to which she feels she should belong but from which she has been made an exile.

Elsewhere, Hall's narrative articulates a broader sense of oppresson in a world that prohibits lesbian desire. In the lonely environs of Paris, where Stephen at last makes contact with a fragile community of like-minded women, she attends a party where two Black men sing spirituals. The opening of the scene is blatantly racist – 'His eyes had the patient, questioning expression common to the eye of most animals and to those of all slowly evolving races' – but the conclusion is one of raised consciousness:

> all the hope of the utterly hopeless in this world, who must live by their ultimate salvation, all the terrible, aching, homesick hope that is born of the infinite pain of the spirit, seemed to break from this man and shake those who listened.[9]

It is Stephen's ability to cross-identify with the prejudice suffered by these Black men, whose music bears the history of slavery, as well as the hope of salvation, that makes *The Well* a political novel – one which anticipates more recent types of radical alliance between subcultures opposing dominant cultures. Yet alliance politics is in itself not so new, as events after the trial against *The Well* illustrate. One debt Hall felt obliged to pay after the events of 1928 was to the miners of South Wales. At the encouragement of the Labour *Daily Herald*, the miners had protested to the Home Secretary about the banning of her book. When the mines were strike-bound early in the following year, Hall sold a John Singer Sargent portrait of her first spiritual guide, mentor, and lover, Mabel Batten, to Glasgow Art Gallery for £1,000. The money was presented to the Lord Mayor of London's Fund for the Relief of Distress in the Coalfields. This event anticipates the support shown by lesbian and gay men and the mining communities to each other during the miners' strike of 1983–4 and the demonstrations against Clause (now Section) 28 five years later.

Stephen Gordon, then, remains indignant at the injustice towards her own kind within a world whose values she largely supports. And her lonely suffering, no matter how deficient the narrative form that represents it, still speaks for the isolating experiences many lesbians and gay men have undergone. But it needs to be borne in mind that Hall's invert, if a predominant figure in writings on homosexuality, was not the only conception of same-sex desire represented in literature during the late nineteenth and early twentieth centuries. Sober and self-critical, Stephen is unlike Oscar Wilde's gothic spectre of degeneration, Dorian Gray. Nor is she outrageously camp, like Wilde and his coterie in the 1890s, or the cast of characters who populate Ronald Firbank's novellas of the 1910s and 1920s. Likewise, Stephen is not altogether akin to Carpenter's 'comrade'. Furthermore Hall shared neither Wilde's nor Carpenter's brands of socialism. In fact, earlier lesbian writers, like the partnership inscribed in the name 'Michael Field', looked not to sexology, as Hall did, but to classical writing for cultural models to express their love. Sappho is the guiding inspiration to the aunt and niece (Katherine Bradley and Edith Cooper) who comprised 'Michael Field'. As Christine White's essay in the present collection demonstrates, the work of 'Michael Field' is closer to the writings of those 'Uranians' who drew on classical myth in praise of boy-love.[10] At a later date, as Diana Collecott shows, H. D. – in her remarkable lesbian rewriting of Modernism – turned to Ancient Greece to discover a language for her love for the women in her life. Such writing was of necessity oblique, and testifies to how lesbian poetry at that time could only speak of a desiring 'unsaid'. Collecott points up both the specificity of H. D.'s mythography and its broader relationships with more recent strategies undertaken by lesbian poets – Adrienne Rich and Audre Lorde – to articulate same-sex desire.

Terry Castle examines a different kind of lesbian textual manouevre in the 'revisionary plot' of Sylvia Townsend Warner's *Summer Will Show* (1936). Lesbian and gay writing often undertakes to revise the heterosexual script, often in apparently heterosexual terms. Hall's novel is a good example. But as *The Well* indicates, Stephen's world of tragic losses is not identical to that of any conventional heroine. *Summer Will Show* similarly enters into the realist plot and – with a detailed understanding of how lesbianism is suggested but cannot surface in nineteenth-century writing – subverts its antecedent narratives from within. Warner picks up motifs from, among other novels, *Great Expectations*, the Brontës' fiction, and aspects of George Eliot's *Daniel Deronda* and *Felix Holt*. Each precursor text is then re-situated in a lesbian context, which is also a period of revolution (1848). Warner's chosen historical setting, if a time of political upheaval, also hints at the historical possibilities in which sexual change might be imagined. In a sense, Warner is reclaiming, and making lesbian, the potentially radical and oppositional subtext of many Victorian women's realist novels. Hall, if far less consciously, was involved in a similar writing practice.

Alan Sinfield investigates a more recent period: the swinging sixties, after the Wolfenden Report (1957; advocating the legalization of homosexual relations) and before the Sexual Offences Act (1967), when Joe Orton's drama came into its own. But if the 1960s celebrated Orton's capacity to shock, they were not, strictly speaking, where his subcultural context lay. Sinfield makes the important point of placing Orton's representation of male homosexuality not within the scope of sixties libertarianism (with which Orton is commonly associated) but into the 1950s (if not earlier), alongside the work of playwrights such as Terence Rattigan and Noël Coward. This was an older, more closeted era which aligned queerness with treachery, and sodomy with spying.

In an essay taken from his full-length study of transgression and subcultures, Jonathan Dollimore celebrates the energy unleashed in the first furious moments of sixties liberation. But in order to show why this heyday of radical militancy was of such cultural significance, Dollimore engages with a particularly revealing and far-reaching strand running through the history of sexuality – that of perversion, all the way from Augustine to Foucault. He points out how, through a passage of many hundreds of years, the determining concepts of theology underpin the assumptions of sexology and psychoanalysis. Tracing an enduring theological trope, which recognizes that what is perverse is central to, even constitutive of, what is spiritually good, Dollimore reveals how and why the pervert consistently becomes the object onto which violent fears are projected and displaced. Freud, after all, begins his study of sexual life with the perversions, only to disclose how these seemingly aberrant drives are sublimated and repressed, but – problematically – never eradicated. They remain, according to Dollimore, 'obscurely yet violently active', within the psyche and, more broadly, within civilization itself, migrating from one powerful discourse to another. As a cure to the murderous history that, perversely, stigmatizes perversion, he suggests that the 'perverse dynamic' that exists at the foundations of culture should not be abandoned but embraced. Since the rise of the Gay Liberation Front (GLF) in 1969, perversion has been proudly practised, and so a range of new lesbian and gay identities (often at odds with each other) have developed within differing subcultures.

IDENTITIES, FUTURES

In the 1960s, a politics of identity arose out of the liberation movements: Black Civil Rights; Women's Liberation; and GLF. And the influence of these movements on radical struggles has been considerable, particularly in transforming the Left's traditional imperative to give precedence to class (sometimes pejoratively referred to as workerism). In the late 1980s, sections of the Left (mostly connected with *Marxism Today*) have, rather belatedly, begun to rethink questions of political agency in relation to the politicization of identity. Consequently, a wide-ranging debate has opened up about the ways in which each of us possesses a multiplicity of allegiances to different identities – of race, of class, of region, and so on. But not all of these often contradictory elements which make us who we 'are' necessarily stand in an equal relationship to one another. Lesbians and gay men, if we identify as such, are likely to view this sexual identity, however we conceive of it and practise it, as taking priority above all other identities we may claim to own.

Above all other things, our sexuality is where we place ourselves; sexuality locates our sense of belonging. And it is within the subculture enabling our forms of sexual expression that our reading and writing primarily belong. It is important to underline this obvious point, since the shared understanding of lesbian and gay writing within our subcultures is inevitably distinct from the discussion of them on a literature syllabus. But this is not to claim that non-lesbian and not gay-identified readers cannot participate in reading, studying, and teaching these works. What must be acknowledged is that such texts possess specific meanings when consumed within their subcultural contexts because they are a crucial part of securing sexual political identifications. The value of these works is not universal but particular to the needs of a specific readership. Should readers not belonging to our subcultures forget this point, then there is the likelihood of a return to a misconceived idea of 'multi-culturalism' (in its widest sense), where a liberal notion of openness comes into play, and so differences are dissolved in the name of a common culture. One culture's commonality, of course, is not always that of another. As Sinfield states: 'A divided society should have a divided culture; anything else must be a mystifying presence, reinforcing prevailing power relations'.[11] He is not advocating separatism. Instead, he is saying that consent to a divided culture may well overcome cultural divisiveness.

One further issue needs to be raised here. To stake a claim on being either lesbian or gay should not necessarily mean subscribing to an essentializing rhetoric of authencity, whereby each of us puts paid to the idea that we really 'are' what we 'choose' to be. This question is, in many ways, central to current debates within lesbian and gay politics. Eve Kosofsky Sedgwick provides an outline of this problematic. General understanding of homosexuality, among 'moderately to well-educated Western people', is, as Sedgwick says, 'organized around a radical and irreducible incoherence':

> It holds the minoritizing view that there is a distinct population of persons who 'really are' gay; at the same time, it holds the universalizing view that sexual desire is an unpredictably powerful solvent of stable identities; that apparently heterosexual persons and object choices are strongly marked by same-sex influences and desires, and vice versa for apparently homosexual ones; and that at least male heterosexual identity and modern masculinist culture may require for their maintenance the scapegoating crystallization of a same-sex male desire that is widespread and in the first place internal.[12]

It has to be said, immediately, that Sedgwick is not exhorting all of us – whatever our sexual identification – to move towards a universally bisexual culture. Rather, her observation probes a conflict between discourses of liberation and those of psychoanalysis. On the one hand, the discourse and practice of emancipation – with its strong Enlightenment roots – encourages us to declare that 'we are lesbians, we are gay', while on the other, psychoanalysis – exerting the force of modernity – makes its reproach by saying 'you only think you are what you claim to be'. Sexuality, then, may be expressed by sexual political identities, but there remain, inevitably, psychical resistances running through and against those chosen identities. It is perhaps through such conflict, between 'minoritizing' and 'universalizing' views of sexuality, that new identities will be formed, and new lesbian and gay texts with them – although these as yet unrealized readers and writers may have remade both lesbian and gay identities to the point of having dispensed with them.

In a divided (rather than divisive) culture, it is possible to see how a new politics of alliances can be imagined to lead us all, whatever our identities, some way towards a sexual political future freed of the contempt provoking the 1857 illustration from *Punch* printed at the start of this Introduction. An alert, generous, and responsive textual practice for the 1990s will have to recognize, historicize, and theorize the differences that remain between us all. As always, we will need to be sensitive to the dangers of appropriating each other's places of belonging marked by subcultural divisions. But as with all forms of progressive debate, we will just as urgently need to learn how to negotiate joint strategies out of a history that would prefer us not to be talking to each other at all. To a limited extent, with this publication and others with a similar project in mind, a new dialogue within literary studies has begun.[13]

Sheffield City Polytechnic

NOTES

1 See, for example, Judith Walkowitz, *Prostitution and Victorian Society: Women, Class and the State* (Cambridge: Cambridge University Press, 1980), and 'Male vice and feminist virtue; feminism and the politics of prostitution in nineteenth-century Britain', *History Workshop*, 13 (1982), pp. 77–93. The present discussion owes much to the analysis of prostitution in the context of the moral panic triggered in 1857 (as represented by Augustus Leopold Egg's painting, *Past and Present*) in Lynda Nead, *Myths of Sexuality: Representations of Women in Victorian Britain* (Oxford: Basil Blackwell, 1988), pp. 71–86.

2 Michel Foucault, *The History of Sexuality*, Volume 1, *An Introduction*, trans. Robert Hurley (1976; Harmondsworth: Penguin Books, 1981), pp. 1–13.

3 Lillian Faderman, *Surpassing the Love of Men: Romantic Friendship and Love between Women from the Renaissance to the Present* (London: Junction Books, 1982). For discussion of Faderman's romantic friendship hypothesis,

see Christine White's essay in this issue, and Sheila Jeffreys, 'Does it matter if they did it?', in Lesbian History Group (eds), *Not a Passing Phase: Reclaiming Lesbians in History 1840–1985* (London: Women's Press, 1989), pp. 19–28. (*Not a Passing Phase* also contains 'An introduction to books for lesbian history studies' by Avril Rolph, Linda Kerr, and Jane Allen (pp. 188–227).) Although not engaged solely with literary history, the following study covers a considerable body of male homosexual fiction and related writings: Jeffrey Weeks, *Coming Out: Homosexual Politics in Britain, from the Nineteenth Century to the Present* (London: Quartet, 1977). Detailed analyses of specific formations of gay literary culture can be found in Simon Shepherd, *Because We're Queers: The Life and Crimes of Kenneth Halliwell and Joe Orton* (London: GMP, 1989), and Alan Sinfield, 'Queers, treachery and the literary establishment', in *Literature, Politics and Culture in Postwar Britain* (Oxford: Basil Blackwell, 1989), pp. 60–85.

4 Cited in Michael Baker, *Our Three Selves: A Life of Radclyffe Hall* (London: Hamish Hamilton, 1985), p. 202.

5 ibid., p. 238.

6 Hall's heroine, Stephen Gordon, discovers the works of Krafft-Ebing in her recently deceased father's library; this discovery amounts to the revelation that her father was aware of her inversion from her earliest days: *The Well of Loneliness* (1928; London: Virago, 1982), p. 207. The comments made on *The Well of Loneliness* in the present essay are indebted to Rebecca O'Rourke, *Reflecting on The Well of Loneliness, Heroines?* (London: Routledge, 1989), and Carolyn Brown, 'Feminist literary strategies in the postmodern condition', in Helen Carr (ed.), *From My Guy to Sci-Fi: Genre and Women's Writing in the Postmodern World* (London: Pandora, 1989), pp. 112–34, and Alison Hennegan's Introduction to the Virago Edition, pp. vii–xvii.

7 Hall, *The Well of Loneliness*, p. 55.

8 ibid., p. 412.

9 ibid., p. 366.

10 See Timothy d'Arch Smith, *Love in Earnest: Some Notes on the Lives and Writings of English 'Uranian' Poets from 1889 to 1930* (London: Routledge & Kegan Paul, 1970).

11 Alan Sinfield, 'Thatcher, culture and the closet', *New Statesmen and Society*, 13 October 1989, p. 31. On the dangers of 'consensus' politics, see Sinfield, *Literature, Politics and Culture in Post Britain*, pp. 277–310.

12 Eve Kosofsky Sedgwick, 'Epistemology of the closet (I)', *Raritan*, 7, 4 (1988), pp. 56–7. Sedgwick's work is in itself an alliance-making project, connecting contemporary feminisms with specific lesbian and gay literary traditions. For a further example of her recent work since the publication of *Between Men: English Literature and Male Homosocial Desire* (New York: Columbia University Press, 1985), see 'Across gender, across sexuality: Willa Cather and others', *The South Atlantic Quarterly*, 88, 1 (1989), pp. 53–72. (This essay appears in an issue entitled 'Displacing Homophobia'.) Sedgwick's essays published in the late 1980s are to be brought together in *Epistemology of the Closet* (Berkeley: University of California Press, 1990). But if highly influential – to the degree that Elaine Showalter has said there is now something resembling an 'École d'Eve' (E. Showalter (ed.), *Speaking of Gender*, London: Routledge, 1989, p. 8) – Sedgwick has been strongly criticized for omissions and potentially harmful constructions; see, for

example, Terry Castle's essay in this issue, on the absence of lesbianism in *Between Men*; and also the debate in *Critical Inquiry* about Sedgwick's 'The beast in the closet: James and the writing of homosexual panic', in Ruth Bernard Yeazell (ed.), *Sex, Politics, and Science in the Nineteenth-Century Novel*, Selected Papers from the English Institute 1983–84, NS no. 10 (Baltimore: Johns Hopkins University Press, 1986), pp. 147–86, anatomized by David Van Leer, 'The beast of the closet: homosociality and the pathology of manhood', *Critical Inquiry*, 15, 3 (1989), pp. 587–605; and the subsequent exchange of comments: Sedgwick, 'Tide and trust', *Critical Inquiry*, 15, 4 (1989), pp. 745–57, and Van Leer, 'Trust and trade', *Critical Inquiry*, 15, 4 (1989), pp. 758–63.

13 Several recent books are relevant here. The following collections of essays place their contents to some degree in dialogue with each other: Alice Jardine and Paul Smith (eds), *Men in Feminism* (London: Metheun, 1987); Linda Kauffman (ed.), *Gender and Theory: Dialogues on Feminist Criticism* (Oxford: Basil Blackwell, 1989) and *Gender and Institutions: Dialogues on Feminist Theory* (Oxford: Basil Blackwell, 1989). In each of these books, contributors can explore and learn to acknowledge each other's differences in the name of feminist literary criticism. A final point: the development of gay studies – in ways paralleled by the increased visibility of a broader-based (implicitly heterosexual) 'men's studies' – has disquieted at least one feminist critic who wonders if 'feminism has had its place in the liberal sun and should move over to leave the victim's space for a greater (male) victim, the homosexual': Janet Todd, *Feminist Literary History: A Defence* (Cambridge: Polity Press, 1988), p. 118 (cited in Showalter, *Speaking of Gender*, p. 13). Todd's remark suggests that there may be a competition between feminists and gay men about who has the most radical sexual politics in literary theory; such a consideration, carrying with it more than a tinge of homophobia, will certainly prove a block to a progressive sexual politics that brings an end to victimization within what remains an extremely violent gender/sexuality hierarchy. Feminist literary criticism clearly needs 'defending' from neutralization within the academy but it does not require this kind of territorial 'defence', implying that there is only one space for a sexual 'victim'.

JONATHAN DOLLIMORE

The cultural politics of perversion: Augustine, Shakespeare, Freud, Foucault

This essay argues that perversion is not only a culturally central phenomenon, but, thereby, also a crucial category for cultural analysis.[1]

In Freud's theory of the sexual perversions the human infant begins life with a sexual disposition which is polymorphously perverse and innately bisexual. It is a precondition for the successful socialization and gendering of the individual – that is, the positioning of the subject within hetero/sexual difference – that the perversions be renounced, typically through repression and/or sublimation. In this way, not only is the appropriate human subject produced but so also is civilization reproduced. But the perversions do not thereby go away: repressed or sublimated, they help to constitute and maintain the very social order; this is one reason why that order requires their repression and sublimation. As such they remain intrinsic to normality and might be said to constitute the cement of culture, helping 'to constitute the social instincts' (11, pp. 437–8)[2] and providing 'the energy for a great number of our cultural achievements' (8, p. 84). Sublimated perversions place 'extraordinary large amounts of force at the disposal of civilized activity' because they are able to exchange their original aims (sexual) for other ones (social) without their intensity being diminished (8, p. 84; 12, pp. 39, 41).

So one does not become a pervert but remains one (8, p. 84); it is sexual perversion, not sexual 'normality', which is the given in human nature. Indeed, sexual normality is precariously achieved and precariously maintained: the process whereby the perversions are sublimated can never be guaranteed to work; it has to be re-enacted in the case of each individual subject, and it is an arduous and conflictual process, a psychosexual development from the polymorphous perverse to normality which is less a process of growth than one of restriction (7, p. 57). Sometimes it doesn't work; sometimes it appears to, only to fail at a later date. Civilization, says Freud, remains precarious and 'unstable' (1, p. 48), as a result.

The clear implication is that civilization actually depends upon that which is usually thought to be incompatible with it, a proposition which has been resisted inside psychoanalysis, and, even more, outside it. At its worst, psychoanalysis has ignored Freud's theories and simply demonized or pathologized the pervert, most notably the homosexual, in ways exhaustively summarized in Kenneth Lewes's recent study.[3] Indeed, it is ironically revealing that this idea of perversion as integral to culture is today not so much associated with Freud's most influential psycho-analytic successors but with one of their most influential critics, Michel Foucault. For Foucault, too, perversion is endemic to modern society, though not in the Freudian sublimated form, nor because of a process of desublimation or some other kind of breakdown in the mechanisms of repression. It is one of the central arguments of Foucault's *History of Sexuality* that perversion is not repressed at all; rather, culture actively produces it. We are living through what he calls, in a chapter heading, the 'perverse implantation'. Perversion is the product and the vehicle of power, a construction which enables it to gain purchase within the realm of the psychosexual: authority legitimates itself by fastening upon discursively constructed, sexually perverse, identities of its own making.[4]

So, though from opposed perspectives, Freud and Foucault discover perversion to be not only central to culture but indispensably so, given the present organization of culture. It is to make this point about the centrality of perversion, and this point alone, that I've begun with Freud and Foucault, and not because my project requires that I begin by adjudicating between them. In fact, the place to begin is much further back. I don't think we can assess either the psychoanalytic theory or its Foucauldian critique until we've recovered the complex and revealing history of perversion in some of its pre-Freudian meanings, which necessarily include its non-sexual meanings. I begin, then, with the early modern period in an attempt to replace the pathological sense of perversion with a political one. Far from wanting to psychoanalyse that period, I want instead to use the Renaissance to help read psychoanalysis and, simultaneously, to use psychoanalysis against its own conservative advocates. In short, I use history to read theory, but in a way enabled by theory.

PATHOLOGY TO THEOLOGY

> In the extreme, life is what is capable of error . . . error is at the root of what makes human thought and its history.[5]

Perversion is a concept signifying: (1) an erring, straying, or deviating from (2) a path, destiny or objective which is (3) understood as natural or right – right because natural (with the natural possibly having a yet 'higher' legitimation in divine law).

Immediately we encounter a paradox: why should the prima-facie innocent activity of *departure* be so abhorrent? Why, for example, in this, the first *OED* definition of 'perverse', is there the rapid slippage from divergence to evil: 'turned away from the right way, or from what is right or good; perverted, wicked'? And – a related question – why should this deviation *from* something be seen also, instantly, as a wicked subversion *of* it? Part of the answer lies in the fact that perversion is regulated by the binary opposition between the natural and the unnatural. Again, it's those like Foucault who have theorized this view in relation to the modern period. But we find ample evidence of the same process in the earlier period. This, for example, is Francis Bacon from 1622: '[for] Women to govern men ... [and] slaves freemen ... [are] total violations and perversions of the laws of nature and nations'.[6] Binary opposites, as Derrida pointed out, and Bacon here confirms, are violent hierarchies. The natural/unnatural opposition has been one of the most violent of all hierarchies. Note how in the Bacon passage just quoted the violence of the hierarchy is displaced, through the concepts of violation and perversion, on to its subordinate terms – women and slaves. As we'll see, the attribution of perversion often involves this process, that is, a displacement of violence, contradiction, and crisis, from the dominant, wherein they are produced, on to the subordinate, especially the deviant.

The pervert deviates from 'the straight and narrow', the 'straight and true'; even such commonplace remarks as these bear the trace of western metaphysics, the epistemological, via metaphor, here picking up with the linear or the teleological. Somewhat over-schematically (and so provisionally) western metaphysics can be represented in terms of three related tenets: the one I've just referred to, teleology, together with essence and universality (these two being the source of essential truth and absolute truth respectively). One reason for recovering the linguistic histories of perversion is because they have often constituted a transgression of normative and prescriptive teleologies. Such transgression was especially feared in the Renaissance, an age obsessed with disordered and disordering movement, from planetary irregularity to social mobility, from the vagrant and masterless men roaming the state, to the womb which supposedly wandered the body of the 'hysterical' woman. All such phenomena contradicted the principles of metaphysical fixity as formulated in those three main categories – essence, universality and teleology – three categories which between them have profoundly fixed the social order in western culture. The charge of perversity was at once a demonizing and a disavowal of an aberrant movement that was seen to threaten the very basis of civilization; that is why time and again metaphysical fixity – fixed origin, nature, identity, development, and destiny – is invoked in the condemnation of that movement. Recall that Othello is described as an erring barbarian, the extravagant and wheeling stranger, and Desdemona as having erred from Nature. I return to *Othello* below.

The sexological sense of perversion does not appear in the *OED* until its 1893 *Supplement*, and then only cautiously. However, in the numerous citations which the *OED* does give for the word and its cognate terms, two *other* kinds of pervert recur: the wayward, assertive woman – the woman on top – whom we've already glimpsed in that quotation from Bacon; and the religious heretic. At the beginning of Christian history, they went together. As Milton put it, justifying the ways of God to man, Satan created the perverted kingdom, and Eve was God's first convert. Or, rather, we should say that she was his first pervert. I'm trying to be precise rather than perverse: in theological discourse the term to describe the opposite of conversion is perversion, and it signifies that terrible deviation from the true religion to the false. It is this use which suggests a central paradox of the perverse, and another reason why perversion is so despised and feared. Perversion has its origins in, or exists in an intimate relation with, that which it subverts. I suppose this is really the case by definition: to err from the right way literally presupposes that one was once in the right place. But it goes deeper than that: in Burton's *Anatomy of Melancholy* (1622), it's not his discussion of what sexologists would later call the sexual perversions that produces the paradoxical sense of the word that interests me – although Burton *does* discuss these – but his discussion of what might be thought to be their opposite. Quite near the beginning of the *Anatomy*, Burton declares that it is not our bestial qualities that are potentially the most dangerous but our civilized ones: 'Reason, art [and] judgement', properly employed, much avail us, 'but if otherwise perverted, they ruin and confound us'.[7] The 'shattering effect' of perversion – and I borrow this description from Leo Bersani[8] – is related to the fact that it originates internally to just those things it threatens. I call this the *perverse dynamic*.

Throughout western culture this paradox recurs: the most extreme threat to the true form of something comes not so much from its opposite or its direct negation, but in the form of its perversion. Somehow the perverse is inextricably rooted in the true and authentic, while being, in spite of (not because of) that connection, also the utter contradiction of it. This paradox begins to suggest why perversion, theological or sexual, is so often conceived as *at once utterly alien to, and yet mysteriously inherent within* the true and authentic. This is related to a further and equally disturbing paradox of the perverse, which suggests that we are created desiring that which is forbidden us. As John Norris put it in 1687: 'What strange perversity is this of Man! When 'twas a Crime to taste th' inlightning Tree, He could not then his hand refrain' (*OED*, 'perversity', p. 740). But long before this Augustine had indicated that Adam and Eve were already fallen before the definitive transgression of Eden: 'the evil act, the transgression of eating the forbidden fruit, was committed only when those who did it were already evil' (XIV.13 (p. 572)).[9] The implication, here and elsewhere (e.g. XI, 13, 17, 18 and 20), is that both the angelic revolt in heaven and the human fall in Eden were predestined.

Hence, of course, the so-called problem of evil in traditional theodicy: God's omnipotence has to be defended, while at the same time exonerating him from responsibility for evil. The impossibility of this task was nicely formulated by the philosopher David Hume paraphrasing Epicurus, as cited by Lactantius: 'Is he [God] willing to prevent evil, but not able? Then he is impotent. Is able but not willing? Then he is malevolent. Is he both able and willing? When then is evil?'[10]

Augustine's influential answer to the problem was the privative theory of evil: evil exists only as a lack, a privation, of good. This was in reaction against the Manichean heresy: to allow, as the Manicheans did, that evil was a real force coexistent with, and opposite to, good, compromised either God's omnipotence (he wasn't in complete control) or his goodness (he created evil). Augustine counters this heresy with the assertion that evil has no real existence. But the idea of evil simply as lack could never explain its destructive power. This is why *at the heart of Augustinian privation is perversion*. Perversion becomes a main criterion of evil, mediating between evil as lack and evil as agency. That is, perversion becomes something utterly inimical to authentic being, yet without authentic being itself.

For Augustine the most pernicious form of evil occurs when the human will deviates from good:

> when the will leaves the higher and turns to the lower, it becomes bad not because the thing to which it turns is bad, but because the turning is itself perverse [*perversa*]. (XII, p (p. 478))

Although such perversity is unnatural, against the order of nature, nothing actually in nature is evil: neither the nature to which the evil-doer turns nor, even, the evil-doer's own nature. Augustine adds, in an extraordinary passage, that 'not even the nature of the Devil himself is evil, in so far as it is a nature; it is perversion that makes it evil [*sed perversitas eam malet facit*]' (XIX.13 (p. 871)). We can begin to see then that for Augustine the perverse turning away from good (itself a perversion of the order of nature) is the essence of evil. Here is the beginning of a theory which will become the rationale for a history of untold violence: '*essentially*', *perversion becomes the negative agency within privation*.

In the words of theologians who have defined the privative theory of evil in our own time: 'the most radical opposition to which being can be subjected is not contrariety but privation'; 'evil is an inverted positivity'.[11] The power of evil is only the power of the good it perverts, and 'the more powerful this good is, the more powerful evil will be, not by virtue of itself, but by virtue of this good. This is why no evil is more powerful than that of the fallen angel'.[12]

The paranoic potential of this theology is considerable. But if we read the fall narrative against the grain – that is, subject it to an aberrant decoding – without much effort we find the reason for the paranoia: after all, in the Christian scheme, evil not only erupts from within a divinely ordained order but, more telling still, it erupts from within the beings closest to God, *those who participate most intimately in divinity* – first the angels, then man, or rather woman – who make, according to another theologian, 'an inexplicably perverse misuse of their god-given freedom'.[13] That is to say, they allegedly pervert their most divine attribute, free will, which then becomes the primary, or for Augustine, the only, source of evil.

In short, a negation/deviation erupts from *within* that which it negates (divinity) only to be then displaced on to the subordinate term of the God/man binary – and then further displaced on to the subordinate within man (i.e. woman). *Proximity, therefore, is the enabling condition of a displacement which in turn marks the 'same' as radically 'other'.*

It may seem strange that this study of perversion should go so far back into Christian history. I haven't space here to fill in many of the connections but let me simply suggest the way several popular notions of sexual perversion in our own time echo the Augustinian theory of evil: (i) evil, says Augustine, is utterly inimical to true existence and yet itself lacks authentic existence (ontological or natural). Likewise with the pervert *vis-à-vis* normality; (ii) evil, says Augustine, is at once utterly alien to goodness and yet mysteriously inherent within it. Likewise sexual perversion is utterly alien to true sexuality yet mysteriously inherent within it, such that perversion must be rooted out by the ever vigilant; (iii) evil, says Augustine, has powers of perversion paradoxically the greater with the goodness and innocence of those being perverted. Likewise with sexual perversion: this being why, presumably, the young and the military are thought to be especially at risk. (I'm alluding to the fact that in the United Kingdom homosexuality in the military and for those under 21 is still illegal.) These echoes suggest a larger argument: as perversion has been retheorized in sexology and psychoanalysis, this earlier conceptual history has been largely obliterated but never entirely lost. In part, this history has been telescoped into a sexological and psychoanalytic narrative where it remains obscurely yet violently active.

NATURE ERRING FROM ITSELF

Augustine deploys and develops the concepts of perversion and deviation, making then definitive criteria of evil. At the same time, these concepts become lodged at the heart of those problems which haunt Christianity, and which ultimately sunder faith itself, most notably the realization (i) that we are created wicked; (ii) that God himself bears 'the ultimate responsibility for evil' – the inevitable conclusion of theodicy;[14] and (iii) that evil is intrinsic to good.

All three of these beliefs have the happy consequence of making the original pervert not Satan but God. But suppose for a moment we let God off the hook; let's concede that he, like successive US Presidents in the face of illegal activities originating from the centre of their governments, was innocent or at least ignorant, and that perversion actually orginated with his one-time deputy, Satan, and that Eve was his first convert. (Or rather pervert.) This is the official line. It is a myth of origin which will help legitimate violence against women, and their subjection, for centuries to come:

> *Othello*: And yet, how nature erring from itself –
> *Iago*: Ay, there's the point, as (to be bold with you)
> Not to affect many proposéd matches
> Of her own clime, complexion, and degree,
> Whereto we see in all things nature tends –
> Foh! one may smell in such a will most rank,
> Foul disproportions, thoughts unnatural.
>
> (*Othello*, III, iii, 227–33)[15]

'Nature erring from itself': the perverse originates internally to, from within, the natural. Here Othello imagines, and Iago exploits, the paradoxical movement of the perverse: a *straying from* which is also a *contradiction of*; a divergence which is imagined to subvert that from *which* it departs in the instant that it *does* depart. In short, from within that erring movement of the first line, a perverse divergence within nature, there erupts by the last line its opposite, the 'unnatural'. Additionally, in the accusation of perversion misogyny and xenophobia are rampant. And so too is racism: Iago demonizes Desdemona and Othello, she as the one who has degenerate desire, he as the object of that desire. Desire and object conjoin in the multiple meanings of 'will most rank' where 'will' might denote at once volition, sexual desire and sexual organ (cf. Sonnets 134–6), and 'rank' may mean lust, swollen, smelling, corrupt and foul. All this in seven terrifying lines which effectively sign Desdemona's death warrant. It's a passage in which (among other things) the natural/un-natural binary is powerfully active. I've tried to represent it diagram-matically (see over page).

The central vertical line represents the binary opposition between the natural and the unnatural: it is in the vertical to signify that the binary is also a violent hierarchy.

The erring/aberrant movement is marked as a deviation to the left; this is not arbitrary: psychoanalysis and, more significantly, anthropology confirm an intriguing cultural connection between deviation and left-sidedness. But our language has always confirmed as much: 'sinister' has, as one of its meanings, 'lying on or towards the left hand' (*Shorter OED*), while the Latin '*sinister*' has 'perverse' as one of its meanings (*Cassell's Latin Dictionary*).

The arcs, A_2 to D, represent the social and psychic processes inseparable from the opposition of the binary but which it cannot acknowledge in its legitimating function. They are also what makes the perverse dynamic possible (though not in this case). Borrowing from Fredric Jameson, we can call them the political unconscious of the binary.

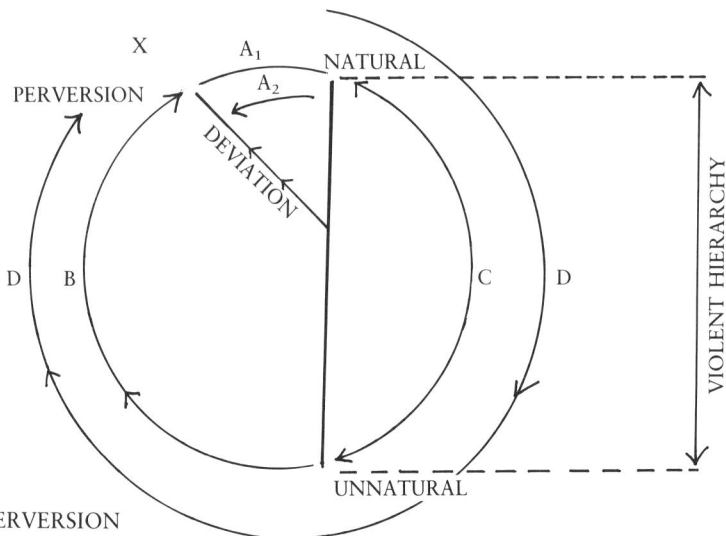

X = PERVERSION

The narrow arc (A_1), running between the natural and the perverse, simply represents the cultural marking or demonizing of difference. It is the identification of a threat which is also a differentiation of it from that which is threatened (the natural). That much wider arc (B), running between the unnatural and the perverse, is the field of displacement. That is, it marks the way in which, when the perverse is identified from the position of the natural, there occurs a simultaneous alignment of the perverse and the unnatural: the unnatural is folded up into, *thereby appearing as*, the perverse. It is this displacement which helps make possible the slippage from 'deviation from' to 'contradiction of' noted earlier in the *OED* definition. And what is marked on that other side of the diagram (C) is really what makes the displacement possible: the natural/unnatural binary is only ever a differential relation – that is, a difference which is always already one of intimate, though antagonistic, interdependence. What is constructed as absolutely other is in fact inextricably related. Hence the double arrow on C.

B and C disclose the operation of A_2: the recognition of the perverse involves a mapping on to the deviation of one part of a split within the natural – 'nature erring from itself'; just as the unnatural is folded up into the perverse (B), so one part of the split natural is folded down into the perverse. This is marked by A_2. B and A_2 can be imagined as the two hands of a clock, each folding towards one another, and meeting across the axis of the perverse. And we should also remember that this double displacement may be mapped on to either an actual deviation or, as here, an imaginary one.

One might say that when the natural, especially in its guise as the normal (or normative), recognizes the perverse (A_1), it is only ever recognizing itself. But this is not to say that the two things are identical, or that one is simply a reflection of the other. In its splitting the natural produces the perverse as a disavowal of itself and as a displacement of an opposite (the unnatural) which, because of the binary interdependence of the two (the natural and the unnatural), is also an inextricable part of itself. This is represented by that clockwise continuum (D) – from the natural, through the unnatural, to the perverse.

The process of displacement (B) often figures in the construction of the perverse and the unnatural, and I want to explore it further, still with reference to the passage from *Othello*. It's extraordinary just how much treachery and insurrection Iago manages to attribute to Desdemona in just six lines. This is a play partly about impending war. Venetian civilization is at stake, at least to the extent that its military has moved to Cyprus to defend the island against the approaching Turks. In 1575 Thomas Newton declared of the Turks: 'They were (indeed) at the first very far off from our clime and region, and therefore the less to be feared, but now they are even at our doors and ready to come into our houses.'[16] It's been shown how the symbolic geography of the play creates just this effect of Cyprus as a beleaguered outpost,[17] while Richard Marienstras shows how, at this time, England's xenophobia was increasing in spite, or maybe because, of the fact that it was also embarking on colonization and expansion.[18] The result was a real conflict between, if you like, the centripetal tendencies of nationalism, and the centrifugal tendencies of colonialist expansion. One consequence of this conflict was a paranoid search for the internal counterparts of external threats.

The famous *Homily Against Disobedience and Wilfull Rebellion* (1571) is obsessed with internal rebellion, the enemy within, weakening the state and rendering it vulnerable to

> all outward enemies that will invade it, to the utter and perpetual captivity, slavery, and destruction of all their countrymen, their children, their friends, their kinsfolk left alive, whom by their wicked rebellion they procure to be delivered into the hands of foreign enemies. (p. 615)

In this *Homily*, the sin of rebellion encompasses *all* other sins in one (pp. 609, 611–12). Racism plays its part: a Royal Edict of 1601 expresses discontent 'at the great number of "Negars" and "blackamoors" which are crept into the realm'; Queen Elizabeth wanted them transported out of the country. The ostensible reason was unemployment among the English, but the representation of Black people 'as satanic, sexual creatures, a threat to order and decency, and a danger to white womanhood' was also a factor.[19] Such considerations meant that, for many in early modern England, the implicit confrontation in *Othello* was between civilization and barbarism. (Although, as Martin Orkin reminds us in *Shakespeare against Apartheid*, the struggle for Cyprus was actually conducted between two imperialist powers.[20])

According to Iago, Desdemona's 'thoughts unnatural' involve a threefold transgression: of 'clime, complexion, and degree'; that is, of region, colour, and rank; or, in our terms, of country, race, and class – three of civilization's most jealously policed boundaries. Is it coincidence, then, that what Desdemona violates – country, race, and class – are all three at risk in the war with the Turks? Country, obviously; race, in the sense that that enemy is, in the terms of the play, racially and culturally inferior; class, or degree, in the sense that it is the indispensable basis both of the culture being defended and of the military doing the defending. So what we witness here is a classic instance of displacement: an external threat recast as an internal deviation; through imagined sexual transgression the perverse subject – the desiring woman – becomes a surrogate alien, a surrogate Turk. And, remarkably, yet in a way all too familiar, the internal deviation which allegedly replicated the external threat is located in the domestic realm, at the most protected central region of the patriarchal order, and at the furthest remove from its beleaguered borders. And it's located within one who is, by any substantial criteria, powerless.

By looking at two instances of the pervert – the religious heretic and the wayward woman – I've been trying to indicate how the pre-sexological and pre-Freudian history of the concept of perversion can be reconstructed as one of struggle and conflict between domination and insubordination, between desire and law, and between transgression and conformity. I have also attempted to demonstrate how this earlier history of perversion figured centrally in the language of paranoia and displacement, and how it could trigger the paradoxes inherent within, and so subvert, the orders which are defined over and against the pervert. Significantly, it is easier to trigger the paradoxes subversively in the case of religious heresy than with the wayward woman. Note how in the Othello passage the paradox – indeed contradiction – has almost surfaced ('nature erring from itself') but not quite. The instability produced by that almost-apparent contradiction is contained, or re-formed, by Iago into a violent hierarchy and its repression. Hence Desdemona's death. It is a powerful reminder that dominant social formations can and do reconstitute themselves around the self-same contradictions that destabil-ize them. Through disavowal and displacement the same instability that destabilizes can become a force of repression much more than a force of liberation.

In the remainder of this essay, I consider the representation of sexual perversion in the modern period in the light of the concept's 'lost history'. I do not want to leave the Renaissance without remarking that there *were* instances of gender struggle at that time in which contradictions were successfully exploited by subordinate groups for subversive ends. (One of the most fascinating instances of all is the controversy in the period over female cross-dressing, which I've discussed elsewhere.[21])

PERVERSION AND PSYCHOANALYSIS

In our own century, the repressive deployment of psychiatry and psychoanalysis has been obvious and notorious, especially with regard to the so-called perversions, and one in particular: homosexuality. As an example I've chosen an essay by Sandor Feldman. He writes: 'As a practitioner, I have learned that, *essentially*, homosexuals want to mate with the opposite sex. In therapy my intention is to discover what kind of fear or distress *diverted* the patient from *the straight line* and made a *devious detour* necessary.' All homosexuals, he continues, started as heterosexuals. Moreover, 'the main part of the therapy ... is to emphasize that the patient's original position is a healthy one, given as a precious gift by nature'. The analyst must:

> bear in mind always that his real goal is to bring up the patient to the biologically given heterosexual relationship which is not created by the therapy but liberated for us. .... The homosexual will, for a while at least, stubbornly insist that ... homosexuality remains for him the only route to sexual gratification. This is all untrue. The more convinced the analyst is that an underlying natural personal relationship in sexual and in other ways is present, the more ... the patient will come to the same conclusion as the analyst: that man is born for woman and woman is born for man.[22]

This is stunningly crass but not untypical in its assumptions. Feldman reproduces a familiar metaphysics of nature: essence/teleology/universality. An essential sexuality moves along a teleologically defined path of psychosexual development (Feldman's 'straight line' – already encoded in the biological origin) to the universal goal: heterosexual union. So in the first instance his theory should be understood not only as a crass appropriation of Freud but also as a containment of the perverse via the traditional metaphysical schema which Freud rejects. Let's be clear about this: Freud had used his account of perversion to *subvert* theories of sexuality growing from the same tradition that Feldman reinvokes in Freud's name. Freud rejects those theories by retaining and developing the paradoxes within the semantic field of perversion, especially that major paradox outlined earlier: the shattering effect of perversion arises from the fact that it is integral to just those things it threatens.

I sketch Freud's theory of the perversions with two aims in mind. Specifically, I want to explore the way he incorporates into his theory the paradoxical dynamic of perversion – what I've called the perverse dynamic. More generally, I simply want to outline a theory which is more challenging than most contemporary versions of psychoanalysis allow. The larger project from which this essay derives argues that the perverse dynamic begins to challenge key aspects of the psychoanalytic project itself, just as with Christianity before it.

Freud says: 'the abandonment of the reproductive function is the common feature of all perversion. We actually describe a sexual activity as perverse if it has given up the aim of reproduction and pursues the attainment of pleasure as an aim independent of it' (1, p. 358). On this account, especially since the arrival of the postmodern, we are presumably all perverts now, actual or aspiring. (I'm reminded of the postmodern anecdote about the foot fetishist who was in love with the foot but had to settle for the whole person.) A more specific definition is clearly required, and Freud provides it: perversions are sexual activities which involve *an extension, or transgression, of limit* with respect 'either to the part of the body concerned or to the sexual object chosen' (8, p. 83). In the first case (namely the part of the body), perversion would involve the lingering over the immediate relations to the sexual object – as might the foot fetishist just invoked – relations which 'should normally be traversed rapidly on the path towards the final sexual aim'. That is, reproduction via heterosexual genital intercourse (7, p. 62). In the second case (sexual object), it would involve the choosing of an 'inappropriate' object – for example, someone of the same sex.

As I indicated at the outset, in the formation of the socialized, gendered subject – that is, the production of the human subject within hetero/sexual difference – the perversions are necessarily repressed, sublimated, and renounced. Sublimated perversion is intrinsic to normality and indeed provides, as it were, the cement of culture. As a consequence, 'some perverse trait or other is seldom absent from the sexual life of normal people' (1, p. 364). As regards homosexuality: *everyone* has made a homosexual object choice, says Freud, if only in their unconscious. In short: 'in addition to their manifest heterosexuality, a very considerable measure of latent or unconscious homosexuality can be detected in *all* normal people' (9, p. 399). Moreover, 'homosexual impulses are invariably discovered in every single neurotic'. Indeed, the repression of perverse desire actually generates neurosis – hence Freud's statement that neurosis is the negative of the perversions (7, p. 163).

Freud is unrelenting in finding perversion, especially homosexuality, in those places where it is conventionally thought to be *most* absent, and where this assumed absence actually constitutes identity. There is, for instance, the inextricable connection between perversion and childhood. It is not only that children are sexual beings but also that their sexuality is quintessentially – one might say, naturally – perverse (8, p. 352). All children, says Freud, may well be homosexuals (8, p. 268). Conversely, there is a quality of childlike innocence about the perversions themselves.

Relatedly, Freud insists on attributing to the perversions precisely the qualities usually thought to be possessed only by their opposite. For instance, far from being 'bestial' or 'degenerate', the perversions are intellectual and idealistic, involving 'an idealization of instinct'. He says of the Wolf Man, one of his most famous patients:

> The process has led to a victory for the faith of piety over the rebelliousness of critical research, and has had the repression of the homosexual attitude as its necessary condition. Lasting disadvantages resulted. . . . His intellectual activity remained seriously impaired after the first great defeat. (9, p. 307)

He says too that love, far from being that which transcends perversion, is that which liberates it: 'Being in love . . . has the power to remove represssions and reinstate perversions' (11, p. 95). Further, the 'omni- ·

potence of love is perhaps never more strongly proved than in such of its aberrations as these'. He continues: '*The highest and lowest are always closest to each other in the sphere of sexuality*' (7, p. 75; my emphasis). And further still, the satisfaction afforded by perverse desire is greater than that afforded by desire which has been socially tamed (12, p. 67).

I hope to have sketched enough for the destructive implications of Freud's theory to be apparent. At the very least, a range of central binary oppositions (spiritual/carnal; pure/degenerate; normal/abnormal) – oppositions upon which the social order depends – are either inverted/ removed or collapsed into a relational interdependence: a deep, mutal, antagonistic implication. But even more is at stake, and Freud is quite explicit about this: there is something chaotic and subversive about perversion. The persistence and ever-threatened re-emergence of perversion means thatcivilization has failed to secure its own reproduction. The represssive organization of sexuality which constitutes normality 'falls apart' (7, p. 156). The perversions, therefore, become a paradigm of the (in)subordinate displacing the dominant (for that read, heterosexual, reproductive, genital intercourse). In their 'multiplicity and strangeness' (1, p. 346), says Freud, the perversions constitute a threatening excess of difference originating from within the same. So Freud attributes to the perversions an extraordinary disruptive power: (i) they subvert the genital organization of sexuality, thereby sabotaging the whole process of normative psychosexual development (or subjection) upon which civilization depends; (ii) they subvert sexual difference itself, whether it be biological (reproduction) or social (sublimation); and (iii) perversion affords more pleasure than those forms of organized desire based on its repression (and this apart from the pleasure of transgression itself, which is a separate issue). Moreover, perversion may be produced by what is conventionally assumed to be at the furthest possible remove from it (that is, love). Finally, perversion cannot be eliminated. It persists in three principal ways: an active practice by some; the repressed constituent of neurosis; and the always unstably sublimated basis of civilization itself.

POLYMORPHOUS PERVERSE TO THE PERVERSE DYNAMIC

I oppose Freud's account of perversion to Feldman's work not in order to return to Freud – to uncover the authentic voice of psychoanalysis – but to follow further the complex history of perversion. As yet, little in my argument depends on the correctness or otherwise of Freud's views. However, via Freud, we can see that the concept of perversion always embodied what has now become a fundamental and crucial proposition – call it deconstructive, poststructuralist, postmodern, whatever. It is the proposition that what a culture designates as alien, utterly other and different, is never so. Culture exists in a relationship of difference with the alien, which is also a relationship of fundamental, antagonistic interdependence. What is constructed as absolutely other is, in fact, inextricably related – most obviously in terms of the binary opposition,

Derrida's violent hierarchy. Freud goes further: civilization is not merely dependent upon perversion; the latter, via sublimation, is integral to the former since civilization is rooted in perversion. The binary is not merely transcended or dissolved. Rather, the different is inscribed within the self-same. One doesn't become a pervert but remains one. Put another way, every inlaw was once, and in a crucial sense remains, an outlaw. It is because culture repeatedly disavows this fact that manifest perversion is made the focus of endless demonizing and displacement. In an article called 'Civilised Sexual Morality' (1908), Freud pushes the process even further, showing how civilization reaches a stage of development where it begins to produce the very perversion it needs to suppress. In Freud, then, there emerges a truly violent dialectic between represssion and perversion, and it is one which suggests that the most terrifying fear may not be of the other but of the same, and that the social is marked by an interconnectedness so radical that it has to be disavowed in most existing forms of social organization.

Above all, Freud brilliantly identifies the psychic basis of what I've been describing; I am thinking especially of his concepts of resistance, disavowal, negation, and splitting. One of the most acute accounts is in his article on 'Repression' (1915):

> [T]he objects to which men give most preference, their ideals, proceed from the same perceptions and experience as the objects which they most abhor, and . . . they were originally only distinguished from one another through slight modifications. . . . Indeed . . . it is possible for the original instinctual *representative* to be split in two, one part undergoing repression, while the remainder, *precisely on account of this intimate connection*, undergoes idealization. (11, p. 150; my emphasis)

Alongside this passage should be read his account of the way negation and disavowal always involve a simultaneous acknowledgement of what is being negated and disavowed (15, pp. 438–40). Such are the processes which produce the perverse and which are in turn destabilized by the perverse dynamic. Freud offers a narrative whereby we begin to understand how and why the negation of homosexuality has been in direct proportion to its centrality; why the culturally marginal position of homosexuality has been in direct proportion to its cultural significance; and, ultimately, why homosexuality is so strangely integral to the self-same heterosexual culture which so obsessively denounces it.

But – and it's a big but – Freud helped to telescope the perverse dynamic into a transhistorical psychosexual narrative, with the consequence that the history – the cultural dynamic of perversion briefly outlined in the first half of this essay – was lost. What that history reveals is a fundamentally different kind of displacement. It reveals not the endless Freudian displacement of sexuality into culture (e.g. via sublimation), but a displacement going the other way: the endless displacement of social crisis and confict into sexuality. Moreover, this may well be the more important kind of displacement. That is why, increasingly, and as a matter of life and death for some, a crucial task for a radical sexual politics for the present is to expose this displacement of the political into the sexual. To expose this structure involves not the familiar task of *liberating* sexuality but rather that task of *taking sexuality apart and revealing the histories within it*, the displacements which constitute it.

Since Freud, the twentieth century has been faced not only with the crassness of Feldman's version of perversion but also, within more sophisticated varieties of psychoanalyis, the suppression of Freud's much more radical concept of the same. What makes both kinds of containment possible is not just the limitations of the psychoanalytic project itself but, as I've tried to show, a much longer metaphysical tradition privileging dominant social formations, sexual and otherwise, in terms of essence, nature, teleology and universality. At the same time, the challenge of the perverse remains inscribed irreducibly within the same tradition, as it does within psychoanalysis.

I've been concerned to make visible a particular cultural dynamic with the aim of retrieving the concept of perversion as a category of cultural analysis. I started with the historically earlier semantic fields of perversion. The etymological histories are significant, partly for what they convey directly but more importantly for the cultural dynamic which the concept of perversion sought to control, repress, and disavow. So we need to go beyond such definitions and, in seeking to recover what is repressed and disavowed (the histories of perversion), to ensure that the concept itself is extended and developed. This procedure – first, attention to a formal definition leading to, second, an historical recovery, which in turn promotes, finally, a conceptual development – is analogous to what has already occurred with, say, the Bakhtinian notions of carnival, inversion, and the dialogic.[23]

I conclude with a word about perversion as a strategy of cultural resistance. In the period of post-war change, a radical sexual politics explored the idea that if we could desublimate the polymorphous perverse, we would not only liberate ourselves from represssion, but also liberate an energy which could transform the entire social domain. I'm reminded of those heady days of liberation in the 1960s when one was urged not just to sit in front of the tanks, but to fuck there as well. This is John Rechy:

> Promiscuous homosexuals (outlaws with dual identities ...) are the shock troops of the sexual revolution. The streets are the battleground, the revolution is the sexhunt, a radical statement is made each time a man has sex within another on a street. . .
>
> Cum instead of blood. Satisfied bodies instead of dead ones. Death versus orgasm. Would they bust everyone? With cum-smeared tanks would they crush all?[24]

Times, of course, change, and sexuality with them. The challenge lies not in the polymorphous perverse but in what I call the paradoxical perverse or the perverse dynamic. It's this concept which I've begun to reconstruct in Augustine, in the Renaissance, and in Freud, that I'd like to see developed for a cultural politics. I've indicated elsewhere how writers like Wilde and Genet embrace the central paradoxes of the perverse, turning and using them against the normative orders which demonize the sexual deviant.[25] In the case of both Wilde and Genet, the perverse dynamic subverts the binaries of which the pervert is an effect, and does so internally. Additionally, the perverse dynamic suggests that we exist in terms of a radical interconnectedness which is not so much the *basis* of social organization, as what that organization must disavow to survive in its existing forms. This dynamic also suggests that if we fear the other we also fear the same, *especially of sameness within the other* (homosexual congress constituted as the other of heterosexuality). Therefore, we see that the other is sometimes only feared because it is structured within an economy of the same. Discriminations like homophobia occur not in spite of, but because of, sameness.

Oscar Wilde knew only too well of, and brilliantly explored, the dynamic, subversive connection between perversity and paradox. He wrote: 'what the paradox was to me in the sphere of thought, perversity became to me in the sphere of passion'.[26] But he wrote that from prison. So, in affirming a politics of the perverse, we should never forget the cost: death, mutilation, and incarceration have been, and remain, the fate of the pervert.

University of Sussex

NOTES

1 The issues and arguments outlined in this essay are explored more fully in Jonathan Dollimore, *Perverse Dynamics Sexuality, Transgression and Sub-cultures* (forthcoming).

2 All quotations from Freud's writings are taken from the Pelican Freud Library. Volume and page numbers are included in the text.

3 Kenneth Lewes, *The Psychoanalytical Theory of Male Homosexuality* (London: Quartet, 1989). Those analysts Lewes cites include Edmund Bergler ('the most important analytic theorist of homosexuality in the 1950s', p. 15), who wrote: 'I have no bias against homosexuality ... [but] homosexuals are essentially disagreeable people ... displaying a mixture of superciliousness, false aggression, and whimpering ... subservient when confronted with a stronger person, merciless when in power, unscrupulous about trampling on a weaker person' (cited by Lewes, p. 15).

4 Michel Foucault, *The History of Sexuality*, vol. 1, *An Introduction* (New York: Vintage, 1978). See especially pt 2, ch. 2.

5 Foucault, 'Introduction' to George Canguilhem, *The Normal and the Pathological* (New York: Zone Books, 1989), p. 22.

6 Francis Bacon, 'Advertisement Touching an Holy Warre', in *Works*, ed. J.

Spedding and R. L. Ellis (1857–61; Stuttgart: Fromann, 1961–3), vol. 7, pp. 33–4.

7 Robert Burton, *The Anatomy of Melancholy*, ed. Holbrook Jackson (London: Dent, 1932), first partition, p. 136.

8 Leo Bersani, *The Freudian Body: Psychoanalysis and Art* (New York: Columbia University Press, 1986).

9 Augustine, *City of God*, trans. Henry Bettenson (Harmondsworth: Penguin Books, 1972). All page references to this edition are given in the text.

10 David Hume, *Dialogues Concerning Natural Religion*, part X, in Steven M. Cahn (ed.), *Classics of Western Philosophy* (Indianapolis: Hackett, 1977), p. 741; Lactantius, 'The Wrath of God' in *Lactantius: The Minor Works* (Washington, DC: Catholic University of America Press, 1962), pp. 92–3. I am grateful to Tony Nuttall for these references.

11 Charles Journet, *The Meaning of Evil*, trans. Michael Barry (London: Geoffrey Chapman, 1963), pp. 43, 46, 66.

12 Jacques Maritain, *St Thomas and the Problem of Evil* (Milwaukee: Marquette University Press, 1942), p. 2.

13 John Hick, *Evil and the God of Love* (Glasgow: Collins, 1968), p. 68.

14 ibid., p. 264.

15 Quotations from *Othello* are taken from the Signet Classic Shakespeare edition, ed. Alvin Kiernan (New York: New American Library, 1963).

16 Cited in Simon Shepherd, *Marlowe and the Politics of Elizabethan Theatre* (Brighton: Harvester Press, 1986), p. 142.

17 Alvin Kiernan, 'Introduction' to *Othello*, Signet Classic Shakespeare, pp. xv–xviii.

18 Richard Marienstras, *New Perspectives on the Shakespearean World*, trans. Janet Lloyd (Cambridge: Cambridge University Press, 1985), chs 5 and 6.

19 On the demonic representation of Black people in Elizabethan England, see Eldred Jones, *Othello's Countrymen* (London: Oxford University Press, 1965); Ruth Cowhig, 'Blacks in English Renaissance drama and the role of Shakespeare's Othello', in David Dabydeen (ed.), *The Black Presence in English Literature* (Manchester: Manchester University Press, 1985), pp. 4–7; and Ania Loomba, *Gender, Race, Renaissance Drama* (Manchester: Manchester University Press, 1989), pp. 42–5.

20 Martin Orkin, *Shakespeare against Apartheid* (Craighall, South Africa: Ad. Donker, 1987), pp. 88–96.

21 Jonathan Dollimore, 'Sexuality, subjectivity and transgression: the Jacobean connection', *Renaissance Drama*, NS 7 (1986), pp. 53–82; and *Radical Tragedy: Religion, Ideology and Power in the Drama of Shakespeare and his Contempories*, 2nd edn (Hemel Hempstead: Harvester-Whetsheaf, 1989), pp. xxxv–xi.

22 Sandor Feldman, 'On homosexuality' in S. Lorand and M. Balint (eds), *Perversions: Psychodynamics and Therapy* (New York: Random House, 1956), pp. 74–5, 93–4 (my emphasis). (Incidentally, this volume also contains an essay co-written by Jacques Lacan.)

23 See, for example, Peter Stallybrass and Allon White, *The Politics and Poetics of Transgression* (London: Methuen, 1986).

24 John Rechy, *The Sexual Outlaw: A Documentary/A Non-Fiction Account, with Commentaries of Three Days and Three Nights in the Sexual Underground* (London: W. H. Allen, 1978), pp. 299, 301.

25 Dollimore, 'Different desires: subjectivity and transgression in Wilde and

Gide', *Textual Practice*, I, 1 (1987), pp. 48–67, and *Genders*, 2 (1988), pp. 24–41; 'The dominant and the deviant', in Colin MacCabe (ed.) *Futures for English* (Manchester: Manchester University Press, 1988), pp. 179–92.

26 *The Letters of Oscar Wilde*, ed. Rupert Hart-Davis (New York: Harcourt, 1962), p. 466.

CHRISTINE WHITE

'Poets and lovers evermore': interpreting female love in the poetry and journals of Michael Field

WHAT'S IN A NAME?

Katherine Bradley and Edith Cooper were poets and lovers from 1870 to 1913. They lived together, converted to Catholicism together, and together developed the joint poetic persona of Michael Field. As aunt and niece their love was socially structured and sanctioned. As Catholics and Classicists they developed a language of love between women. As Michael and Henry their life together is recorded in the surviving manuscript journals. And as Michael Field they presented themselves to the world as Poets. (The capitalization, and the sense of the importance of this activity, is theirs.) But were they lesbians in any recognizable sense? This question relates to a developing orthodoxy in lesbian history and politics, in particular the influential thesis of Lillian Faderman in *Surpassing the Love of Men* where she discusses Michael Field, an analysis which I will attempt to interrogate in this essay.[1] I want to make an intervention in the interpretative practice employed by Faderman, whereby all loving relationships between women before the 1920s are viewed as romantic friendships, and not as sexualized or erotic. Through connecting questions of homosexual history, politics, and desire, this essay will suggest a more radical theory of lesbian desire and lesbian history than Faderman's, by focusing on a specific body of writing.

In their relationship and their work, Katherine and Edith typify many of the difficulties in deciphering the meaning and nature of love between women. Faderman's comments are based only on published extracts (a slender volume concerned primarily with their lives as Catholics) from their extensive journals covering the years 1869–1914. The scale of this material is, in fact, enormous: thirty-six foolscap volumes, with several others consisting of correspondence and notes.[2] It is a remarkable resource, but it is neither assimilable to a linear narrative nor capable of being easily represented here. (There is also the problem that some words and phrases are indecipherable.) It would be a mistake, however, to assume that these journals offer anything like a straightforward access to the 'truth' about the relationship or Katherine and Edith's understanding of it, even given all the usual reservations about the mediated status of autobiography.[3] The journals were left with instructions that they might be opened at the end of 1929, and that the editors, T. and D. C. Sturge Moore, should publish from them as they saw fit. It hardly needs pointing out, therefore, that at some point the journals became directed towards publication. When that was, or whom the journals are addressed to, is never clear. There is, I must assume, no truly 'private' record.

There are in the journals and the poetry copious references that may be read as lesbian. These texts are dotted with the words 'Sapphic', 'Beloved', 'Lover' and 'Lesbian'.[4] Although it is possible to infer that such terms indicate a same-sex relationship, Faderman insists that they are not at all sexual. I intend to demonstrate that these references are not simply definable as 'sexual' or 'non-sexual', but have their origins in more diverse sources. Any such analysis must be hedged around by considering the historically specific treatment of the Sapphic and the Lesbian.

Classical Greek literature and culture provided one way for nineteenth-century homosexual writers to talk about homosexuality as a positive social and emotional relationship. These authors appropriated the works of Plato and the myths of male love and comradeship to argue for social tolerance of same-sex love. For homosexual writers, a culture that was in the nineteenth century regarded as one of the highest points of civilization provided a precedent that was both respectable and sexual. This deployment of a Greek cultural precedent appears in Katherine and Edith's volume *Bellerophôn*, published under the pseudonyms Arran and Isla Leigh, in the poem 'Apollo's Written Grief', on the subject of Apollo and Hyacinth. This poem may be understood as a homo-political appeal for tolerance and an expression of the search for the right way of conducting a homosexual relationship:

> Men dream that thou wert smitten by the glow
> Of my too perilous love, not by the blow
> Of him who rivalled me.[5]

Apollo's love for his 'bright-eyed Ganymede' (p. 160) is presented as the best option for the boy, since he would otherwise have been consumed by Zephyrus or Zeus 'in greed' (p. 160). Apollo's love would not have proved dangerous to Hyacinth who, in 'panting for the light' (p. 159) of the sun-god, 'sufferedest the divine/Daring the dread delight' (p. 159). This poem, therefore, employs the already existing construction and terminology for homosexual love and desire. These myths remained available to readings as homoerotic archetypes or ideals.[6] But where a whole canon of male-male bondings and loves exists, women had only one classical equivalent to draw upon for expressions and strategies of female-female love – in the poetry of Sappho. This classical antecedent must, moreover, be recuperated from male appropriations, salaciousness or prurience.

Katherine and Edith wrote at a time when treatments of Sappho's verse were numerous and diverse. There are instances of deliberate suppression of the female pronouns, as in T. W. Higginson's translation published in

1871. In the novels of Alphonse Daudet, Theophile Gautier and Algernon Charles Swinburne, Sappho and Sapphic women were constructed as sadistic, predatory corrupters of innocent women. A standard work on Greek culture describes Sappho as 'a woman of generous disposition, affectionate heart, and independent spirit ... [with] her own particular refinement of taste, exclusive of every approach to low excess of profligacy'.[7] Alternatively, another academic author declared that there was 'no good early evidence to show that the Lesbian standard was low'[8] (that is, sexual). In other versions, Sappho was portrayed as a woman falling in love with the fisherman Phaon, committing suicide when that love was unreciprocated.[9] The plurality of depictions and appropriations of Sappho indicate the extent to which Sappho became a cultural battleground, much more so than any male homosexual equivalent. Where some writers attempt to recuperate at all costs the great poet from accusations of lewdness, and others concede the love between women, but deny it as being passion of a base nature, Michael Field holds her up as a paragon among women, and puts the passion back into the poet's community of women. Michael Field's 1889 volume *Long Ago*, a series of poems based on and completing Sappho's fragments, explores the heterosexual version of Sappho, alongside poems on passion between women:

> Come, Gorgo, put the rug in place,
>   And passionate recline;
> I love to see thee in thy grace,
>   Dark, virulent, divine.[10]

This is no sexless romance between friends, but rather a dangerous eroticism. 'Virulent' may relate in part to the appearances of Gorgo in Sappho's poetry. Fragment 44 reads 'I have had quite enough of Gorgo', and fragment 47 '[I cannot bear it;] ... Archeanassa is Gorgo's lover ...'[11] Gorgo is a figure in Sappho's poetry who evokes despair and resentment in the poet, not sisterly feelings.

If this is one version of Sappho, there are at least two other Sapphos in *Long Ago*. One is a woman at the centre of a loving community of women, a community which she must keep safe from the intrusions of men. In poem LIV, 'Adown the Lesbian Vales', Sappho is in possession of a 'passionate unsated sense' which her maids seek to satisfy. The relationship between Sappho and her maids is premised upon a need to keep the women away from marriage: 'No girls let fall/Their maiden zone/At Hymen's call' (p. 96). The third Sappho is the heterosexual lover of Phaon:

> If I could win him from the sea,
> Then subtly I would draw him down
> 'Mid the bright vetches; in a crown
> My art should teach him to entwine
> Their thievish rings and keep him mine.[12]

This is a possessive heterosexual desire, springing from a manipulative battle to win him in a destructive competition with the fisherman's work at sea.

The second and third versions of Sappho come into conflict over the issue of virginity and poetry. The love of Phaon and the inviolate women of the Lesbian community are combined in poem XVII: 'The moon rose full, the women stood'. Sappho calls to her virginity, her 'only good', to come back, having been lost to Phaon. The inviolate state is 'that most blesséd, secret state/That makes the tenderest maiden great', not the possession of a male's sexual attention. Sappho's loss of virginity effectively puts an end to her poetic gift:

> And when
> By maiden-arms to be enwound
>   Ashore the fisher flings,
> Oh, then my heart turns cold, and then
>   I drop my wings.
>
>   (*Long Ago*, XX, p. 33)

The connection between poetry and virginity is broached in *The New Minnesinger and Other Poems*, published by Katherine under the pseudonym of Arran Leigh. The title-poem discusses the craft of the woman-poet, 'she whose life doth lie/In virgin haunts of poesie'.[13] The virgin woman poet, by virtue of her freedom from men, possesses the potentiality to be 'lifted to a free/And fellow-life with man' (p. 12). But whatever 'realm' a woman endeavours to enclose, she must 'ever keep/All things subservient to the good/Of pure free-growing womanhood' (p. 13). This version of femininity offers an ambiguous challenge to the terms of patriarchal culture. It exists apart from patriarchal dictates, but includes fellowship and equality with men. It embraces the productiveness of womanhood and an all-woman community, but concedes the reality of an attraction to men, destructive as that is.

It is this construction of femininity that makes the Michael Field relationship assimilable to Faderman's model of romantic friendship (or what I will label the Romantic Friendship Hypothesis). However, this construction is more complex than an unequivocal embrace of a non-sexual friendship. Michael Field represents Sappho as a wise old(er) woman who remembers the rejections of youth and deplores the fickleness of younger women and their susceptibility to men. Her constancy to women, 'Maids, not to you my mind doth change' (*Long Ago*, XXXIII, p. 52), is contrasted with her reaction to the men whom she will 'defy, allure, estrange, /Prostrate, made bond or free'. To her maids she is a maternal or passionate lover, and to men she is manipulative and fickle. (The attitude to men is complicated by virtue of the poems being authored under the name of a man. The 'male' poet relates sexually to both men and women.) The volume concludes with poem LXIX, 'O free me, for I take the leap', where Sappho flings herself from a cliff with a prayer to Apollo for a 'breast love-free'.

Michael Field's Sappho, therefore, is not the denizen of a lesbian or Lesbian idyll. Rather, she is the subject of a contradiction which emerges from those versions described above. On the one hand, Sappho the poet must be defended from accusations of immorality, while, on the other, Sappho the Lesbian must be salvaged from the Phaon myth. The Lesbian community of women is more than a society of friendship, but is also a site of poetic production and, moreover, the production of the Poet identity. Both are threatened by men and heterosexuality. Sexuality is not, therefore, the only interpretative category in play in *Long Ago*. The practice of Poetry is equally as important, and it interweaves with sexuality. In the preface to *Long Ago* there is an ambiguous appeal to 'the other woman'. The volume is jointly authored, yet the voice of the preface is in the first person singular. This prefatorial voice advocates worship for, and the apprehension of, an ideal of the Poet and the lover in the poetry and person of Sappho. There is a direct connection made between Sappho's prayer and the prayer of this first-person voice:

> Devoutly as the fiery-bosomed Greek turned in her anguish to Aphrodite, praying her to accomplish her heart's desires, I have turned to the one woman who has dared to speak unfalteringly of the fearful mastery of love, and again and again the dumb prayer has risen from my heart –
>
> σὺ δαντα
> συμμαχος εσσο[14]

Here, the Greek is translated as 'you will be my ally'. The 'one woman' is either Sappho, a lover or a writing partner. This ambiguity of identity is central to this volume of poetry. In *Long Ago* Michael Field are writing with Sappho the Poet, and working with Sappho, Aphrodite and the partner in an imaginary alliance. The preface does not specify who that mastery of love is directed to. But perhaps that is the point. In order to speak 'unfalteringly' of woman's love for woman, it is necessary for Michael Field to work in alliance with other women and other women's formulations of such love. The construction in the preface is both strategic and passionate, not a privatized emotion which continues detached from historical and social concerns. It is political, creating changes in the presentation of love between women on the basis of the available cultural models. Finally, Michael Field's appeal to 'the one woman' does not rest upon a strategic image of monogamous romance, which while apparently neutral and ahistorical is intimately connected with bourgeois values and patriarchal family structures, and which lesbianism has the potential to sidestep or remake.

'THE FEARFUL MASTERY OF LOVE'

If, in the late twentieth century, contemporary lesbians are determined to write our own dictionary of lesbian love and desire, there appears to be no such imperative behind the writings of Michael Field. Current debates within lesbian politics take two principal forms: first, by reclaiming names that have been used derogatively, such as 'dyke'; second, by developing an entirely new framework of naming and reference. In *Another Mother Tongue: Gay Words, Gay Worlds*, Judy Grahn begins from a rejection of the so-called expert discourses of science, medicine, and law, and moves on to a rewriting/reinvention of a different, specifically gay cultural dictionary, since 'my little list of taboo words turned out to be keys to knowledge'.[15] Language, and specifically names, are decisive for Grahn in developing a political critique of gay oppression. By contrast, Pat Califia's book *Sapphistry: The Book of Lesbian Sexuality* premisses its development of a lesbian cultural framework upon sexual fantasy and practice.[16] All of these activities are brought under the heading of 'sapphistry', another indicator of the significance of the Lesbian poet for our cultural and political understandings. In the introduction to her book Califia writes:

> The majority culture controls us by limiting our vision and denying us all possible images of the women we might become. This book carries a subversive message. . . . Our sexuality can be a source of pleasure, nourishment and strength. This book is an attack on the repression and colonisation of women's sexuality. It is intended to strengthen us and prepare us for a long, difficult struggle for liberation. (pp. xiii–xv)

Sapphistry seeks to name the spectrum of lesbian sexual experience, while *Another Mother Tongue* concentrates on the relationship between the dominant culture and suppressed gay history, but both are concerned with developing a distinct conceptual and political framework in which to talk about gay or lesbian culture and history, albeit from very different political perspectives: Califia as a sado-masochist dyke; Grahn as a lesbian-feminist.

Michael Field, rather than inventing a vocabulary with an unmistakable precision of meaning, deploys the language of classical scholarship, the language of love belonging to heterosexuality, the language of friendship (but never noticeably the language of blood-relatives), and later the language of Catholicism. These differing languages represent a series of modulations both chronologically within their *œuvre* and in the different forms of writing they practised. There is no single language which they employ to talk about each other and their relationship. Consequently, there is enough imprecision or ambiguity in the slippage around their words of love and desire for Faderman, misleadingly, to find sufficient material in their writings to call them romantic friends. It is, of course, equally misleading to call them lesbians. Although the term 'lesbian' is historically available, it is not a word they ever used of themselves to indicate a sexual relationship. They did, however, have other terms and metaphors.

In comparing themselves to Elizabeth Barrett Browning and Robert Browning, Michael Field assert *'we are closer married'*.[17] Marriage was an available metaphor or conceptualization for both women to apply to their relationship. Following Edith's death, Katherine invoked the words of the marriage service when making an approach to the literary periodical the *Athenæum* to 'write a brief appreciation of my dead Fellow-Poet, not separating what God has joined, yet dwelling for her friends' delight on her peculiar & most rare gifts'.[18] In the preface to *Works and Days* God is said to have joined Michael Field both as the Poet and as 'Poets and lovers evermore' (*Works and Days*, p. xix). And, as a last example, to Havelock Ellis, on the subject of his attempts to discover who wrote which piece, they asserted 'As to our work, let no man think he can put asunder what God has joined.'[19] Faderman refuses any sexual meaning to these statements, insisting that since 'they were generally so completely without self-consciousness in their public declarations of mutual love' (p. 210), their love must have been 'innocent'. In addition to this, Faderman makes the error of deciding that their love for one another '*caused* them to convert to Catholicism' (p. 211; my emphasis), since this conversion was a way to guarantee being together eternally. These two statements are in contradiction with one another, since if their love were innocent, they surely would not deliberately have planned for a united eternity. Faderman's specious theory appears to be based wholly upon one paragraph in the published journals, written by Edith: 'It is Paradise between us. When we're together eternally, our spirits will be interpenetrated with our loves and our art under the benison of the Vision of God' (p. 324). Faderman derives the whole of their Catholic experience from this brief extract, which was written when Edith was dying. Moreover, Faderman ignores the evidence of the rest of the journals, which reveal their faith as being a good deal more than a mere instrumentalist insurance policy, and the history and pattern of Catholic conversion at that time, with many literary figures joining the Church and some, notably John Gray and Frederick Rolfe, becoming or attempting to become priests.

Faderman bases the Romantic Friendship Hypothesis on a specific construction of femininity. She presents it as the sole form of the relationship between loving women before the development of a female homosexual identity and pathology through political and scientific discourses, such as the work of the sexologists and the gay rights movements in Germany and France. Consequently, Faderman applies a modern version of relations between women to the late nineteenth century which precludes any consciousness of sexual interest. In doing so, she constructs all female friendships along the lines of the dominant culture. Faderman argues that, since sexual relationships between women were unacceptable to the dominant, and since women were constructed as the passionless gender and ignorant of sex, they could not possibly have had the knowledge, language, or experience of lesbian *desire*. Any Victorian woman, she maintains, would have been profoundly shocked by any such interpretation of their feelings, and therefore every woman's expression of love or passion must of necessity have been free from the taint of homosexual desire. Faderman does not even entertain the possibility that these women, knowing that the dominant culture condemned such feelings and relationships, could have developed their own strategies for talking about and explaining such expressions of sexuality. Instead she presumes that innocence is a superior form of loving compared to sexual experiences between women. She practices the condescension of history, and in doing so attempts to dodge the revelation of her own political agenda. Of course, Katherine and Edith did not have available to them the language, politics, and structures of contemporary lesbianism and feminism. But Faderman's insistence that they could not have known any better rests upon a belief in linear progress from one age to the next. Contemporary lesbians, so the argument goes, are much wiser than their nineteenth-century sisters because they of course can see through the mechanisms used to oppress and limit women. Therefore, by practising this evolutionary politics, Faderman manages to read over the top of all the strategies and devices that Michael Field, among many others, did deploy in order to create a cultural space for themselves. That these strategies did exist is beyond question, and they were various, from the appropriations of Greek culture to Carpenter's assertion that 'homogenic love', encompassing both male and female homosexuality, was a potentially superior social force to heterosexuality.[20]

Before going further, I want to make it clear that I am disquieted by the project of going into print criticizing another lesbian. This is an unsisterly thing to do, particularly given the open nature of this forum. Such debates ought not to be conducted in public and in a manner belonging to the practices of non-feminist, gentlemen's club scholarship. *Surpassing the Love of Men* is an invaluable catalogue of the works of hundreds of lesbians which have been suppressed or ignored. But opposition to the political agenda of the book's thesis and the new orthodoxy, which is finding such currency amongst lesbians, academic and non-academic, is in my view of paramount importance. This version of lesbianism appropriates to itself lesbian history and makes of it a reactionary sexual politics. In the introduction to *Surpassing the Love of Men* Faderman makes this claim:

> In lesbian-feminism I have found an analog to romantic friendship . . . I venture to guess that had the romantic friends of other eras lived today, many of them would have been lesbian-feminists. (p. 20)

My guess is that in 'romantic friendship' she found an analogue to radical lesbian-feminism. She displays yet another methodological error in her making of history into analogues, since this works to deny the material specificity of the past as well as the present. Both romantic friendship and lesbian-feminism are positions distinguished by the desexualized nature of relations between women. This denial of lesbian sexual practice is spelt out by Elizabeth Mavor in *The Ladies of Llangollen: A Study in Romantic Friendship*, a work which in many respects provides the conceptual framework of Faderman's study:

Much that we would now associate solely with a sexual attachment was contained in romantic friendship: tenderness, loyalty, sensibility, shared beds, shared tastes, coquetry, even passion.[21]

This reading of love declarations between women and accounts of women living together as wholly non-sexual is explained by Faderman as follows:

Women in centuries other than ours often internalised the view of females as having little sexual passion. . . . If they were sexually aroused, bearing no burden of proof as men do, they might deny it even to themselves if they wished. (p. 16)

Undoubtedly, women internalized the prescriptions of dominant ideology, but the leap from saying they took on board these prescriptions to the assumption that this internalization defined and limited all they believed and practised is quite breathtaking. In particular, it seems hardly credible that simply because women did not have penile erections they would not have recognized how sexual arousal felt and what it meant. Yet this is the outcome of the position adopted by Faderman and Mavor, which argues for a female nature utterly distinct from all things male and masculine. Both writers construct a time that is both more innocent and more separatist than our own. The radical lesbian-feminist position maintains that 'Lesbian separatism is feminism carried to its logical conclusion'.[22] Accordingly, heterosexual feminists are said to be 'sleeping with the enemy', and the aim of every true feminist should be lesbianism, to stop participating in patriarchy by engaging in any way with men and to confront the very basis of society, heterosexuality. Lesbianism is not seen as a matter of sexual preference or political choice, but a political imperative, since 'it should be impossible to analyse any type of oppression without making the connection that lesbianism signifies the eventual destruction of the heterophallocratic system'.[23] Adrienne Rich formulates a slightly different lesbianism in her essay 'It is the lesbian in us':

I believe it is the lesbian in every woman who is compelled by female energy, who gravitates towards strong women. . . . It is the lesbian in us who drives us to feel imaginatively, render in language, grasp, the full connection between woman and woman.[24]

Lesbian separatists construct lesbianism and lesbians as superior, more creative, more sensitive and more human. Romantic friendship is an expression of lesbian separatism which takes the form of a relationship that is, in Mavor's words, 'more liberal and inclusive and better suited to the more diffuse feminine nature' (p. xvii) – not concentrated in an erect penis – and which, according to Faderman, 'had little connection with men who were so alienatingly and totally different' (p. 20). The prescriptions of lesbian-feminism extend even into what happens sexually between women. Two women together escape the oppression of phallic heterosexuality, but to arrive in a utopian region of non-sexual romance and intimacy they must never behave in a manner which in any way reflects that in which men behave towards women.

Paradoxically, the Romantic Friendship Hypothesis is a celebration of many of the conventional attributes of femininity as it has been constructed by patriarchy, such as passivity, gentleness, domesticity, creativity and supportiveness, and which condemns as irretrievably phallic other characteristics generally labelled masculine, including strength, capability, activity, success, independence and lust. In claiming women-loving women as romantic friends, the hypothesis annihilates from history all those lesbians/lovers who gave histories to (or recognized themselves in the works of) sexologists such as Havelock Ellis,[25] or who, alternatively, formed part of lesbian subcultures based on sexual preference and emotional commitment.[26] Faderman's model consigns lesbian sexual activity to a male fantasy that routinely appears in pornographic writing. She opposes the pornographic image of women's sexuality to the 'true', non-sexual history of women's relationships which, it is claimed, appears in their diaries and writings. Having lighted upon male pornographic images of lesbian sex, Faderman concludes that if men talk about women having sex through a particular discourse, then since that discourse does not appear in women's writings, then women did not have sex together or relate sexually to each other.

I am not arguing that every close relationship between women was a sexual one. Rather, the point is, that the evidence should be looked at without the limitations of lesbian-feminist presuppositions. The political imperative behind my argument is to avoid having lesbian and gay histories misappropriated yet again, and this time from within the ranks of gay writers. Faderman's work is a revisionist project whose critique is focused, in Gayle Rubin's words, on 'non-routine acts of love rather than routine acts of oppression, exploitation or violence.[27] On the basis that these women lovers did not behave like or pretend to be men, this position concludes that they are 'nice girls', not lesbians. As an alternative to this revisionism, I want to propose a 'pro-sex' history of lesbianism that gives such women as Michael Field at least some credit for awareness and strategic practice, and which has the potentiality to include within its frame of reference class, race, and power. This pro-sex investigation into lesbian history will reject the lesbian-feminist invention of a realm and an age of harmonious femininity where all women are equal, provided they do not indulge in politically right-off sexual activity.

FLESHLY SIN AND FLESHLY LOVE

In order to develop a framework in which to place the pro-sex history of lesbianism, I will now go on to look at the references to desire between women in the works of Michael Field, and examine the plurality of ways in which they talked about their understanding of sexual and emotional love between women. In analysing the treatment of sexuality in Michael Field's journals I will use 'fleshly sin' to denote practice which they did not recognize as having anything to do with their own relationship; and I will refer to 'fleshly love' to describe how they might have organized their understanding of the physical aspects of their relationship. Two instances of fleshly sin and fleshly love between women appear in the journals. Travelling through Europe, Edith fell ill in Dresden, and wrote: 'My experiences with Nurse are painful – she is under the possession of terrible fleshly love [which] she does not conceive as such, and as such I will not receive it.'[28] Clearly the nurse does not recognize her experience. Edith, however, does conceive of this love as fleshly. It is certainly within Edith's conceptual framework to apprehend one woman's feelings of physical desire for another woman. This instance of fleshly love does not belong to the imagination of a pornographer. In the extract, the use of the words 'possession' and 'terrible' cannot be simply read as condemnatory, since any unwelcome sexual attentions may appear to be a terrible possession of the harasser. It is not clear, though, if it is the case that Edith would not accept fleshly love in any context, or that this particular instance is unwelcome.

The second example concerning fleshly sin appears in the manuscript journal for 1908, referring to a painting they saw.

A man named Legrand – a monstrous charlatan – who can by a clever trick give the infamies of the worldly Frenchwoman – especially in unconscious self-conscious exposure to her own sex . . . [as manuscript] female friends together. What is to be expressed is of Satan – and the means as ugly as the matter. The people round me say 'He must be a Genius' – I answer to myself A Demon-Spawned Charlatan.[29]

I have yet to trace this painting, but it obviously enraged Edith. She can read this picture as false and disgusting. The exposure is apparently to the female gaze, but actually for the male gaze. The prurience of that gaze is expressed through that 'unconscious self-consciousness', a wink at the audience, inviting the viewer in to enjoy the scene. This 'clever trick' is that of the pornographer. Two women apparently exist for their own pleasure, but they are actually on offer as double pleasure for the male viewer.[30] The unreality of the scene is evident to Edith. Her racism is evident in her ascribing of infamies to Frenchwomen (and German women too, as evidenced by her comments on the nurse). The point is, she recognizes that Legrand's painting is a false image of how women behave to one another as 'female friends'. Edith repudiates the way in which patriarchal values frame and perceive relations between women. Legrand is a charlatan; his representation bears no relation to the truth. Yet this rejection is not the same thing as denying the existence of desire between women. However, what that truth is cannot easily be deduced from the writings.

Outside the treatment of Sappho, which is a minefield of interpretative complexity, there is in the journals very little explicit analysis of the relationship between Katherine and Edith. Katherine and Edith's primary concern is always with Michael Field the Poet, and it is the name itself I want to focus on now because it reveals to a large extent how they conceived of their practice as poets. That male-authored publications are usually better received and taken more seriously than female-authored works is a truism. Before the adoption of the joint persona they used the pseudonyms Arran and Isla Leigh, which brought them more favourable reviews than they ever had as Michael Field, and also the assumption that they were either a married couple or a brother and sister. Perhaps this misinterpretation is what led them to adopt the single pen-name. Although Katherine and Edith used metaphors of marriage to describe their love, it would be surprising if they had wanted to be publicly portrayed as a heterosexual couple. However, 'Michael Field' cannot be regarded as a true pseudonym, since it was widely known in a literary circle that included John Gray, George Meredith, and Oscar Wilde, as well as their friends Charles Ricketts and Charles Shannon, that they were two women. Much of their correspondence is addressed to them both under the heading of Michael Field and they often signed themselves with the joint name. The name contains a compelling contradiction: they both deploy the authority of male authorship and yet react against such camouflage. Michael Field is not a disguise. Nor is it a pretence at being a man.

None the less, they were appalled when they became known to their Catholic congregation as the women behind Michael Field. Edith confronted her confessor Goscommon:

> I say I regret it is known; but that in the same way, I am glad he, as my Confessor, knows, for it will help him to understand some things I feel he has somewhat misunderstood, & also it is for a poet with his freedom of impulse to submit to the control & discipline of the Church.[31]

This anxiety for concealment is in marked contradiction to their previous willingness to be known. Wayne Koestenbaum offers the explanation that 'their aliases gave them a seclusion in which they could freely unfold their "natures set a little way apart"'.[32] Yet that desired seclusion became impossible when they submitted to the authority of the Church. Even though their attempts to develop a framework in which to talk about their love and desires in part depended upon a screen from the world, this effort did not rest wholly upon the use of a male pen-name. Rather, the development of the poetic persona Michael Field gave them another role in which to play out their understandings of their relationship. The persona is distinct from Katherine and Edith, and separate from their pet names Michael and Henry, which were in common currency among friends. Michael Field the Poet is always presented as the highest point of their work.

Complicated shifts took place when they converted to Catholicism. Entering the Roman Catholic Church evokes from Edith the two explicit references to sexuality I have found. In the 1907 volume of the journals she wrote: 'Since I have entered the Holy Catholic Church, I have never fallen into fleshly sin',[33] which presupposes that before she joined she had succumbed to such fleshly temptation. Here fleshly sin may be a reference to masturbation, but I am doubtful, given the second reference in 1908: 'When I came into this Church a year ago [I gave] a gift that was a vow of chastity.'[34] Not practising masturbation may constitute abstinence from fleshly sin, but chastity in this context seems to involve another person. This may be an indication that before conversion there had been a sexual or erotic relationship between Katherine and Edith.

Edith, in one of her last entries before her death, wrote: 'We have had the bond of race, with the delicious adventure of the stranger nature, introduced by the beloved father.'[35] Since the word father is not capitalized, I hazard to guess that this is a reference to John Gray, a poet, a convert, a priest, Katherine's one-time confessor and spiritual adviser to them both. He was also the long-time lover of the poet Marc-André Raffalovich.[36] The word 'race' here is intriguing, but again there is the notion of natures that are different. Although they had been in correspondence with Havelock Ellis,[37] there is no evidence in their work of any belief or interest in sexology, inversion and the 'third sex'. That said, these remarks do seem to resonate with the notion of belonging to a 'breed apart'.

Their strategies for making sense of their love do not take the shape of pretending to be or believing themselves to be men, nor of understanding themselves to be romantic friends. In their account of their role as Michael Field and of their love for each other, Katherine and Edith construct a position of opposition against the misapprehensions and prejudices of the world. That opposition relies upon their alliance with one another, and with specific cultural formations that they recognize as expressive or reflective of that alliance. This is the impulse behind their declaration of 1893:

My Love and I took hands and swore
Against the world, to be
Poets and lovers evermore.[38]

The roles of poet and lover are both integral to one another and essential to their rejection of the judgement of 'the world'. This is an implicitly political understanding of women as lovers, rather than a private and personal retreat from the world into romantic friendship.

There is no strategy or organizing principle that they use to define themselves, a point which is demonstrated in the difference between the poem from 1893 and the prefatory poem from the 1875 volume The New Minnesinger by Arran Leigh (alias Katherine Bradley). 'To E. C.' refers to the 'mast'ring power' of the other woman's love, and the writer's need of that love which is 'forever voiceless' (p. vii). The 'lighter passions' will find a way 'into rhythm', and the voiceless need is premissed upon the assertion that 'Thou hast fore-fashioned all I do and think' (p. vii). This difference marks the shift from a virtual silence about the love to the opening up of a framework in which to talk about that love.

Edith and Katherine's methods of explaining their love and desire are difficult to decipher because they are so unlike our own modes of explanation. But the fact that we have that trouble does not mean that they encountered the same problem. It is, then, necessary to beware of failing or refusing to recognize the complexity of the negotiations these women-loving women made. If we do, as Faderman has done, then all those negotiations made within a hostile dominant culture would lead to a particularly restricted view – a homogeneous and desexualized version – of lesbian and gay history which can produce such idiocies as this:

> [Before the nineteenth century] most people . . . were ignorant of the existence of the phenomenon of tribady. . . . Practically no women did know any examples of sexual relations between women and few, at any rate of the common people, had ever heard of them. Sexual desire and love was thought of as something that could only be experienced with a male. We can therefore assume that most women who fell in love with other women could not place or identify those feelings. Therefore, it is logical that those women would think: if I covet a woman, I must be a man.[39]

This is an appropriation by two apparently straight historians. How do they know? Were they there to ask all these anonymous people? It is this version of gay and lesbian history, where lesbians and gays are reduced to mere pseudo-men or pseudo-women respectively, that is being passed on from academics to non-academics. I have heard feminist lesbians trot out this account of lesbians in previous centuries as if it were gospel truth, without their realizing that this story serves very specific political ends, in the construction of a correct lesbian-feminism *now*. Much of the history of lesbianism remains to be written, and much of that which has already been written is wrong-headed and dishonest. What I have attempted to do here is to begin the process of mapping out the complicated processes whereby the discourses of lesbianism might have been inscribed in the nineteenth century, and not to fall into a simplistic one-theory-fits-all position.

University of Nottingham

NOTES

1 Lillian Faderman, *Surpassing the Love of Men: Romantic Friendship and Love between Women from the Renaissance to the Present* (1981; London: Women's Press, 1985). Page references are included in the text.

2 The journals are held in the British Library under the title 'Works and Days' from 1870 on. All manuscript reference numbers and folio numbers indicate these texts. The published journals appeared as *Works and Days*, ed. T. and D. C. Sturge Moore (London: John Murray, 1933).

3 See, for example, Domna C. Stanton and Jeanine F. Plottel (eds), *The Female Autograph: Theory and Practice from the Middle Ages to the Present*

(Chicago: University of Chicago Press, 1987), and Liz Stanley and Sue Scott (eds), *Writing Feminist Biography* (Manchester: University of Manchester, Department of Sociology, 1986).

4 Please note the distinction between my use of 'Lesbian' (referring to people and things pertaining to Lesbos) and 'lesbian' (referring to sexual and emotional relationships between women).

5 Arran and Isla Leigh, *Bellerophôn* (London: Kegan Paul, 1881), p. 159. Further page references are included in the text.

6 Examples of homosexual treatments of Greek literature and culture include William Cory, 'Heraclitus', in *Ionica* (London: Smith, Elder, 1858); Charles Kains-Jackson, 'Antinous', in the *Artist and Journal of Home Culture*, 12 (1891); Walter Pater, *Greek Studies: A Series of Lectures* (1894); and John Addington Symonds, *A Problem in Greek Ethics* (1883). This material is documented in Timothy d'Arch Smith, *Love in Earnest: Some Notes on the Lives and Writings of English 'Uranian' Poets from 1889 to 1930* (London: Routledge & Kegan Paul, 1970).

7 William Mure, *Critical History of the Language and Literature of Antient Greece* (1850–57), cited in Richard Jenkyns, *Three Classical Poets: Sappho, Catullus and Juvenal* (London: Duckworth, 1982).

8 Gilbert Murray, *Ancient Greek Literature* (1897), cited in Jenkyns, op. cit., p. 2.

9 The version of Sappho as heterosexual lover appeared in ironized form as early as 1848 in Christina Rossetti's suppressed poem, 'What Sappho would have said had her leap cured instead of killing her'.

10 Michael Field, *Long Ago* (London: Bell, 1889), XXXV, p. 56. Roman numerals, referring to the sequence of poems in this volume, are included with page numbers in the text.

11 Translations of Sappho's poetry are taken from Josephine Balmer, *Sappho: Poems and Fragments* (London: Brilliance Books, 1984).

12 Poem V, 'Where with their boats the fishers land'.

13 Arran Leigh, *The New Minnesinger and Other Poems* (London, 1875), p. 2.

14 Preface to *Long Ago*, p. iii; a translation of this poem appears in Balmer (unpaginated edition [p. 58]).

15 Judy Grahn, *Another Mother Tongue: Gay Words, Gay Worlds* (Boston: Beacon Press, 1984), p. xiii.

16 Pat Califia, *Sapphistry: The Book of Lesbian Sexuality* (Tallahassee: Naiad Press, 1983).

17 Mary Sturgeon, *Michael Field* (London: Harrap, 1922), p. 47.

18 British Library, Add. MS 46803, ƒ100ᵛ.

19 Sturgeon, op. cit., p. 47.

20 Edward Carpenter, *Homogenic Love, and its Place in a Free Society* (Manchester: Manchester Labour Society, 1894).

21 Elizabeth Mavor, *The Ladies of Llangollen: A Study in Romantic Friendship* (1971; London: Penguin Books, 1973), p. xvii.

22 Lesbian Separatist Group, *Amazon Analysis* (1973–4), cited in Ariane Brunet and Louise Turcotte, 'Separatism and radicalism: an analysis of the differences and similarities', in *Lesbian Ethics*, 2, 1 (1986), p. 43.

23 Brunet and Turcotte, op. cit. p. 48.

24 Adrienne Rich, 'It is the lesbian in us', in *On Lies, Secrets and Silence: Selected Prose 1966–1978* (London: Virago, 1980), p. 201.

25 Case histories of female sexual inverts contained in H. Havelock Ellis, *Studies*

in the Psychology of Sex, vol. 1, *Sexual Inversion* (1897) included Edith Ellis and Renée Vivien.

26 See Sonja Ruehl, 'Sexual theory and practice: another double standard', in Sue Cartledge and Joanna Ryan (eds), *Sex and Love: New Thoughts on Old Contradictions* (London: Women's Press, 1983), p. 219.

27 Gayle Rubin, 'Thinking sex: notes for a radical theory of the politics of sexuality', in Carole S. Vance (ed.), *Pleasure and Danger: Exploring Female Sexuality* (London: Routledge & Kegan Paul, 1984), p. 301.

28 *Works and Days*, p. 63.

29 British Library MS 46798 ʃ25ᵛ.

30 See E. Ann Kaplan, 'Is the gaze male?', in Ann Snitow, Christine Stansell, and Sharon Thompson (eds), *Desire: The Politics of Sexuality* (Virago, 1984), pp. 321–38.

31 British Library MS 46797, ʃ52ᵛ.

32 Wayne Koestenbaum, *Double Tale: The Erotics of Male Literary Collaboration* (London: Routledge, 1089), p. 173; he is citing Sturgeon, op. cit., p. 23.

33 British Library MS. 46797, ʃ52ᵛ.

34 British Library MS. 46797, ʃ77.

35 *Works and Days*, p. 326.

36 See, with reservation and suspicion, Brocard Sewell, *Footnote to the Nineties: A Memoir of John Gray and André Raffalovich* (London: C. & A. Woolf, 1969), and *In the Dorian Mode: A Life of John Gray 1866–1934)* (Padstow: Tabb House, 1983).

37 Sturgeon, op. cit., p. 47.

38 *Works and Days*, p. xix.

39 Rudolf M. Dekker and Lotte C. van der Pol, *The Tradition of Female Transvestism in Early Modern Europe* (London: Macmillan, 1989), p. 57.

TERRY CASTLE

Sylvia Townsend Warner and the counterplot of lesbian fiction

What is a lesbian fiction? According to what we might call the 'Queen Victoria Principle' of cultural analysis, no such entity, of course, should even exist. In 1885, after the passage of the Criminal Law Amendment Act outlawing homosexual acts in Great Britain, it was pointed out to Queen Victoria that the amendment only dealt with 'acts of gross indecency' between men; women, alas, were not covered. The queen responded – as if to a *non sequitur* – 'No woman would ever do that.' Desire between men was conceivable, indeed, could be pictured vividly enough to require policing. Desire between women was not.[1] The love of woman for woman, along with whatever 'indecency' it might entail, simply could not be represented. According to this primal (il)logic, it would follow, therefore, that 'lesbian fiction' is also inconceivable: a non-concept, a nothingness, a gap in the meaning of things – anything but a story there to be read.

We pride ourselves nowadays on having made some intellectual advances on the Victorian position. We know that lesbian fiction, like lesbianism itself, exists; we may even be able to name a few celebrated (or reviled) lesbian novels – *The Well of Loneliness*, *Nightwood*, *Orlando*, *The Desert of the Heart*, *The Female Man*, and so on. And yet on what theoretical basis do we make such denominations? What characteristics inform our definition of 'lesbian fiction' itself? Is a 'lesbian novel' simply any narrative depicting sexual relations between women? If this were the case, then any number of works by male writers, including Diderot's *La Religieuse*, for example, or some of the other pornographic or semi-pornographic texts of male voyeurism, would fall under the rubric of lesbian fiction. Yet this does not feel exactly right. Would a lesbian novel be a novel, then, written by a lesbian? This can't be the case, or certain of Willa Cather's novels, say, or Marguerite Yourcenar's, would have to be classed as lesbian novels, when it is not clear that they really are. 'A novel written by a lesbian depicting sexual relations between women' might come closer, but relies too heavily on the opacities of biography and eros, and lacks a certain psychic and political specificity.

The concept of 'lesbian fiction', one has to conclude, remains somewhat undertheorized. It remains undertheorized, paradoxically, even in those places where one might expect to see it brought under the most intense scrutiny – in criticial studies specifically dealing with the subject of homosexual desire in fiction. To date the most provocative and influential study on this theme has undoubtedly been Eve Kosofky Sedgwick's *Between Men: English Literature and Male Homosocial Desire* (1985). This brilliant meditation on 'homosociality' in literature, which Sedgwick wrote, as she recounts in her introduction, out of a specifically 'antihomophobic and feminist' position, can justly be said to have galvanized the world of gay literary studies, at least as far as that world is presently constituted in the United States.[2]

And yet how is the question of lesbian fiction handled in this book? The answer, simply, is not at all. To be fair to Sedgwick, she is aware of the omission and candidly acknowledges it in her introduction. 'The absence of lesbianism from the book', she writes, 'was an early and, I think, necessary decision, since my argument is structured around the distinctive relation of the male homosocial spectrum to the transmission of unequally distributed power relations.'[3] In other words, the very terms of Sedgwick's argument do not allow for any consideration of lesbian desire or its representation. But how can this be so?

Put in the most basic form, Sedgwick's thesis (which will already be familiar to many readers) is that English literature, at least since the late seventeenth century, has been structured by what she calls the 'erotic triangle' of male homosocial desire. Drawing on the work of René Girard, Claude Lévi-Strauss, and especially Gayle Rubin, whose classic feminist essay, 'The traffic in women', underpins much of the thinking here, Sedgwick constructs the argument that just as patriarchal culture has traditionally been organized around a ritualized 'traffic' in women – the legal, economic, religious, and sexual exchange of women between men (as in the cherished institutions of heterosexual love and marriage), so the fictions produced within patriarchal culture have tended to mimic, or re-present, the same triangular structure. English literature is 'homosocial', according to Sedgwick, to the extent that its hidden subject has always been male bonding – the bonding mediated 'between' two men through, around, or over, the body and soul of a woman. In fiction as in life, the 'normative man', she writes, uses a woman 'as a "conduit of a relationship" in which the true *partner* is a man' (p. 26).

In a series of bravura readings Sedgwick traces the persistence of the male-female-male 'homosocial paradigm' in English writing from Shake-speare and Wycherley through the novels of Sterne, Hogg, Thackeray, Eliot, and Dickens. What she discovers along the way is that homosociality also has its discontents. These arise, not unexpectedly, from the ambiguous relationship between homo*sociality* and homo*sexuality*. The system of male domination, according to Sedgwick, depends on the maintenance of highly charged attachments between men. 'It is crucial to every aspect of social structure within the exchange-of-women framework', she writes, 'that heavily freighted bonds between men exist, as the backbone of social form or forms' (p. 86). At the same time, she points out, when these male-male attachments become *too* freighted – that is, explicitly sexual – the result is an ideological contradiction of potentially crippling magnitude. If a man can become 'like' a woman in the act of homosexual intercourse, what is to distinguish such a man from any woman? By doing away with the 'female middle term' and blurring the putative difference between 'male' and 'female', the overt eroticization of male bonds undermines the very conceptual distinction on which modern patriarchy is founded.

How then to separate 'functional' male bonds – those which bolster the structure of male domination – from those which weaken it? In Sedgwick's insinuating rereading of patriarchal cultural history, literature itself has been a primary means of resolving, or of attempting to resolve, this potentially disruptive ideological problem. Its solution has been to emphasize, with an almost paranoiac insistence, the necessity of triangulation itself – of preserving the male-female-male 'erotic paradigm' precisely as a way of fending off the destabilizing threat of male homosexuality. The plots of classic English and American fiction, according to Sedgwick, are blatantly, often violently, homophobic: in Hogg's *Confessions of a Justified Sinner*, or Dickens's *Our Mutual Friend* – to take two of her more memorable examples – the homoerotic desire of man for man is shown to lead, as if by gothic compulsion, to morbidity, persecution, mania, and murder. By activating what she calls the standard plot mechanisms of 'homosexual panic', these novels, along with many others, reveal themselves as none-too-subtly disguised briefs on behalf of the mediated eros of male homosocial desire. The triangular male-female-male figure returns at the conclusion of each story – triumphantly reinstalled – as a sign both of normative (namely, heterosexual) male bonding and of a remobilization of patriarchal control.

The obsession with vindicating male homosociality at the expense of male homosexuality has not been confined, writes Sedgwick, to the works of the English literary tradition. Indeed, in the most ambitious formulation of her argument, she asserts that the entire European literary canon since the Renaissance might be considered a massively elaborated (and ultimately coercive) statement on male bonding. What makes a literary work 'canonical', in her view, is precisely in fact the degree of its absorption in the issue of male homosociality. She makes this provocative claim in a crucial passage – once again from the introduction – in which she explains the somewhat idiosyncratic assortment of texts to which individual chapters of *Between Men* are dedicated:

The choices I have made of texts through which to embody the argument of the book are specifically *not* meant to begin to delineate a separate male-homosocial literary canon. In fact, it will be essential to my argument to claim that the European canon as it exists is already such a canon, and most so when it is most heterosexual ... I have simply chosen texts at pleasure from within or alongside the English canon that represented particularly interesting interpretive problems, or particularly symptomatic historical and ideological modes, for understanding the politics of male homosociality. (p. 17)

Literature canonizes the subject of male homosociality; in return, it would seem, the subject of male homosociality canonizes the work of literature.

Within such a totalizing scheme, with its insistent focus on relations 'between men', what place might there be for relations between women? Sedgwick is aware, or at least half-aware, that her theory in some way fails 'to do justice to women's own powers, bonds, and struggles' (p. 18). She freely acknowledges that her reluctance to distinguish between what she calls 'ideologizing' and 'de-ideologizing' narratives may have led her to present 'the "canonical" cultural discourse in an excessively protean and inescapable . . . form'. Yet at the same time she makes it clear that she can offer little in the way of comment on 'women's own cultural resources of resistance, adaptation, revision, and survival'. She is content to send out a somewhat perfunctory appeal to her readers for 'better analyses of the relations between female-homosocial and male-homosocial structures' (p. 18).

If the subject of female bonding sets up a kind of intellectual or emotional 'blockage' in Sedgwick's argument, the specialized form of female bonding represented by lesbianism seems to provoke in her, interestingly enough, even deeper resistance. In the one or two somewhat strained paragraphs of *Between Men* that Sedgwick *does* devote to women's bonds, she more or less summarily dismisses 'lesbianism' as a useful category of analysis. In contrast to spectacularly polarized arrangement she finds in the realm of male desire, she can see no real cultural or ideological distinction, in the case of women, between homosociality and homosexuality:

> The diacritical opposition between the 'homosocial' and the 'homosexual' seems to be much less thorough and dichotomous for women, in our society, than for men. At this particular historical moment, an intelligible continuum of aims, emotions, and valuations links lesbianism with the other forms of women's attention to women: the bond of mother and daughter, for instance, the bond of sister and sister, women's friendship, 'networking', and the active struggles of feminism. The continuum is crisscrossed with deep discontinuities – with much homophobia, with conflicts of race and class – but its intelligibility seems now a matter of simple common sense. However agonistic the politics, however conflicted the feelings, it seems at this moment to make an obvious kind of sense to say that women in our society who love women, women who teach, study, nurture, suckle, write about, march for, vote for, give jobs to, or otherwise promote the interests of other women, are pursuing congruent and closely related activities. (pp. 2–3)

Lesbians, defined here, with telling vagueness, only as 'women who love women', are really no different, Sedgwick seems to imply, from 'women promoting the interests of other women'. Their way of bonding is so 'congruent' with that of other women, it turns out, that one need no longer call it homosexual. 'The adjective "homosocial" as applied to women's bond', she concludes, '*need not be pointedly dichotomized as against "homosexual"; it can intelligibly denominate the entire continuum*' (p. 3; my emphasis). By a disarming sleight of phrase, an entire category of women – lesbians – is lost to view.

In the face of these rhetorically tortured and – for Sedgwick – uncharacteristically sentimental passages, one's immediate impulse may be to remark, somewhat uncharitably, that she has not 'gotten the point', so to speak, of pointedly dichotomizing lesbian from straight existence. What may appear 'intelligible' or 'simple common sense' to a non-lesbian critic will hardly seem quite so simple to any female reader who has ever attempted to walk down a city street holding hands with, let alone kissing or embracing, another woman. The homosexual panic elicited by women publicly signalling their sexual interest in one another continues even, alas, 'at this particular historical moment', to be just as virulent as that inspired by male homosexuality, if not more so.[4] To obscure the fact that lesbians are women who have sex with each other – and that this is not exactly the same, in the eyes of society, as voting for women or giving them jobs – is, in essence, not to acknowledge the separate peril and pleasure of lesbian existence.

Are we then simply to blame Sedgwick for succumbing, albeit belatedly, to the Queen Victoria Principle? I think not – for what I am calling, perhaps too tendentiously, the 'blockage' in her theory, is intimately related, paradoxically, to its strength. It is precisely because Sedgwick has recognized so clearly the canonical power of *male-male* desire – and has described so well its shaping role in the plots of eighteenth- and nineteenth-century English and American literature – that she does not 'get the point' of *female-female* desire. For to do so would mean undoing, if only imaginatively, the very structure she is elsewhere at such pains to elaborate: the figure of the male homosocial triangle itself.

To theorize about female-female desire, I would like to suggest, is precisely to envision the taking apart of this supposedly intractable patriarchal structure. Female bonding, at least hypothetically, destabilizes the 'canonical' triangular arrangment of male desire, is an affront to it, and ultimately – in the radical form of lesbian bonding – displaces it entirely. Even Sedgwick's own geometrical model intimates as much. As the diagram below suggests, the male-female-male erotic triangle remains stable only as long as its single female term is unrelated to any other female term. Once two female terms are conjoined in space, however, an alternative structure comes into being, a female-male-female triangle, in which one of the male terms from the original triangle now occupies the 'in between' or subjugated position of the mediator (see Fig. 1 on p. 218).

Within this new *female* homosocial structure, the possibility of male bonding is radically suppressed: for the male term is now isolated, just as

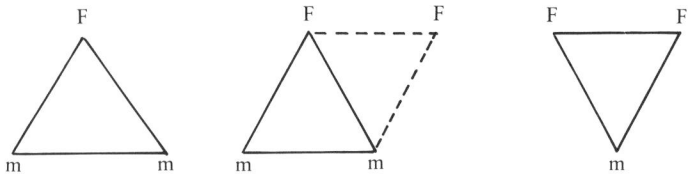

Figure 1

the female term was in the male homosocial structure.

But one can go still further. In the original male-female-male configuration, we may recollect, the relationship between the dominant male terms was not static. Indeed, this was the inherent problem in the structure from the patriarchal perspective: that the two male terms might hook up directly, so to speak, replacing the heterosexual with an explicitly homosexual dyad. Yet exactly the same dynamism is characteristic of the female homosocial triangle. In the most radical transformation of female bonding – i.e. from homosocial to *lesbian* bonding – the two female terms indeed merge and the male term drops out. At this point, it is safe to say, not only is male bonding suppressed, it has become impossible – there being no male terms left to bond.

A pleasing elaboration of the Sedgwickian model, perhaps – but does it have any literary applications? If we restrict ourselves, as Sedgwick herself does, to the canon of eighteenth- and nineteenth-century English and American fiction, the answer would have to be no, or not really. Indeed, one might easily argue that just as the major works of realistic fiction from this period constitute a brief against male homosexuality (Sedgwick's point), so they also constitute, even more blatantly, a brief against female homosociality. Even in works in which female homosocial bonds are depicted, these bonds are inevitably shown giving way to the power of male homosocial triangulation. In Charlotte Brontë's *Shirley*, for example, a novel which explicitly thematizes the conflict between male and female bonding, the original female homosocial bond between Shirley Keeldar and Caroline Helstone (a bond triangulated through the character of the mill owner Robert Moore) is replaced at the end of the novel by not just one, but two interlocking male homosocial triangles, symbolized in the marriages of Robert with Caroline and of Robert's brother Louis with Shirley. True, *Shirley* represents an unusually tormented and ambivalent version of the male homosocial plot: but even Brontë, like other Victorian novelists, gives way in the end to the force of fictional and ideological convention.[5]

But what if we turn our attention to twentieth-century writing? Are there any contemporary novels that undo the seemingly compulsory plot of male homosocial desire? It will come as no surprise that I am about to invoke such a work, and that I propose to denominate it, without further ado, an exemplary 'lesbian fiction'. The work I have in mind is Sylvia Townsend Warner's 1936 *Summer Will Show*, an historical fiction set in rural Dorset and Paris during the revolution of 1848. What makes this novel paradigmatically 'lesbian', in my view, is not simply that it depicts a sexual relationship between two women, but that it so clearly, indeed almost schematically, figures this relationship as a breakup of the supposedly 'canonical' male-female-male erotic triangle. As I shall try to demonstrate in what follows, it is exactly this kind of subverted triangulation, or erotic 'counterplotting', that is in fact characteristic of lesbian novels in general.

Summer Will Show is not, I realize, a well-known piece of fiction – indeed quite the opposite. Even among Townsend Warner devotees it is still a relatively unfamiliar work, despite a Virago reprint in 1987. Warner's earlier novel *Lolly Willowes* (1926) remains generally better known; later works, such as the novel *The Corner That Held Them* (1948), the biography of T. H. White (1967), and the short story collection *The Kingdoms of Elfin* (1977) have attracted more critical attention.[6] What notice *Summer Will Show* has received has tended to be condescending in nature: because Townsend Warner wrote the novel during the period of her most passionate involvement with the British Communist Party and intended it in part as an allegory of the Spanish Civil War, it has often been dismissed as a 'Marxist novel' or leftist period piece. While not entirely an *un*read work of modern English fiction, *Summer Will Show* is at the very least an *under*read one.

Yet some of the resistance the work has met with must also have to do, one suspects, with its love story, which challenges so spectacularly the rigidly heterosexual conventions of classic English and American fiction. This story begins deceptively simply, in a seemingly recognizable literary landscape – that of nineteenth-century fiction itself. The tall, fair-haired heroine, Sophia Willoughby, is the only daughter of wealthy landed gentry in Dorset, the heiress of Blandamer House (in which she resides), and the wife of a feckless husband, Frederick, who, after marrying her for her money and fathering her two small children, has abandoned her and taken a mistress in Paris. At the start of the novel, Sophia is walking with her children, a boy and a girl, on a hot summer's day to the lime-kiln on the estate, in the hope that by subjecting them to a traditional remedy – lime-kiln fumes – she can cure them of the whooping-cough they have both contracted.

Already in these opening pages, given over to Sophia's reveries on the way to the lime-kiln, we have a sense of her proud, powerful, yet troubled nature: like another Gwendolyn Harleth or even a new Emma Bovary, she broods over her unhappy marriage and yearns ambiguously for 'something decisive', a new kind of fulfilment, some 'moment when she should exercise her authority' (p. 11).[7] While devoted to her children, she also feels constricted by them and infuriated at her husband for leaving them entirely to her care. As for Frederick himself, she harbours no lingering romantic illusions there, only 'icy disdain', mixed with a sense of sexual grievance. It is not so much that she is jealous – their marriage has been devoid of passion – but that she resents his freedom and his predictably chosen 'bohemian' mistress:

For even to Dorset the name of Minna Lemuel had made its way. Had the husband of Mrs. Willoughby chosen no other end than to be scandalous, he could not have chosen better. A byword, half actress, half strumpet; a Jewess; a nonsensical creature bedizened with airs of prophecy, who trailed across Europe with a tag-rag of poets, revolutionaries, musicians and circus-riders snuffing at her heels, like an escaped bitch with a procession of mongrels after her; and ugly; and old, as old as Frederick or older – this was the woman whom Frederick had elected to fall in love with, joining in the tag-rag procession, and not even king in that outrageous court, not even able to dismiss the mongrels, and take the creature into keeping. (p. 31)

At the same time, however, Sophia feels an odd gratitude to the other woman: thanks to Minna, Sophia reminds herself, she is 'a mother, and a landowner; but fortunately, she need no longer be counted among the wives' (p. 20).

All this is to change as a result of the lime-kiln visit itself. With Sophia looking on, the lime-kiln keeper – a silent, frightening-looking man with sores on his arms – suspends each of the children over the kiln. Though terrified, they inhale the fumes and Sophia takes them home. In the next few weeks her attention is distracted by the arrival of her nephew Caspar, the illegitimate mulatto child of an uncle in the West Indies. At her uncle's request, she takes Caspar to Cornwall to place him in a boarding-school. Returning home, she finds her own children mortally ill: the lime-kiln keeper was in fact carrying smallpox and has infected both children. Sophia delays writing to her husband to inform him; yet Frederick comes anyway, having been recalled by a letter written by the doctor who is attending the children.

At once Sophia senses a subtle change in her husband, a mystifying new refinement, which she attributes – balefully, yet also with growing curiosity – to the influence of his unseen mistress. Listening to him repeat the words 'Ma fleur' over his dying daughter's sickbed, it seems to Sophia as if a stranger were speaking through him: someone possessed of 'a deep sophistication in sorrow'. The intrusive cadence, she reminds herself angrily, must be copied from 'that Minna's Jewish contralto'. Yet afterwards, when both of the children are dead and Frederick has gone back to Paris, Sophia finds herself haunted by a memory of the voice – one that seems, 'according to her mood, an enigma, a nettle-sting, a caress' (p. 83).

With the death of Sophia's children, the crucial action of the novel commences. Distraught, grief-stricken, yet also peculiarly obsessed with her husband's other life, Sophia decides to seek him out in Paris, for the purpose (she tells herself) of forcing him to give her more children. Yet, as if driven by more mysterious urgings, she finds herself, on the very evening of her arrival, at the apartment on the Rue de la Carabine where Minna holds her salon. Entering the apartment unobserved, Sophia joins the crowd of guests (including Frederick himself) who are listening to their hostess tell a story.

The story, which is presented as an embedded narrative, is a hypnotic account of Minna's childhood in Eastern Europe – of the pogrom in which her parents were killed, of her own escape from the murderers, and of her eventual rescue by a vagrant musician. The experience of persecution has made her an artist, a story-teller, a romantic visionary, and a political revolutionary. As Sophia listens, seemingly mesmerized by the Jewish woman's charismatic 'siren voice', she forgets entirely about Frederick and the putative reason why she has come. Suddenly the tale is interrupted: barricades are being put up outside in the streets; the first skirmishes of what will become the February Revolution are about to begin. Minna's listeners, mainly artists and intellectuals who support the revolt, depart, along with Frederick, who has not yet seen his wife. And Sophia, still as if under a spell, finds herself alone in the room with Minna.

She is utterly, heart-stoppingly, captivated. Not by Minna's beauty – for Frederick's mistress is a small, dark, and sallow woman, with 'a slowly flickering glance' and 'large supple hands' that seem to 'caress themselves together in the very gesture of her thought' (p. 127). Yet something in this very look, 'sombre and attentive', alive with tenderness and recognition, ineluctably draws Sophia to her. ('I cannot understand', Sophia finds herself thinking, 'what Frederick could see in you. But *I* can see a great deal' (p. 154).) Minna in turn seems equally delighted with her lover's wife. Together they look out on the barricades: Frederick is below and now sees Sophia; he is piqued when she refuses his offer of a cab. Minna also ignores him, so he leaves. Minna then confides in Sophia her hopes for the success of the insurrection. Sophia, entranced yet also exhausted, falls asleep on Minna's sofa. When she awakens the next day her hostess is sitting beside her. Inspired by the strange 'ardour' of the Jewish woman's attention, the normally reticent Sophia suddenly finds herself overcome by an urge to recount the story of *her* own life. As if freed from an invisible bondage, she finds herself talking for hours. When Frederick returns that afternoon, he is momentarily 'felled' to discover his wife and mistress 'seated together on the pink sofa, knit into this fathomless intimacy, and turning from it to entertain him with an identical patient politeness'. For 'neither woman, absorbed in this extraordinary colloquy, had expressed by word or sign the slightest consciousness that there was anything unusual about it' (p.157).

Nor, might it be said, does Townsend Warner. The attraction between Sophia and Minna is treated, if anything, as a perfectly natural elaboration of the wife–mistress situation. The two women, it is true, separate for several weeks, in part because Sophia is afraid of the depth – and complication – of her new attachment. While the political turmoil in the city grows, she stays with her wealthy, superannuated French aunt, Léocadie, who tries to reconcile her with Frederick. Yet she is drawn back into Minna's orbit soon enough, when she hears that Minna has given away almost all of her money to the striking workers and is destitute. Outraged with Frederick for 'casting off' his mistress (which is how

Sophia describes the situation to herself), she determines to fulfil his 'obligations' herself. She returns to the now-shabby apartment on the Rue de la Carabine, and finding Minna weak with cold and hunger, decides to stay and care for her. As her absorption in the other woman grows – and is reciprocated – Sophia gradually feels her old identity, that of the heiress of Blandamer, slipping away. As if 'by some extraordinary enchantment', she is inexorably caught up in Minna's world and in the revolutionary activity in which Minna is involved.

Meanwhile Frederick, incensed by the alliance between his wife and his (now) ex-mistress, cuts off Sophia's allowance in order to force her to return to him. Yet his machinations serve only to intensify – indeed to eroticize – the intimacy between the two women. When Sophia tells her friend that Frederick has told the bank not to honour her signature 'as he is entitled to do being my husband', they suddenly comprehend their desire for what it is:

> 'You will stay? You must, if only to gall him.'
> 'I don't think that much of a reason.'
> 'But you will stay?'
> 'I will stay if you wish it.'
> It seemed to her that the words fell cold and glum as ice-pellets. Only beneath the crust of thought did her being assent as by right to that flush of pleasure, that triumphant cry.
> 'But of course', said Minna a few hours later, thoughtfully licking the last oyster shell, 'we must be practical.' (p. 274)

Townsend Warner, to be sure, renders the scene of their passionate coming together elliptically – with only a cry (and an oyster) to suggest the moment of consummation – yet the meaning is clear: Sophia has severed all ties with the past – with her husband, her class, and with sexual convention itself.

In the final section of the novel spring gives way to summer; the popular insurrection, dormant for several months, flares once again. Inspired by her new-found love for Minna, Sophia throws herself into political activity, becoming a courier for a group of communists who are collecting weapons in preparation for open civil war. Her last contact with her husband comes about when her nephew Caspar suddenly turns up in Paris, alienated and sullen, having run away from the school in Cornwall: Sophia is forced to ask Frederick for money to pay for the youth's schooling in Paris. Without her knowledge Frederick, who now cynically supports the government, instead buys Caspar a place in the Gardes Mobiles, the force opposing the now-imminent July revolution.

Returning from one of her courier missions, Sophia finds that street fighting has begun in the neighborhood around the Rue de la Carabine. Minna is already on the barricades. Together they join in the battle, loading and reloading the workers' rifles. The Gardes Mobiles launch an attack on the barricade and Sophia, to her surprise, recognizes Caspar in their midst. He plunges a bayonet into Minna, who falls, apparently mortally wounded. Sophia shoots Caspar in retaliation, but is herself captured and taken away with some other prisoners to be executed, only to be freed the next day because she is a woman. She searches frantically for Minna but cannot discover if she is alive or dead. The revolt has been put down and the workers' hopes seemingly destroyed. Returning to Minna's apartment, yet still harbouring a hope that her lover will return, Sophia opens one of the pamphlets that she had been delivering the previous day. It is Marx's *Communist Manifesto*. As she settles down to read it – exhausted but also arrested by its powerful opening words – the novel comes ambiguously to an end.

I will return to this somewhat curious denouement in a moment: I would like to draw attention first, however, to the more obviously revisionist aspects of Townsend Warner's narrative. For *Summer Will Show* – as I hope even my highly compressed account of its characters and incidents will have indicated – is a work obsessed with 'revising' on a number of counts. In the most literal sense the novel is a kind of revisionist fantasia: in recounting the story of her pseudo-Victorian heroine, Sophia Willoughby, Townsend Warner constantly pastiches – yet also rewrites – Victorian fiction itself. The opening scene at the lime-kiln, for example, both recalls and traduces the episode in *Great Expectations* in which Pip is dangled over a lime-kiln by the infamous Orlick: the 'great expectations' here belong, ironically, to the observer, Sophia herself. The early episodes involving the mulatto Caspar and the uncle in the West Indies likewise rework and subvert elements from *Wuthering Heights* and *Jane Eyre*. After Sophia's arrival in Paris, a curiously erotic scene in which Minna shows her her duelling pistols (pp. 154–6) is an almost direct parody of a similar moment in *Shirley*: Minna's guns are about to be given up to the striking workers of Paris; the guns that Caroline Helstone shows to Shirley Keeldar are their protection *against* the striking workers of Briarfield. Minna herself is a kind of revolutionary variant on a George Eliot heroine. Her Jewishness and political radicalism bring to mind characters and situations from *Daniel Deronda* and *Felix Holt*; her appearance – and passionate intelligence – may be modelled on Eliot's own. Yet she is far more deviant than any Eliot heroine is ever allowed to be. Tellingly, her very name appears to originate in the famous passage in *The Mill on the Floss* in which Maggie Tulliver declares her wish to 'avenge' all the unfortunate dark-haired heroines of English literature – 'Rebecca, and Flora MacIvor, and Minna, and all the rest of the dark unhappy ones.'[8] Maggie's Minna is the hapless heroine of Sir Walter Scott's *The Pirate*, abandoned by her lover on a frigid Scottish beach. By contrast, Townsend Warner's Minna – with her freedom from convention, sexual charisma and survivor's instinct – is at once a satirical rewrite of the first Minna and a more resilient version of Maggie herself.

But it is not only English fiction that Townsend Warner is rewriting in *Summer Will Show*. In a somewhat tongue-in-cheek note composed in the 1960s, she revealed that in order to write the book she 're-read Berlioz's *Mémoires*, and with an effort put the French novelists out of my mind'.[9]

Berlioz is certainly there, but so too are the French novelists. The scenes at Minna's Parisian salon have the flavour of Staël and Hugo, as well as of Stendhal and Balzac; Sophia's right-wing aunt Léocadie, along with her egregious confessor Père Hyacinthe, are straight out of *La Comédie humaine*. But it is Flaubert, obviously, and *his* novel of 1848, that Townsend Warner is most deeply conscious of displacing. Anyone who doubts the subterranean importance of *L'Education sentimentale* to *Summer Will Show* need only consider the name Frédéric – or Frederick – and the parodistic relationship that exists between Flaubert's anti-hero, Frederic Moreau, and Townsend Warner's comic villain, Frederick Willoughby.[10]

To invoke Flaubert's masterpiece, however, is also to return – with a vengeance – to the Sedgwickian issue of erotic triangulation. For what is *L'Education sentimentale* if not a classic work, in Sedgwick's terms, of male homosocial bonding? Flaubert's Frédéric, we recall, acts out his emotional obsession with his friend Arnoux by falling in love first with Arnoux's wife, then with his mistress. Townsend Warner's Frederick, by contrast, not only has no male friend, his wife and his mistress fall in love with each other. In the very act of revising Flaubert – of substituting her own profoundly 'anti-canonical' fiction in place of his own – Townsend Warner also revises the plot of male homosocial desire itself. Indeed, all of her revisionist gestures can, I think, be linked with this same imaginative impulse: the desire to plot *against* the seemingly indestructible heterosexual narrative of classic European fiction.

This work of counterplotting can best be figured, as I suggested at the outset, as a kind of dismantling or displacement of the male homosocial triangle itself. Granted, at the beginning of *Summer Will Show*, the hoary Sedgwickian structure still seems firmly in place: Sophia is more or less mired in the 'in between' position that patriarchal society demands of her. As the only heiress of Blandamer, 'the point advancing on the future, as it were, of that magnificent triangle in which Mr. and Mrs. Aspen of Blandamer House, Dorset, England, made up the other two apices' (p. 3), she has functioned, we are led to deduce, as the social mediator between her own father, who has been forced to give her up in marriage in order to perpetuate the Aspen family line, and Frederick, the son-in-law, who has enriched himself by allying himself with the Aspen patrimony.

Yet instabilities in this classic male-female-male triad soon become apparent. The deaths of Sophia's children are the first sign of a generalized weakening of male homosocial bonds; these deaths, we realize, are not just a transforming loss for Sophia, but for Frederick also, who loses, through them, his only remaining biological and symbolic connection to Sophia's dead father, his partner in the novel's original homosocial triangle. Significantly, perhaps, it is the son who is the first of the children to die: in a way that prefigures the symbolic action of the novel as a whole, the patrilineal triangle of father-mother-son here disappears, leaving only a female-male-female triangle, composed of Sophia, Frederick, and their daughter. Even at this early stage, one might argue, Townsend Warner represents the female-dominant triangle as 'stronger', or in some sense more durable, than the male-dominant one.

Yet other episodes in the first part of the novel suggest a disintegration of male homosocial structures. When Sophia delays writing to Frederick during the children's illness, her doctor, thinking the absence of her husband a scandal, writes to him without her knowledge. The letter is intercepted, however, by the doctor's young wife, who brings it to Sophia and offers to destroy it. 'Why should all this be done behind your back?' exclaims the outraged Mrs Hervey, 'what right have they to interfere, to discuss and plot, and settle what they think best to be done? As if, whatever happened, you could not stand alone, and judge for yourself! As if you needed a man!' (p. 72). Admittedly, Sophia decides in the end to let the letter be sent, but the intimation here of an almost conspiratorial bonding between the two women – against *both* of their husbands – directly foreshadows the more powerful bonding of Sophia with Minna. And as will be true later, a strong current of erotic feeling runs between the two women. 'She might be in love with me', Sophia thinks after Mrs Hervey 'awkwardly' embraces her during one of their first meetings. Now, as she looks at the letter 'lying so calmly' on Mrs Hervey's lap, it suddenly seems only a pretext: 'some other motive, violent and unexperienced as the emotions of youth, trembled undeclared between them'. Later, they walk hand in hand in a thunderstorm, and Sophia briefly entertains a fancy of going on a European tour with Mrs Hervey – 'large-eyed and delighted and clutching a box of watercolour paints' – at her side (p. 78).

With the love affair between Sophia and Minna, one might say that the male homosocial triad reaches its point of maximum destabilization and collapses altogether. In its place appears a new configuration, the triad of *female* homosocial desire. For Frederick, obviously, is now forced into the position of the subject term, the one 'in between', the odd one out – the one, indeed, who can be patronized. Sophia and Minna do just this during their first supper together, following the memorable colloquy on the pink sofa. Sophia takes it upon herself to order the wine, a discreetly masculine gesture that inspires Minna to remark, 'How much I like being with English people! They manage everything so quietly and so well.' Sophia, catching her drift, instantly rejoins, 'And am I as good as Frederick?' 'You are much better', Minna replies. After a short meditation on Frederick's shortcomings, the two women subside into complacent amity. 'Poor Frederick!' says one. 'Poor Frederick!' says the other (pp. 161–2).

We might call this the comedy of female-female desire: as two women come together, the man who has brought them together seems oddly reduced, transformed into a figure of fun. Later he will drop out of sight altogether – which is another way of saying that in every lesbian relationship there is a man who has been sacrificed. Townsend Warner will call attention to this 'disappearing man' phenomenon at numerous points, sometimes in a powerfully literal way. When Sophia returns, for example, to the Rue de la Carabine to help the poverty-striken Minna, only to find her lying chilled and unconscious on the floor, she immediately lies down to warm her, in 'a desperate calculated caress'. Yet this first, soon-to-be eroticized act of lying down with Minna also triggers a reverie – on the strangeness of the season that has brought them together, on the vast distance each has traversed to arrive at this moment, and on the man 'between them' who is of course not there:

> It was spring, she remembered. In another month the irises would be coming into flower. But now it was April, the cheat month, when the deadliest frosts might fall, when snow might cover the earth, lying hard and authentic on the English acres as it lay over the wastes of Lithuania. There, in one direction, was Blandamer, familiar as a bed; and there, in another was Lithuania, the unknown, where a Jewish child had watched the cranes fly over, and had stood beside the breaking river. And here, in Paris lay Sophia Willoughby, lying on the floor in the draughty passage-way between bedroom and dressing-closet, her body pressed against the body of her husband's mistress. (p. 251)

The intimacy, here and later, is precisely the intimacy enjoined by the breakup of monolithic structures, indeed, by the breakup of triangulation itself. For what Sophia and Minna discover, even as they muse over 'poor Frederick', is that they need him no longer: in the draughty passageway leading to a bedroom, the very shape of desire is 'pressed' out of shape, becoming dyadic, impassioned, lesbian.[11]

What is particularly satisfying about Townsend Warner's plotting here is that it illustrates so neatly – indeed so trigonometrically – what we might take to be the underlying principle of lesbian narrative itself: namely, that for female bonding to 'take', as it were, to metamorphose into explicit sexual desire, male bonding must be suppressed. (Male homo*social* bonding, that is; for lesbian characters in novels can, and do, quite easily coexist with male homo*sexual* characters, as Djuna Barnes's *Nightwood*, or even *Orlando* in its final pages, might suggest.)[12] Townsend Warner's Frederick has no boyhood friend, no father, no father-in-law, no son, no gang, *no novelist on his side* to help him re-triangulate his relationship with his wife – or for that matter, with his mistress either. To put it axiomatically: in the absence of male homosocial desire, lesbian desire emerges.

Can such a principle help us to theorize in more general ways about lesbian fiction? Obviously, I think it can. It allows us to identify first of all two basic mimetic contexts in which in realistic writing plots of lesbian desire are most likely to flourish: the world of schooling and adolescence (the world of pre-marital relations) and the world of divorce, widowhood, and separation (the world of post-marital relations). In each of these mimetic contexts male erotic triangulation is either conspicuously absent or under assault. In the classically gynocentric setting of the girls' school, for example, male characters are generally isolated or missing altogether: hence the powerfully female homosocial/homosexual plots of Colette's *Claudine à l'école*, Dorothy Strachey's *Olivia*, Christa Winsloe's *The Child Manuela* (on which the film *Mädchen in Uniform* is based), Lillian Hellman's *The Children's Hour*, Muriel Spark's *The Prime of Miss Jean Brodie*, Catherine Stimpson's *Class Notes* or more recently, Jeannette Winterson's *Oranges are Not the Only Fruit*, in which the juvenile heroine woos her first love while attending a female Bible study group.

Yet the figure of male homosociality is even more pitilessly compromised in novels of post-marital experience. In the novel of adolescence, it is true, male homosocial desire often reasserts itself, belatedly, at the end of the fiction: the central lesbian bond may be undermined or broken up, usually by having one of the principals die (as in *The Child Manuela* or *The Children's Hour*), get married (as in *Oranges are Not the Only Fruit*) or reconcile herself in some other way with the erotic and social world of men (as in *Claudine à l'école* or *The Prime of Miss Jean Brodie*). We might call this 'dysphoric' lesbian counterplotting. To the extent that it depicts female homosexual desire as a finite phenomenon – a temporary phase in a larger pattern of heterosexual *Bildung* – the lesbian novel of adolescence is almost always dysphoric in tendency.[13]

In post-marital lesbian fiction, however, male homosocial bonds are generally presented – from the outset – as debilitated to the point of unrecuperability. Typically in such novels, it is the very failure of the heroine's marriage or heterosexual love-affair that functions as the pretext for her conversion to homosexual desire. This conversion is radical and irreversible: once she discovers (usually ecstatically) her passion for women, there is no going back. We might call this 'euphoric' lesbian counterplotting: it is an essentially comic, even utopian plot pattern. A new world is imagined in which male bonding has no place. Classic lesbian novels following the euphoric pattern include Jane Bowles's *Two Serious Ladies*, Jane Rule's *The Desert of the Heart*, and Claire Morgan's *The Price of Salt*, as well as numerous pulp romances of recent vintage, such as Anne Bannon's *Journey to a Woman* and Katharine V. Forrest's *An Emergence of Green*. In that it too begins with a failed marriage (that of Robin Vote and Felix Volkbein) even such a baroquely troubled work as *Nightwood*, paradoxically, might be considered euphoric in this respect: though its depiction of lesbian love is often malign, the novel takes for granted a world in which female erotic bonds predominate – so much so that the very possibility of male homosociality seems negated from the start.[14]

With its insouciant, sometimes coruscating satire on male bonding, *Summer Will Show* typifies the post-marital or conversion fiction: its energies are primarily comic and visionary. It is a novel of liberation. As Minna says to Sophia at one point: ' "You have run away. . . . You'll never go back now, you know. I've encouraged a quantity of people to run away, but I have never seen any one so decisively escaped as you" '

(p. 217). Yet is this the whole story? Given that the novel concludes with Minna herself apparently slain on the barricades, a victim of Caspar (who in turn is the pawn of Frederick), how complete, finally, is what I am calling, perhaps too exuberantly, its 'undoing' of the classic male homosocial plot?

That the ending of *Summer Will Show* poses a problem cannot be denied: Wendy Mulford, one of Townsend Warner's most astute critics, calls it an unconvincing 'botch' – though not, interestingly, for any purely narratological reason. For Mulford, Minna's bayoneting by Caspar is symptomatic of Townsend Warner's own emotional confusion in the 1930s over whether to devote herself to her writing or to revolutionary (specifically Marxist) political struggle. To the extent that Minna, the story-telling romantic, represents the potentially anarchical freedom of the artist, she has to be 'sacrificed', Mulford argues, in order to 'free the dedicated revolutionary' in Sophia, who functions here as a stand-in for the novelist herself. At the same time, she conjectures, '[Townsend Warner's] unconscious was unable to consent to such a move' – hence the novel's descent into bathos and melodrama at this point.[15]

Yet Mulford already oversimplifies, I think, in assuming without question that Minna is dead. Granted, Minna seems to be dead (during the onslaught on the barricade Sophia sees Caspar's bayonet 'jerk' in Minna's breast) yet in a curious turnabout in the novel's final pages, Townsend Warner goes out of her way – seemingly gratuitously – to hint that she may in fact still be alive. Though unsuccessful, Sophia's attempts to locate Minna's body raise the possibility that her lover has survived: a witness to the scene on the barricades, Madame Guy, concedes that Minna was indeed alive when she was dragged away by soldiers; her daughter confirms it (pp. 397–8). Later visits to 'all the places where enquiries might be made' turn up nothing, but the man who accompanies Sophia reminds her that the officials in charge may be misleading her on purpose – the implication being that her friend may in fact be held prisoner somewhere (p. 399). The ambiguity is hardly resolved even at the last. When Sophia returns to Minna's apartment and takes up the *Communist Manifesto*, her peculiarly composed attitude seems as much one of waiting as of tragic desolation: far from being traumatized by seeing 'the wine that Minna had left for her' or Minna's slippers on the floor, she merely sits down to read, as though Minna were at any moment about to return. The utopian tract she peruses in turn hints symbolically at the thematics of return: if we take seriously the analogy that Townsend Warner has made throughout the novel between her heroine's political and sexual transformation, the inspiriting presence of the *Manifesto* here, with its promise of revolutionary hope resurrected, may also portend another kind of resurrection, that of Minna herself.

The novelist here seems to test how much implausibility we are willing to accept – for according to even the loosest standard of probability (such as might hold, say, in Victorian fiction) the possibility that Minna should survive her bayoneting by Caspar, an event which itself already strains credibility, must appear fanciful in the extreme. Yet it cannot be denied that Townsend Warner herself seems drawn back to the idea – almost, one feels, because it *is* incredible. Having offered us a plausible (or semi-plausible) ending, she now hints, seemingly capriciously, at a far more unlikely plot turn, as if perversely determined to revert to the most fantastical kind of closure imaginable.

Without attempting to diminish any of the ambiguity here, I think Warner's restaging of her conclusion – this apparent inability to let go of the possibility of euphoric resolution however improbable such a resolution must seem – can tell us something useful, once again, about lesbian fiction. By its very nature lesbian fiction has – and can only have – a profoundly attenuated relationship with what we think of, stereotypically, as narrative verisimilitude, plausibility, or 'truth to life'. Precisely because it is motivated by a yearning for that which is, in a cultural sense, implausible – the subversion of male homosocial desire – lesbian fiction characteristically exhibits, even as it masquerades as 'realistic' in surface detail, a strongly fantastical, allegorical or utopian tendency. The more insistently it gravitates toward euphoric resolution, moreover, the more implausible – in every way – it may seem.

The problem with Townsend Warner's novel – if in fact it is a problem – is not so much that it forfeits plausibility at the end but that it forfeits it from the start. There is nothing remotely believable about Sophia Willoughby's transformation from 'heiress of Blandamer' into lover of her husband's mistress and communist revolutionary, if by 'believability' we mean conformity with the established mimetic conventions of canonical English and American fiction. The novelist herself seems aware of this, and without ever entirely abandoning the framing pretense of historicity (the references to real people and events, the 'Berliozian' local colour), often hints at the artificial, 'as if' or hypothetical nature of the world her characters inhabit. Metaphorically speaking, everything in the novel has a slightly suspect, theatrical, even phantasmagorical air. Revolutionary Paris resembles a stage set: the rebels near Minna's house are arrayed like 'comic opera bandits' (p. 177); a bloody skirmish in the streets is a 'clinching raree-show' (p. 171). Trying to convince her to return to her husband, Sophia's aunt Léocadie becomes a 'ballerina', with Frederick 'the suave athletic partner, respectfully leading her round by one leg as she quivered on the tip-toe of the other' (p. 203). Elsewhere Frederick is a 'tenor' plotting with the 'basso' Père Hyacinthe (p. 192). The captivating Minna, in turn is a 'gifted tragedy actress' (p. 217), a 'play-acting Shylock' (p. 212), or someone 'in a charade' (p. 268. Sometimes she leaves the human realm altogether, metamorphosing into something from fairy-tale or myth – a 'Medusa', a 'herb-wife', a 'siren', a 'sorceress' – or a creature out of beast fable or Grandville cartoon. She is a 'macaw', Sophia thinks, a 'parrot', 'some purple-plumaged bird of prey, her hooked nose impending', or perhaps the 'sleekest' of cats (p. 326). Her passion for Minna, Sophia concludes, is like the poet's – 'of a birth as rare/As 'tis of object strange and high ... begotten by despair/Upon impossibility' (p. 289).

These built-in intimations of artifice and romance, of delight and high fakery, present on almost every page of *Summer Will Show*, work against the superficial historicism of the narrative, pushing it inexorably toward the fantastic. Of course a hankering after the fantastic is present elsewhere in Townsend Warner's writing: *Lolly Willowes*, we recall, begins as a seemingly straightforward tale about a spinster in an ordinary English village, but swerves abruptly into the marvellous when the spinster joins a coven of witches led by the Devil. Indeed the development of Townsend Warner's writing career as a whole suggests a progressive shifting away from realism toward the explicitly anti-mimetic modes of allegory and fable: in her last published stories, collected in *The Kingdoms of Elfin*, she dispensed with human subjects entirely, choosing to commemorate instead the delicate passions of a race of elves.

Yet the fantastical element in *Summer Will Show*, is not, I think, simply a matter of authorial idiosyncracy. Other lesbian novels display the same oscillation between realistic and fabulous modes. One need only think again of *Orlando* or *Nightwood*, or indeed of Joanna Russ's *The Female Man*, Elizabeth Jolley's *Miss Peabody's Inheritance*, Lois Gould's *The Sea Change*, Sarah Schulman's *After Delores*, Margaret Erhart's *Unusual Company*, Michelle Cliff's *No Telephone to Heaven*, or any of Jeannette Winterson's recent novels, to see how symptomatically lesbian fiction resists any simple recuperation as 'realistic'. Even as it gestures back at a supposedly familiar world of human experience, it almost invariably stylizes and estranges it – by presenting it parodistically, euphuistically or in some other rhetorically heightened, distorted, fragmented, or hallucinatory way. Indeed, in the most extreme manifestations of this tendency, the pretense of mimesis collapses completely. In Monique Wittig's *Les Guérillères* or Sally Gearheart's *The Wanderground*, for example, two explicitly utopian lesbian novels, the fictional world itself is fantastically tranfigured, becoming a kind of sublime Amazonian dream space: the marvellous inversion, in short, of that real world – 'between men' – the rest of us inhabit.[16]

What then *is* a lesbian fiction? Taking Sylvia Townsend Warner's *Summer Will Show* as our paradigm, we can now begin to answer the question with which we started. Such a fiction will be, both in the ordinary and in a more elaborate sense, non-canonical. Like Townsend Warner's novel itself, the typical lesbian fiction is likely to be an under-read, even unknown, text – and certainly an under-appreciated one. It is likely to stand in a satirical, inverted or parodic relationship to more famous novels of the past – which is to say that it will exhibit an ambition to displace the so-called canonical works which have preceded it. In the case of *Summer Will Show*, Townsend Warner's numerous literary parodies – of Flaubert, Eliot, Brontë, Dickens and the rest – suggest a wish to displace, in particular, the supreme texts of nineteenth-century realism, as if to infiltrate her own fiction among them as a kind of subversive, inflammatory, pseudo-canonical substitute.

But most importantly, by plotting against what Eve Sedgwick has called the 'plot of male homosociality', the archetypal lesbian fiction decanon-izes, so to speak, the canonical structure of desire itself. In so far as it documents a world in which men are 'between women' rather than vice versa, it is an insult to the conventional geometries of fictional eros. It dismantles the real, as it were, in a search for the not-yet-real, something unpredicted and unpredictable. It is an assault on the banal: a re-triangulating of triangles. As a consequence it often looks odd, fantastical, implausible, 'not there' – utopian in aspiration if not design. It is, in a word, imaginative. This is why, perhaps, like lesbian desire itself, it is still difficult for us to acknowledge – even when (Queen Victoria notwith-standing) it is so palpably, so plainly, there.

Stanford University

NOTES

1 To judge by how frequently it is repeated, the story of Queen Victoria's pronouncement has taken on, alas, the status of cultural myth – the 'truth' of which is that lesbians don't really exist. Whenever it is retold – even seemingly jokingly, by anti-homophobic historians and critics – it almost always prefigures the erasure of lesbianism from the discourse that is to follow, usually through some equation of homosexuality with male homosexuality only. For an example of this phenomenon see Richard Ellmann's *Oscar Wilde* (New York: Vintage Books, 1988), p. 409n, in which lesbianism – and Queen Victoria's views thereupon – are mentioned in a footnote, then never referred to again.

2 Theoretical writing on lesbian fiction remains sparse. Since Jane Rule's somewhat impressionistic *Lesbian Images* (New York: Doubleday, 1975), no Anglo-American writer or scholar has attempted a major book on lesbian fiction; most of the miscellaneous criticism written on the subject has tended to be either biographically oriented or focused on lesbian readers, as in Judith Fetterley's 'Writes of passing', *Gay Studies Newsletter*, 14 (March 1987). Several important exceptions must be noted, however: Monique Wittig's 'The straight mind', *Feminist Issues*, 1 (1980), pp. 103–11; Catherine Stimpson's 'Zero degree deviancy: the lesbian novel in English', *Critical Inquiry*, 8 (1980), pp. 363–80; Bonnie Zimmerman's 'Is "Chloe liked Olivia" a lesbian plot?', *Women's Studies International Forum*, 6 (1983), pp. 169–75, and 'The politics of transliteration: lesbian personal narratives', *Signs*, 'The Lesbian Issue', 9 (1984), pp. 663–82; Marilyn R. Farwell's 'Toward a definition of the lesbian literary imagination', *Signs*, 14 (1988), pp. 100–18; and Sherron E. Knopp's '"If I saw you would you kiss me?": Sapphism and the subversiveness of Virginia Woolf's *Orlando*', *PMLA*, 103 (1988), pp. 24–34. The most useful bibliographic study of lesbian fiction is still Jeannette Foster's classic *Sex Variant Women in Literature* (1955; New York: Diana Press, 1975).

3 Eve Kosofsky Sedgwick, *Between Men: English Literature and Male Homosocial Desire* (New York: Columbia University Press, 1985). Page numbers of citations are noted in parentheses. Since the publication of *Between Men*, it is true, Sedgwick has begun to explore the subject of

lesbianism (and of lesbian authorship) more fruitfully, notably in relation to what she calls 'the epistemology of the closet' – the peculiar way in which the reality of homosexuality is at once affirmed and denied, elaborated and masked, in modern cultural discourse. Two of her recently published essays – to be included in her forthcoming book *Epistemology of the Closet* (Berkeley: University of California Press, 1990) – are relevant here: 'Privilege of unknowing' (on Diderot's *La Religieuse*), *Genders*, 1 (1988), pp. 102–24; and 'Across gender, across sexuality: Willa Cather and others', *The South Atlantic Quarterly*, 88 (1989), pp. 53–72. Even in these seemingly more encompassing pieces, however, Sedgwick's unwillingness to separate herself from the spectacle of male bonding is still in evidence. In the case of the Diderot essay, Sedgwick chooses a work which can be labelled 'lesbian' only problematically, if at all: as Sedgwick herself says at one point, 'because of the mid-eighteenth-century origin of the novella and because of its conventual venue, the question of lesbian sexual desire – *is* what is happening sexual desire, and will it be recognized and named as such? – looks, there, less like the question of The Lesbian than the question of sexuality *tout court*'. This may be true, but Sedgwick's immediate and seemingly reflexive transformation of the 'lesbian sexual desire' she admits to seeing in *La Religieuse* into a figure for 'sexuality *tout court*' – the site at which the 'privilege of unknowing' is manifest – might also be taken as a symptom of a certain 'unknowingness' regarding lesbianism itself: whatever *it* (lesbianism) is, Sedgwick implies, it is not worth bothering about in and of itself; it is simply a metaphor for other things that can't be talked about, such as (no surprise here) *male* homosexuality. Having disposed, at least theoretically, of any lesbian element in *La Religieuse*, Sedgwick then proceeds to slot the novel comfortably back into the framework of male homosocial desire. Citing approvingly Jay Caplan's observation that 'this novel has the form of a message addressed by one father to another about their symbolic (and hence, absent) daughter', Sedgwick concludes that *La Religieuse* displays the 'distinctively patriarchal triangular structure' of male homosocial bonding (p. 119) – thus foreclosing any more complex reading of its erotic relations. Tellingly, Sedgwick wonders at one point whether her own resistance to lesbian desire may perhaps have limited her understanding of the novel, but decides that this can't be so: 'it would not be enough', she reassures her reader, 'to say that it is my fear of my own sexual desire for Suzanne [Diderot's heroine] that makes me propulsively individuate her as an "other" in my reading of this book' (p. 120). In the Cather piece, Sedgwick's resistance to lesbianism manifests itself less openly but is still palpable: she is interested in Cather, whom she refers to as 'the mannish lesbian author', primarily to the extent that Cather exemplifies a 'move toward a minority gay identity whose more effectual cleavage, whose more determining separatism, would be that of homo/hetero*sexual* choice rather than that of male/female *gender*' (pp. 65–6). In choosing in the story 'Paul's Case' to depict a young homosexual man sympathetically, argues Sedgwick, Cather at once performed an act of symbolic contrition for writing a hostile editorial in her youth about Oscar Wilde ('cleansing', in Sedgwick's lurid phrasing, 'her own sexual body of the carrion stench of Wilde's victimization') and provided a wholesome model of 'cross-gender liminality'. That Sedgwick prefers such 'liminality' to what she disdainfully labels 'gender separatism' (of which lesbian separatism is a sub-category) is obvious: Cather is praised, because like 'James, Proust,

Yourcenar, Compton-Burnett, Renault' and others she is part of the 'rich tradition of cross gender inventions of homosexuality of the past century' (p. 66). Sedgwick concludes with a swooning paean to Cather's *The Professor's House*, that 'gorgeous homosocial romance of two men on a mesa in New Mexico' (p. 68). Lesbian authors, it seems, are valuable here exactly to the extent that they are able to imagine and represent – what else? – male homosocial bonding. Thus the elevation of Cather, Yourcenar, Compton-Burnett and Renault (significant choices all) to an all-new lesbian pantheon: of lesbians who enjoy writing about male-male eros, triangulated or otherwise, more than its female equivalent. What is missing here is any room for the lesbian writer who *doesn't* choose to celebrate men's 'gorgeous homosocial romances' – for whom indeed such romances are anathema, precisely because they get in the way, so damagingly, of women's homosocial romances.

4 Witness one of the findings of a survey conducted by lesbian sex therapist Joanne Loulan among 1,566 lesbians between 1985 and 1987. While 80 per cent of all lesbians surveyed reported that they liked to hold hands with their partners, only 27 per cent said they felt able to hold hands in public. This 'poignant' finding, writes Loulan, is 'a statement about the oppression of lesbians in our culture. Heterosexuals assume they have the right to hold hands with their partner in public; most lesbians do not.' See Loulan, *Lesbian Passion: Loving Ourselves and Each Other* (San Francisco: Spinsters/Aunt Lute, 1987), p. 205.

5 The 'interlocking male homosocial triangles' at the end of *Shirley* can be visualized as follows:

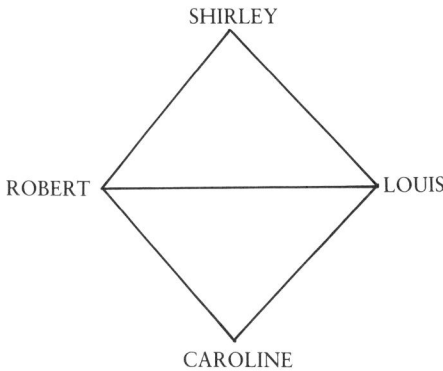

Figure 2

– in which the line linking Robert and Louis separates Caroline and Shirley. One might imagine, of course, some hypothetical renewal of erotic bonding between the two women that would recross, so to speak, the line of male bonding; but one would be on the way then to writing a lesbian 'post-marital' sequel to Brontë's novel.

6 Townsend Warner's brilliant and varied writings, many of which touch on the theme of homosexuality, have been sorely neglected since her death in 1978 – not least by gay and lesbian readers and critics. Her most enthusiastic admirer, somewhat unexpectedly, remains George Steiner, who in the pages of the *TLS* (2–8 December 1988) recently pronounced *The Corner That Held Them* a 'masterpiece' of modern English fiction. Claire Harman's recent

biography, *Sylvia Townsend Warner* (London: Chatto & Windus, 1989), will no doubt help to rectify this curious situation, as should Wendy Mulford's *This Narrow Place – Sylvia Townsend Warner and Valentine Ackland: Life, Letters and Politics, 1930–1951* (London: Pandora, 1988), a superb study of the relationship between Townsend Warner and the poet Valentine Ackland, her lover of thirty years. Also of great interest is Townsend Warner's correspondence, edited by William Maxwell (London: Chatto & Windus, 1982). Besides displaying Townsend Warner's matchless wit and unfailingly elegant style, the letters also demonstrate that she was capable of imagining Queen Victoria's sex life, even if Queen Victoria could not have imagined hers (see letter to Llewelyn Powys, 7 December 1933).

7 Townsend Warner, *Summer Will Show* (1936; London: Virago, 1987). All page numbers noted parenthetically refer to this edition.

8 George Eliot, *The Mill on the Floss*, bk. 5, ch. 4.

9 Townsend Warner, *Letters*, p. 40. Townsend Warner seems to have had Berlioz in mind – and his despairing comment on the hardships suffered by artists and musicians during the 1848 revolution – when she created the character of Guitermann, the impoverished Jewish musician befriended by Sophia late in the novel. See *The Memoirs of Hector Berlioz*, ed. and trans. David Cairns (London: Victor Gollancz, 1969), pp. 44–5.

10 Frederick Willoughby is condemned by his name on two counts of course: if his first name recalls the stooge of Flaubert's *L'Education sentimentale*, his last he shares with the unprincipled villain of Austen's *Sense and Sensibility*. In Austen's novel, we recall, the more hapless of the two heroines is abandoned by (John) Willoughby in favour of a rich heiress. To the extent that (Frederick) Willoughby – now married to his rich heiress – is himself abandoned by wife and mistress both, one might consider Warner's novel a displaced sequel to Austen's: a kind of comic postlude, or 'revenge of Marianne Dashwood'.

11 A very similar plot twist occurs, interestingly, in a novel that Townsend Warner certainly knew – and paid homage to in *Summer Will Show* – Colette's *L'Autre*, first published in 1929 and translated into English (as *The Other One*) in 1931. In Colette's novel as in Townsend Warner's, a wife and mistress discover to their mutual delight that they vastly prefer each other's company to that of the man they are supposedly competing for. Colette, it is true, does not eroticize the relationship between her two women characters as explicitly as Townsend Warner does, but her depiction of their alliance (scandalous to the husband) is exhilarating none the less. The Colettian 'wife-husband-other woman' configuration turns up again in Townsend Warner's writing, in the slyly comic short story 'An Act of Reparation' in *Stranger with a Bag* (London, Chatto and Windus 1961). Here a divorced woman named Lois accidentally meets the young, somewhat befuddled new wife of her former husband while out shopping. After the young woman confesses her anxiety about cooking, Lois goes home with her and shows her how to make oxtail stew. The husband, returning home, smugly concludes that Lois is trying to win him back by showing off her superior culinary skills; but Lois herself knows she is merely performing an 'act of reparation' to the young wife, whom she now pities, with unexpected tenderness, for being stuck with the boorish ex-husband.

12 That overtly lesbian and gay male characters often end up inhabiting the same fictional space makes a kind of theoretical as well as mimetic sense: if

the imperative toward heterosexual bonding in a fictional work is weak enough to allow one kind of homosexual bonding, chances are it will also allow the other. Two recent lesbian novels lending support to this idea are May Sarton's *Mrs. Stevens Hears the Mermaids Singing* and Jane Rule's *Memory Board*, both of which include important male homosexual characters.

13 I borrow the euphoric/dysphoric distinction from Nancy K. Miller, who in *The Heroine's Text* (New York: Columbia University Press, 1980) uses the terms to refer to the two kinds of narrative 'destiny' stereotypically available to the heroines of eighteenth- and nineteenth-century fiction. A euphoric plot, Miller argues, ends with the heroine's marriage; a dysphoric plot with her death or alienation from society. That the terms undergo a dramatic reversal in meaning when applied to lesbian fiction should be obvious: from a lesbian viewpoint, marriage can only be dysphoric in its implications; even death or alienation – if only in a metaphoric sense – may indeed seem preferable.

14 The reader may object, rightly, that the most famous lesbian novel of all, Radclyffe Hall's *The Well of Loneliness*, does not seem to fall clearly into either the euphoric or the dysphoric category. It may well be that we need to devise a new category – that of 'lesbian epic' – to contain Hall's manic-depressive extravaganza. True, in that it manages to work unhappy variations on both the pre-marital and the post-marital plot types (Stephen's first love, Angela, is a married woman who refuses to leave her husband; her second, Mary, leaves her in order to marry a male friend), *The Well of Loneliness* often leans in a dysphoric direction. Yet the introduction near the end of the novel of the Natalie Barney character, Valérie Seymour, and Hall's tentative limnings of a larger lesbian society in Paris, also seem to promise an end to Stephen's intolerable 'loneliness' – if only in some as yet ill-defined, unknown future. With its multiplying characters and sub-plots, constant shifts in setting and mood and powerfully 'ongoing' narrative structure, *The Well* seems more a kind of Homeric or Tennysonian quest-fiction – a lesbian *Odyssey* – than a novel in the ordinary sense.

15 Mulford, *This Narrow Place*, pp. 121–2.

16 That lesbian novelists have been drawn to science fiction should come as no surprise; to the degree that science fiction itself is a form of utopian fantasy, one that posits a fictional world radically different from our own, it lends itself admirably to the representation of alternative sexual structures.

DIANA COLLECOTT

What is not said: a study in textual inversion

Silences shape all speech.
> Pierre Macherey, *A Theory of Literary Production*

SILENCE = DEATH
> ACT UP (AIDS Coalition to Unleash Power) slogan, USA

What are the words you do not yet have? What do you need to say?
> Audre Lorde, 'The transformation of silence into language and action',
> *Sister Outsider*

You will not find in what I say ... any semblance of a woman whom you can love.
> Virginia Woolf, 'Reminiscences', Chapter 1, *Moments of Being*

Where does the body come in? What is the body?
> H. D., *Notes on Thought and Vision*

TURNING IN

Sexual Inversion is the second volume of Havelock Ellis's *Studies in the Psychology of Sex*, and the one which caused him most embarrassment. In the preface to the first American edition, he apologizes for publishing a study of the 'abnormal manifestations of the sexual instinct before discussing its normal manifestations', and presents this as compensatory behaviour for his own inclination to 'slur it over as an unpleasant subject'.[1] The same unease may be responsible for his stuttering insistence on the syllable *in* in his definition of *inversion* as 'the turning in of the sexual instinct towards people of the same sex' and his conclusion that this instinct is 'inborn'. Linguistic contortions such as these suggest that Ellis is teetering between the obligation to present homosexuality (of whatever kind) as unnatural and abnormal, and the awareness that this instinct 'to those persons who possess it appears natural and normal'. As a scientist he was conscious of the uncertainty principle that is active in different perceptions of the same phenomenon, and he passively incorporates this principle in his writing by citing authorities other than himself – most notably 'several persons for whom I felt respect and admiration who were the congenital subjects of this abnormality'. How is the 'normal' reader to take such statements, and is a different interpretation permissible to the reader constructed as 'abnormal' according to Ellis's pathology? Where men are the norm, are all women abnormal? Or is the 'female invert' so doubly defined by her abnormality as to be excluded from discussion?

In this same preface, Ellis demurs to the 'normal' (heterosexual male) reader when he writes: 'If I had not been able to present new facts in what is perhaps a new light, I should not feel justified in approaching the subject of sexual inversion at all.' It is tempting to imitate this doctor's presumption of objectivity and to write here as an academic, concealing my other identities as a woman and a lesbian. Yet it is as a subject conscious of the discontinuities between these positions that I write. Should my text try to 'pass' as a 'straight' essay, or turn in on itself, using deliberate word-play to subvert the pre-Freudian norms of academic discourse? Should it display its embarrassing openings to other possibilities of interpretation, or of interpenetration between different systems of meaning? What degree of co-operation can it expect from the reader, in its eccentricity, double talk, interruptions, hesitations, scholarly presentations of 'new facts'? So much turns upon the reader, whose position is – what? He . . . She. . . 'The other who knows'.[2] And if not?

LESBIAN SILENCE

Monique Wittig insists, in her Author's Note to *The Lesbian Body*, on the difference between homotextualities. Her book, she says,

> has lesbianism as its theme, that is, a theme which cannot even be described as a taboo, for it has no real existence in the history of literature. Male homosexual literature has a past, it has a present. The lesbians, for their part, are silent – just as all women are as women at all levels.[3]

Wittig's statement is as relevant now, in the late 1980s, as when it was written, in the early 1970s. During the intervening decade, many women in the academy have 'come out' as feminists, but few have come out as lesbians. Feminist critical attention to women's silences has itself been largely silent concerning the taboo on female homosexuality and its effects on literature. So long as gays pass as men and lesbians pass as feminists, heterosexism will be normative in education. This sustains a situation summed up by Adrienne Rich in 1975:

> Women's love for women has been represented almost entirely through silence and lies. . . .
>
>   Heterosexuality as an institution has also drowned in silence the erotic feelings between women. . . .[4]

The last sentence quoted here contains two words that are especially charged for lesbian writers and readers: 'silence' and 'erotic'. In the 1970s, (hetero)sexuality became a permissible subject for discourse, while (homo)sexuality was still subject to taboo. In the 1980s, a curious inversion of meaning has taken place, whereby (hetero)sexuality has been naturalized so that (homo)sexuality is marked as non-domestic and hence erotic. Yet, to reiterate Wittig, 'The lesbians, for their part, are silent': 'gay' means 'male' in most contexts, just as 'invert' means 'male' throughout most of Ellis's text. Even today, few speakers or writers on homosexuality bother to differentiate between those whom the culture constructs as men and those whom it constructs as women. The male body dominates current discussion in gay studies, while the female body is doubly deleted: is deleted as a maternal body, and as both subject and object of lesbian desire. This reduplicates the silence that Audre Lorde once broke with her cry: 'We have been raised to fear the *yes* within ourselves, our deepest cravings . . .'[5]

This situation leaves the lesbian conscious of herself as an absence from discourse, and the lesbian writer, teacher, or theorist in an historical position that does not synchronize with the relative recognition and the relative freedom of gay men to write, teach, and theorize. Wittig has suggested that 'The fascination for writing the never previously written and the fascination for the unattained body proceed from the same desire.'[6] While, under the shadow of AIDS, 'the unattained body' has become a figure of mourning for gay men, it remains a figure of absence for lesbians in most parts of the contemporary world. Let us not share the North American delusion that most lesbians are 'out', or that economic independence is not a *sine qua non* of homosexual expression. Virginia Woolf recognized these 'facts' in the 1920s. Although *A Room of One's Own* is now a canonical text for Women's Studies, few feminists are aware that in it Woolf identifies the task of articulating lesbian desire as one that involves re-reading, as well as writing in previously unknown ways:

And I began to read the book again, and read how Chloe watched Olivia put a jar on a shelf and say how it was time to go home to her children. That is a sight that has never been seen since the world began, I exclaimed. And I watched too, very curiously. For I wanted to see how Mary Carmichael set to work to catch those unrecorded gestures, those unsaid or half-said words, which form themselves, no more palpably than the shadows of moths on the ceiling, when women are alone, unlit by the capricious and coloured light of the other sex. She will need to hold her breath, I said, reading on, if she is to do it; for women are so suspicious of any interest that has not some obvious motive behind it, so terribly accustomed to concealment and suppression, that they are off at the flicker of an eye turned observingly in their direction. The only way for you to do it, I thought, addressing Mary Carmichael as if she were there, would be to talk of something else, looking steadily out of the window, and thus note, not with a pencil in a notebook, but in the shortest of shorthand, in words that are hardly syllabled yet, what happens when Olivia . . .[7]

Is this assumption of silence, this habit of 'concealment and suppression', this necessary obliquity, outmoded in most lesbians' experience of both living and writing? I suspect not, despite Adrienne Rich's confident assertion that 'it is the lesbian in us who drives us to feel imaginatively, render in language, grasp, the full connection between woman and woman.'[8] Rich writes here as an out American lesbian with a surprisingly unproblematic sense of the writer's task, and indeed of the nature of language. Both of the effective verbs in this statement can be read in a double sense. 'Drives' reads grammatically as a singular verb ('She *drives* a car'); but it can also be read ungrammatically as a plural noun (as in the 'libidinal *drives*' of popular psychology). 'Grasp' means, literally, to have direct physical contact with; figuratively, to comprehend or understand. Whether conscious or unconscious on Rich's part, these double meanings override what other writers have felt to be a gap between experience and representation. There is even a deliberate implication that, given 'full connection between woman and woman' – a connection that is presumably physical as well as symbolic – signs and their meanings will also achieve full connection.

For her part, and in her time and place, Virginia Woolf was convinced that felt or perceived experience cannot be fully rendered in words, least of all in patriarchal language. In her 'Reminiscences', Woolf addressed her nephew Julian Bell in a passage that implicitly positions itself in relation to the *Mausoleum Book* of her father and his grandfather, Leslie Stephen.

> Written words of a person who is dead or still alive tend most unfortunately to drape themselves in smooth folds annulling all evidence of life. You will not find in what I say, or again in those sincere but conventional phrases in the life of your grandfather, or in the noble lamentations with which he fills the pages of his autobio-graphy, any semblance of a woman whom you can love . . .[9]

Death marks Woolf's writing here, as it marks much writing by gay men in our time. In 'Reminiscences' Woolf mourns a lost body: the body of her mother. Her metaphor for written language turns the traditional figure of speech as dress to clothe the bare body of meaning into a shroud 'annulling all evidence of life'. By a similar inversion of meaning, the contemporary poet James Merrill, in 'Investiture at Cecconi's (for David Kalstone)', makes words perform in such a way that they represent the speaker's grieving dream for his friend.[10] Here the metaphor modulates from tailor's fitting to mourning robe. Merrill seems to be more confident than Woolf that language can convey, and not merely cover, lived experience. Yet Woolf wants 'written words' to stand for, or recover, what is lost; her passage continues:

> It has often occurred to me to regret that no one ever wrote down her

sayings and vivid ways of speech, since she had the gift of turning words in a manner peculiar to her, rubbing her hands swiftly, or raising them in gesticulation as she spoke.

Woolf's own style turns here, from the 'conventional phrases' she associates with her father ('It has often occurred to me', etc.), to her mother's 'peculiar' manner of expression. As she recalls her mother's 'vivid ways of speech', her mother's actions become vivid too; articulation joins with 'gesticulation' and both manner and movement enter the writing: 'turning words . . . rubbing her hands . . . or raising them . . . as she spoke'. Thus written words are the means by which the mother's body is recovered, or at least represented, in the daughter's text. But the gestures of Julia Stephen also mark Virginia Woolf's recognition that words are only signs and that the body, though not 'annulled', is indeed lost.

DIFFERENCE = SAMENESS

In the title essay of her volume, *In Search of Our Mother's Gardens*, Alice Walker criticizes Virginia Woolf for omitting, from her discussion of women's freedom to write, any consideration of women bound to silence by slavery and racial as well as economic oppression.[11] In the face of such facts as the history of African-American women, we are justified in affirming what Adrienne Rich called 'the lesbian continuum', or should we focus on discontinuity, the absence of a universal lesbian identity? Ann Ferguson has suggested that, given differences of class and race, as well as historical differences, lesbians can be defined only by their opposition to the cultural norms of their time and place.[12]

Audre Lorde's memoir, *Zami: A New Spelling of My Name*, is a text vitally aware of its own oppositionality to the representative tradition of African-American autobiography. Moreover, its subject – the author's experience as a Black lesbian in New York in the 1950s and 1960s – defines itself through verbal and epistemological oppositions. Mapping the contradictions of her life as a student at Hunter College, and in Manhattan's lesbian bars, Lorde writes:

> Downtown in the gay bars I was a closet student and an invisible Black. Uptown at Hunter I was a closet dyke and a general intruder. . .[13]

This double life, with its different silences, is recalled in language that doubles back on itself in punning repetition:

> Lesbians were probably the only Black and white women in New York City in the fifties who were making any real attempt to communicate with each other; we learned *lessons* from each other, the values of which were not *lessened* by what we did not learn. (my italics)[14]

Another passage recalling the gay-girls' bars of Greenwich Village is curiously reminiscent of Woolf's English fantasy of Chloe and Olivia:

Sometimes we'd pass Black women on Eighth Street – *the invisible but visible sisters* – or in the Bag or at Laurel's, and our glances might cross, but we never looked into each other's eyes. We acknowledged our kinship by passing in silence, looking the other way. Still, we were always on the lookout, Flee and I, for that tell-tale flick of the eye, that certain otherwise prohibited openness of expression, that definiteness of voice which would suggest, I think she's gay. *After all, doesn't it take one to know one?* (author's italics)[15]

Here African-American practices of double-talk come into play. The verb 'to pass' is a key-word, denoting mere passing in the street as well as the significant transition from Uptown (Black) to Downtown (White) Manhattan. For light-skinned 'blacks' who could *pass* as 'white', this was the traditional route to economic and social betterment: Nella Larsen's novella *Passing* counts the cost of such a transition across the colour line, for a woman who must deny kinship with her darker sister to sustain the fiction that she herself is white.[16] By contrast, Lorde's sisters 'acknowledged our kinship by passing in silence'. This inversion of usual social behaviour is introduced by a contradiction: 'the invisible but visible sisters' which compacts several levels of meaning. It reminds the reader that Black women are visible in the white community, while treated as invisible. So such sisters are women whose racial difference is marked by colour, while their sexual difference is unmarked, because perceived (both inside and outside the Black community) as more dangerous: so dangerous that the women cannot acknowledge it even to each other. Nevertheless, where Woolf writes of the 'half-said words' of women who are 'off at the flicker of an eye turned observingly in their direction', Lorde records a paradoxical 'openness of expression' and 'definiteness of voice' between women whose shared identity as lesbians was otherwise suppressed.

In a later polemical essay, Lorde recalls this chilling 'message . . . to Black women from Black men': 'if you want me, you'd better stay in your place which is away from one another, or I will call you "lesbian" and wipe you out'.[17] The fear of being 'wiped-out' is taken into much lesbian writing and may account for many of its self-contradictions and obliquities. But when this fear is counterbalanced by lesbian desire, in works like *Zami* or the poetry of Gertrude Stein, it accounts for the erotics of these texts: their word-play, subversion of grammatical rules, resistance to literal reading or single-minded interpretation.

Black American speech has a rich range of practices known as *signifyin'*, which include opposite meanings for common words; hence, as fans of Michael Jackson know, 'bad' means 'good'.[18] The poet and polemicist June Jordan has defended Black English as distinctly different from White English, and equally valid for written use, including literary expression. She demonstrates this in her poem 'Getting Down to get Over (dedicated to my mother)' by signifyin' on idioms such as White Welfare jargon and Black Brother talk.[19] A poem like this requires diachronic as well as synchronic reading: it includes history, and obliges the reader to recognize that, historically, signifyin' has been a form of indirect or silent speech used by a people powerless within a particular cultural economy. Slaves, women, homosexuals, oppressed ethnic and religious groups, have always used forms of double-talk to elude punishment, censorship, or mere ridicule. Such talk can be interpreted only by another who is also 'other' – in Sedgwick's phrase 'the other who knows', for , in Lorde's inversion of the heterosexist sneer, 'doesn't it take one to know one?'

In the prose of *Zami*, Lorde is both more explicit about the political context of her writing, and more relaxed in her use of figures of speech, than Jordan is in her poem. However, a longer quotation from *Zami* will allow Lorde's text to speak with its own urgency.

> In the gay bars, I longed for other Black women without the need ever taking shape on my lips. For four hundred years in this country, Black women have been taught to view each other with deep suspicion. It was no different in the gay world.
>
> Most Black lesbians were closeted, correctly recognizing the Black community's lack of interest in our position, as well as the many more immediate threats to our survival as Black people in a racist society. It was hard enough to be Black, to be Black and female, to be Black, female and gay. To be Black, female, gay, and out of the closet . . . was considered by many Black lesbians to be suicidal . . .[20]

The alternative to individual suicide, as Lorde presents it, is a shared sense of difference. Her emphatic statement '*We were different*' is reiterated in a chant, preparing the reader for the writer's discovery of another Black woman whom she can love. 'We were different' is a complex statement, signifying two kinds of difference (between 'Black' and 'white' women, and between homosexual and heterosexual Black women); it also signifies sameness (between Black women, and between homosexual women), so that 'difference' is a sign of otherness that can be shared. Thus difference of colour may unite Black Women of different sexual orientation, while another difference unites lovers of the same sex. This paradoxical sense of sameness within alienation is enforced by Lorde's repeated use of two phrases, 'each other's' [*sic*] and 'our own' in the following passage:

> The Black gay-girls in the Village gay bars of the fifties knew each other's names, but we seldom looked into each other's Black eyes, lest we see our own aloneness and our own blunted power mirrored in the pursuit of darkness.[21]

Her witty expression 'the pursuit of darkness' may well have Conrad's colonialist depiction of Africa in the corner of its eye. It plays on conventional notions of otherness: the general cultural association of blackness with evil, and the specific cultural association of lesbianism with witchcraft and proscribed desires. Recovering her longing for other Black women from the denigration of racists, anthropologists, and sexologists, Lorde celebrates difference as sameness, and renames herself as a lesbian whose African heritage validates female power and spirituality. Moreover, the passages that re-present, in 'written words', Zami's love-making with Black women, consciously use incantatory rhythms and expressions associated with witchcraft. In one of these passages, the triple repetition of 'each other' provides the kind of override that Rich experienced in language charged with lesbian desire:

> *Our bodies met again, each surface touched with each other's flame, from the tips of our curled toes to our tongues, and locked into our own wild rhythms, we rode each other across the thundering space, dripped like light from the peak of each other's tongue . . .* (author's italics)[22]

In the climactic description of Zami's love for Afrekete, the trope of witchcraft is even more explicit. Introducing the 'crossroads' as a traditional sign of intersection between natural and supernatural powers, Lorde recalls the transition between Uptown and Downtown that was reversed when she met this Black female lover, and turns her words into a ritual of exorcism:

> *I remember the full moon like white pupils in the center of your wild irises. . . .*
>
> *Afrekete, Afrekete, ride me to the crossroads where we shall sleep, coated in the woman's power. The sound of our bodies meeting is the prayer of all strangers and sisters, that the discarded evils, abandoned at all crossroads, will not follow us upon our journey.* (author's italics)[23]

COMING OUT

On the last weekend of October, 1989, the Lesbian and Gay Studies Center at Yale University held its third annual conference, this time entitled 'Outside/Inside'. Over 500 people attended – perhaps four times as many men as women. They included scholars from other American universities and gay activists from New York. On the first evening of the conference, most participants were watching Vito Russo's *The Celluloid Closet*, while a member of ACT UP was in the Yale Law School putting up posters for a presentation scheduled for the next day. A woman teacher at the Law School (who was not attending the conference) saw these genitally explicit posters and reported them to the Yale police as 'obscene'. The Yale Police arrested the man responsible, and when members of the film audience protested at the arrest, they called in the New Haven police and eight more men were arrested. Bystanders, as well as those taken to the police station, were subjected to verbal and physical harrassment by the police. All those arrested were charged with breach of the peace and 'interfering' with a police officer in the course of his duty.

A statement issued by the Lesbian and Gay Studies Center concluded:

> The threat of violence we live with every day was realized in an instant

in the middle of the street. Gay people assaulted and taken prisoner for bringing their sex to light and for voicing anger.

The President of Yale, called to account for the action of the University's own security corps, promised to hold an inquiry and blandly defended the rights of homosexuals to freedom of expression. A slip of the tongue – he referred to 'lays and gesbians' – hinted at his own difficulties with this concept. A week passed during which those arrested appeared in court in New Haven with full media coverage and were released on bail pending trial. Unidentified sympathizers with the police posted the Yale campus with the slogan, 'When gays act up, lock 'em up.'

On the Friday after the conference, a rally was held by the core of active lesbians and gays who remained on campus; no gay members of the University staff who had participated in the conference attended. Cameras and reporters from local and national TV networks were present. The rally was held in front of the President's office on Beinecke Plaza, right outside the library in which I was writing this article. I stopped writing to join in; we listened to speeches urging the President to 'come out' and make good the University's stated policy of non-discrimination. We applauded the students who insisted that the issue was our own bodies, our right to exist as gay or bisexual women and men. And we chanted slogans: 'Lesbian, lesbian, gay, gay/ These words aren't so hard to say'; 'Hey, hey hey, ho, ho ho,/ Homophobia's got to go'; 'No more violence/ End the silence.' Most of us now wore badges showing a pink triangle on a black ground and the legend 'SILENCE = DEATH'.

A week later, there was a further court appearance in New Haven, and the charges against all nine of those arrested were dropped. The *Yale News* published a lengthy self-justification from the woman teacher who had complained about the posters, and the University released a transcript of her taped telephone conversation with the police which exposed the homophobia she denied. The President and his publicity officers held a press conference with one eye on the University's reputation for freedom of expression and inquiry, one on feminist protests against pornography and both on homophobic alumni on whom it depended for endowment. Dismissing the demand of the Lesbian and Gay Studies Center that the police of both forces involved in the action be disciplined or fired, the President and the local Chief of Police agreed to some form of 'sensitivity training' for their men, and announced that the uniforms of the Yale Police would in future be of a different colour to distinguish them from the New Haven police.

'LOVE POEM'

For literate women of my generation, either inside or outside the academy, who came alive to both lesbianism and feminism in the 1970s, two Americans were deeply influential: Audre Lorde and Adrienne Rich. In their essays and speeches, they made statements that were 'hardly syllabled yet' in our conscious minds, and formulated questions that we did not dare to utter. Such is Rich's statement about her earlier poetry: 'I hadn't found the courage yet to do without authorities, or even to use the pronoun "I"';[24] or Lorde's challenge to other women-oriented women: 'What are the words you do not yet have? What do you need to say?'[25] In their different ways, they placed both feminism and lesbianism within a political arena and radicalized our understanding of the institutions of racism and heterosexism. Rich's book *On Lies, Secrets and Silence* inspired many of us to revise our own lives, and the lives and works of earlier women writers. Her own poetry – for instance, the sequence 'Twenty-one Love Poems' – created a context for the rereading of poets as diverse as Emily Dickinson and H. D. Lorde's exploration, in *Sister Outsider*, of the oppositions black/white, female/male, gay/straight was a polemical matrix for her own poetry.

Sister Outsider contains a conversation between Audre Lorde and Adrienne Rich which is also a record of Lorde's coming out as a 'Black lesbian poet'.[26] She connects this historic moment with the power of speech:

> Speaking up was a protective mechanism for myself – like publishing 'Love Poem' in *Ms* magazine in 1971 and bringing it in and putting it on the wall of the English Department.[27]

Notably, the poem appeared in a feminist magazine, but not in Lorde's next volume of poetry, *From a Land Where Other People Live* (1973). She tells Rich:

> My publisher called and literally said he didn't understand the words of 'Love Poem'. He said, 'Now what is this all about? Are you supposed to be a man?' And he was a poet! And I said, 'No, I'm loving a woman.'[28]

This example of 'speaking up' remains ambiguous: the speaker's 'I' can refer to either sex, unless uttered in a female voice. This is also the case with Lorde's 'Love Poem', which is explicit about the sex of the person loved but masks the sex of the lover under a neutral pronoun. It is this masking that the male publisher exploits, concealing his distaste for a woman loving a woman under a cover of what? Subjective misunderstanding or covertly objective critique? The result is the same: censorship.

Is self-censorship already present in Lorde's decision, as a Black lesbian, to write in the anonymous tradition of white male lyricism? Love poems have, for centuries, been addressed from 'I' to 'you', with the sex of both partners unidentified. Masculist traditions of interpretation assume that the poet or speaking subject is male, and the beloved object is female, unless there is internal evidence to the contrary. Heterosexism must also account for the sex-changing of names in nineteenth-century translations of Sappho, and the suppression of Shakespeare's homoeroticism. Yet it is these very conventions that have allowed homosexual writers to publish love poems with impunity. Few teachers discuss the gender of W. H.

Auden's lover in 'Lay your sleeping head my love', or mention Amy Lowell's masculine impersonation in her love poems to Ada Russell. Contextual information of this kind has often been concealed by the writers themselves: Lowell's will instructed Russell to burn her love letters.[29] By contrast, Audre Lorde's autobiography *Zami: A New Spelling of My Name*, offers a context in which her 'Love Poem' must be understood – differently. Here is the full text of the poem:

> Speak earth and bless me with what is richest
> make sky flow honey out of my hips
> rigid as mountains
> spread over a valley
> carved by the mouth of rain.
>
> And I knew when I entered her I was
> high wind in her forests hollow
> fingers whispering sound
> honey flowed
> from the split cup
> impaled on a lance of tongues
> on the tips of her breasts on her navel
> and my breath
> howling into her entrances
> through lungs of pain.
>
> Greedy as herring-gulls
> or a child
> I swing out over the earth
> over and over
> again.[30]

When the lesbian context of this poem is not suppressed but assumed, details that might be misunderstood leap into meaning. The words 'I entered her', which must have disturbed Lorde's publisher, take their place in a pattern of spatial metaphors that maps the female body: '*sky . . . mountains . . . valley . . . forests . . .*'; '*hips . . . mouth . . . fingers . . . tongues . . . breasts . . . navel . . .*'.[31] The descriptions in the first stanza, which precede 'I entered her', must refer to the body of the woman speaking ('I'), and those which follow must refer to the body of the woman loved ('her'). The poem's meaning – and the reader's confusion – arise from the fact that these are, in a sense, the *same* body. Lorde's ecstatic last stanza reinforces this, reminding us in a mere simile ('Greedy . . . as a child') that this same body is the maternal body, the 'earth' from which we come and from which we are freed in love.

TEXT/ CONTEXT/ INTERTEXT

The term 'lesbian context' has an extended meaning, beyond the biography of the writer. It brings into play writings by other lesbians, whether covert or overt, indeed any writing by women that gets its energy from erotic attraction between women. Hence Lorde's metaphors resonate unintentionally with those of Amy Lowell's poetic sequence 'Two Speak Together', as well as with the texts of poems by contemporaries such as Adrienne Rich and Olga Broumas. Moreover, when her 'Love Poem' is brought together with Monique Wittig's *The Lesbian Body*, the lesbian reader will recognize a shared eroticism that the heterosexual reader might categorize as violence. This body of material provides a common matrix for new lesbian writing, and for older writing by homosexual or bisexual women that has survived – often in isolation from its significant others. Indeed, the publication of contemporary lesbian poetry in the 1970s was part of a coming-out process for writings whose homotextuality was forgotten or unknown.

In 1982, when Audre Lorde's 'Love Poem' appeared in her first important selection, H. D.'s poem 'I Said' was printed for the first time, some twenty years after the poet's death.[32] It had been written in 1919 and inscribed 'To W. B.', that is, to Winifred Bryher, the young British writer who had fallen in love with H. D. the previous year. In 1919, aged twenty-five, Bryher was working on her first autobiographical novel, *Development*, and trying desperately to free herself from her parents in order to establish her own identity. In the same year, both H. D. and Bryher separately consulted Havelock Ellis about their sexuality. By the winter of 1919, when H. D.'s poem was written, Bryher had threatened suicide: a form of self-silencing still chosen by many homosexual men and women. 'I Said' is H. D.'s response to that threat – a threat specifically addressed to her as the beloved who must save W. B. from death in one form or another.[33]

As it is now presented to us, in the 1983 edition of H. D.'s *Collected Poems, 1912–1944*, 'I Said' is detached from this history. At the back of the book, an editorial note simply states that earlier typescripts are entitled 'To W. B.' In fact, these initials encode part of the history: they reflect the gender-free signature over which Hilda Doolittle chose to publish, and mark a stage in Winifred Ellerman's transition from her family name to her adoption by deed-poll of the pen-name Bryher. In 1920, *Poetry* published a trio of love poems under the title 'Hellenics' by 'W. Bryher': this 'new spelling' of her name will have concealed the poems' Sapphic content from readers who missed an editorial note mentioning the visit to America of 'Miss Bryher and H. D. (Mrs. Richard Aldington)'.[34] Earlier that year, the two women had visited Greece together, accompanied as far as Athens by Havelock Ellis.[35]

Why do I trouble you, my reader, with such 'new facts'? Is it to remind us, as scholars and textual critics, of our own responsibilities for 'concealment and suppression'? Is it because the facts disturb me – like the phone call threatening suicide that tore me from the library where I wrote this? What are the critical implications of reinserting this poem in its lesbian contexts: the contexts of actual lives, then and now, and the literary contexts? In an attempt to respond to these questions, I want to postpone quotation from 'I Said', in order to consider further the problem of 'What is not said'.[36]

In his *A Theory of Literary Production*, Pierre Macherey argues that what is important in a literary work is 'what [it] cannot say'; he urges the reader to 'investigate the silence' behind the work, to ask ourselves:

> Can we make this silence speak? What is the unspoken saying? . . . To what extent can dissimulation be a way of speaking? Can something that has hidden itself be recalled to our presence?[37]

Macherey's theory was formulated for consideration of unconscious suppression. Does it have any application to the deliberate dissimulation of homosexual writers, and the condition of silence which the taboo on homosexual activity forces on their readers? Its usefulness, surely, is in drawing our attention to contradictions between what is said and what is not said in a given literary text. For Macherey, the signs of such contradictions will be, precisely, silence and dissimulation, and his method of interrogating these silences involves a shift to an ideological intertext where the 'unspoken' speaks.

We have already seen how Virginia Woolf, as imaginary reader of Mary Carmichael's as yet unwritten text, conspires with her to create a space for 'words that are hardly syllabled yet'. For Woolf, the markers of this joint enterprise between writer and reader will be a necessary obliquity: in writing of Chloe and Olivia, Carmichael will have to 'hold her breath', 'talk of something else' and use 'the shortest of shorthand'. For Michael Riffaterre, as for Woolf and Macherey, the reader has a crucial role in producing meaning. Riffaterre identifies the reader as 'the only one who makes the connections between text, interpretant and intertext', and he defines *intertext* as: 'any one of the various matrices that is active in the writing of a passage and vital to the reading of it'.[38] The word *matrix*, with its connotations of the maternal womb, is a resonant one for women readers, and especially those influenced by Julia Kristeva's claim that 'pregnancy still constitutes the ultimate limit of meaning'.[39] In the passage from *A Room of One's Own* cited above, Woolf substitutes for Kristeva's 'archaic . . . mother', an archetypal woman writer named Mary: it is she who is entrusted to record the love of Chloe for Olivia, which exists as yet only in Woolf's text. Some readers will identify the lost maternal body of Woolf's 'Reminiscences' as the intertextual matrix of all her writings, the matrix capable of almost endless extension.

The implications of this way of thinking are so extensive that I want to take them up in another essay on literary (re)production and lesbian collaboration. What matters here is how far the concept 'intertext' will stretch. If, as Catharine Stimpson has so nicely stated, 'Lesbianism partakes of the body', then the matrices of lesbian writing must embrace what have been described as 'the intertexts of relation and desire'.[40] An intertextual approach to lesbian texts thus requires us to acknowledge the silences within society's 'heterosexual presumption', and to acquire forbidden knowledge of writers' lives. It also requires a revision of reading practices, and especially the New Critical convention that a literary text contains within itself all the information necessary to its interpretation.

Where Macherey focuses on ideological contradictions between a text and its matrix, Riffaterre introduces the idea of the *ungrammatical*, arguing that 'any ungrammaticality within the poem is a sign of grammaticality elsewhere'. He goes on to say that this half-hidden relationship between the 'textually grammatical' and the 'intertextually ungrammatical' is so disturbing that 'the reader continually seeks relief by getting away from the dubious words, back to safe reality (or to a social consensus as to reality)'.[41] With texts like Audre Lorde's 'Love Poem' or H. D.'s 'I Said', such a retreat to safety is only done at the cost of reinforcing the social taboo on lesbian identity: the alternative, for readers and editors, is to encounter meaninglessness, as lesbians must in their daily existence. However, once such poems are identified as intertexts for each other, their contradictions and instances of ungrammaticality may, paradoxically become meaningful.

'I SAID'

H. D.'s poem 'I Said' has more fugitive intertexts than Lorde's poem: these include letters between Bryher, H. D. and their friends, including Havelock Ellis, and unpublished prose and poetry found among Bryher's papers after her death.[42] In Bryher's fictional versions, the same episode is replayed in dialogues between two shifting characters: the lover's death-threat and the response of the beloved. In H. D.'s poetry, we find high rhetoric in place of naturalistic prose; this is the opening stanza of the four-part poem:

> I said:
> 'think how Hymettus pours divine honey,
> think how dawn vies
> in the shelter of Hymettus,
> with the clusters of field-violet,
> (rill on rill of violets!
> parted and crested fire!)
> think of Hymettus
> and the tufted spire of thyme,
> hyacinth, wild wind-flower,
> think of Hymettus
> beyond mist,' I said, 'and rain,'
> and you,
> ''twere better, better being dead.'[43]

The repeated Greek name, (Mount) Hymettus, is a key to this stanza's patterns of assonance, and a means of displacing the drama from its actual context. When it is set aside, we find here elements that are also present in Lorde's 'Love Poem': *mountain . . . honey . . . rain*. These suggest a shared physical intertext, acknowleged only as landscape in H. D.'s poem. In 'Love Poem', metaphor is used to reveal rather than to conceal erotic experience; in 'I Said', breathless metonymies hint at what is not said. Thus, in a different lesbian poem, the same signs may mark what Macherey calls 'dissimulation as a way of speaking'.

To hear what the 'unspoken' is saying in this poem, we must attend to ruptures or interruptions; for instance, the abrupt parenthesis – '(rill on rill of violets!/ parted and crested fire!)' – makes a rift in the text as if the mountain itself were breaking open like a volcano. H. D. was aware, from her reading of Pausanias' *Guide to Greece*, that Mount Hymettos is renowned for its flowers and honey-bees. She also thought it was an extinct volcano; an early holograph version of these lines reads: 'in the *crater* of Hymettus, rill on rill of violets – parted fire . . .' [my italics].[44] In the final version, the exclamation marks draw attention to the break in syntax, and we seem to be in the presence of metaphors for the female genitals rather than celebrations of an absent Greek landscape. 'Every peak is a crater. This is the law of volcanoes,' writes Adrienne Rich, 'making them eternally and visibly female.'[45] In later poetry, H. D. will syllable her sexuality in lines like these:

I did not know how to differentiate
between volcanic desire
anemones like embers
and purple fire
of violets
like red heat
and the cold
silver
of her feet . . .[46]

Flower imagery has been used by both men and women to encode eroticism; it is essential to H. D.'s earlier poetry, and connects it with the tradition of homoerotic 'decadence' represented in England by A. C. Swinburne and Oscar Wilde: 'They talked of Greeks and flowers' is her veiled comment on these writers in the novel *Asphodel*, whose own title pays tribute to the Victorian classicism of W. S. Landor. Ros Carroll comments on H. D.'s use of the term 'Lesbian iris' in her essay on Sappho:

The flower is both a metaphor for something which cannot be named, and a signifier for something that H. D. dare not name, not only because of social prohibition, but because it touches upon her own deepest fears, H. D. has absorbed the connections . . . between witchcraft, lesbianism and hysteria, all associated in some way with 'excessive sexual drive'.[47]

If H. D.'s fears about her own sexual desires and sexual ambivalence, reinforced by Ellis's pathological account of the female 'invert', act as unconscious censors on what is said, she is also skilful in consciously constructing a hermetic discourse that will contain meanings not stated in her text. In the lines from 'I Said' quoted above, two words of Greek origin stand out: *Hymettus* and *hyacinth*; they share a common first syllable, and 'hyacinth' can be read, like 'Hymettus', as a proper name. As a mere flower-name it is 'textually grammatical' with the poetic description of place; as the name of the beautiful young man with whom the god Apollo was in love, it directs the reader to a homosexual intertext that resonates in complex ways with the occasion of H. D.'s poem. In Greek legend, Hyacinth was killed, either accidentally or because of Zephyr's jealousy, by a wind-blown discus thrown by Apollo. In Farnell's *Cults of the Greek States*, which H. D. was reading along with Pausanias in 1919, Hyakinthos is identified as a vegetative divinity, like Kore or Adonis; his hero cult was celebrated each spring with flowers and mourning songs. This knowledge enlarges the meaning of the line ''twere better, better being dead', by covertly introducing the idea of rebirth and the theme of heroic death.

Both ideas are present in the second stanza of the poem, where the speaker continues:

> 'But what grave heart,' I said,
> 'of beauty dies if you die:
> at Marathon there bled
> souls such as yours,
> such souls as yours
> stained those pale violets red,
> her violets beyond Athens . . .'

The intertextual matrix of these lines includes the myths of both Hyacinth and Adonis, whose blood was shed as a result of passionate entanglements. The blood of Adonis sprang up as anemones, while Hyacinth's marked the wild iris with Greek letters spelling out his suffering: *ai ai*. In 1918, Bryher published her own translation of Bion's *Lament for Adonis*. Here is a heterosexual text offering florid versions of the same tropes that H. D. will use in 'I Said'; In Bion's poem, it is Aphrodite who mourns, the young man lost to love:

> The Paphian weeps as Adonis bleeds and blood and tears change to flowers upon the earth. Roses are born out of the blood but the tears are windflowers . . .[48]

'Windflowers' follow 'hyacinth' in H. D.'s poem, either through unconscious association with the wind-blown discus, or because Greek poets such as Sappho and Ibycus connect Eros with flowers and liken him to a sudden wind, that shakes the lover's limbs. H. D.'s 'purple hyacinth' ('Heliodora') is not the cultivated species, but the wild Greek iris. Lorde, too, may have the 'Lesbian iris' in mind, when she puns on the 'wild irises' of her lover's eyes. If so, she may also share with H. D. this image of Sappho's: '. . . as the shepherd men trample the hyacinth on the mountain with their feet, and on the ground the purple flower.' H. D. turned this fragment into a description of Sappho's poetic style that alludes to her actual writing: 'violets, purple woof of cloth, scarlet garments . . . the lurid, crushed and perished hyacinth, stains on cloth and flesh and parchment'.[49] Flowers were not only strewn on the graves of men and heroes; they were worn, according to Farnell, as signs of the earth-mother, signifying birth as well as death. Their juices stain like ink or menstrual blood; their petals bruise like passionate flesh, 'lurid' in H. D.'s version of Sappho, as in the writings of Lorde and Wittig, as in the 'hyacinths like famished kisses' in the autobiographical prose of *Asphodel*.

Hyacinth and Adonis are both figures of eternal youth; indeed, Farnell tells us that the word *hyakinthos* 'in form and meaning corresponds to our word "young"'.[50] Dying, they re-enter the earth, like heroes killed in battle, and like their female counterpart, Kore, who returns with the flowers each spring to Demeter her mother. H. D.'s later poem, 'The Mysteries', celebrates the seasonal cycle of death and rebirth with imagery drawn from the rites of Adonis:

the grain
lifts its bright spear-head
to the sun again;
behold,
behold,
the dead
are no more dead . . .[51]

The word 'spear-head' is common to this poem and 'I Said', where it refers to Athene's weapon, 'glittering' at the head of the Athenian army and responsible for their victory at Marathon. Athene Nike is the unnamed she of the line 'her violets beyond Athens', and the goddess whom H. D. identifies elsewhere as 'my own especial sign or hieroglyph'.[52] In this way, Greek myth and legend are serving H. D. as what Woolf called 'the shortest of shorthand': signs or hieroglyphs poised between the text and its concealed intertexts.

Another such sign is the place-name Marathon. If *Hymettus* evokes the Greek world in an ideal serenity, *Marathon* is a site of struggle: the battleground where the Athenian spearsmen defended Greece against a vaster army of invading Persians. Marathon is remembered in English as the name of a foot-race that commemorated the endurance of the solitary runner who carried the news of the victory to Athens, then died of exhaustion. In H. D.'s poem the word connotes victorious resistance, heroic death, and *brotherhood*. When she wrote the poem, the 1914–18 war, in which she lost her dearest brother, was only just over. Even when they hated modern warfare, women envied serving soldiers' close bonds with their own sex, their youthful high-mindedness. War is idealized in H. D.'s references to Marathon so that the poet can praise W. B. for her courage and self-sacrifice. Here her literary intertext is the *Persae* of

Aeschylus, himself said to have been wounded at the battle of Marathon, and defeated by Simonides of Ceos in the poetry competition to celebrate the victory. Poetry, too, may be a site of struggle.

The struggle of 'I Said' is between W. B.'s denial of her own courage ('"I am no Greek", you said') and H. D.'s insistence that there is heroism in resistance to social pressures. In her reply to the suicidal younger woman, the overt target is philistinism, but she covertly implies that living as a lesbian involves an inversion of heterosexual values, a re-reading of words and meanings. Under such conditions, 'lies' may be 'true':

> . . . it seems to me Greek rather
> to live as you lived,
> outwardly telling lies,
> inwardly without swerving or doubt –
> 'if I can not have beauty about me
> and people of my own sort,
> I will not live,
> I will not compromise' –
> and though I have heard many people
> talk about life
> and the indubitable comfort of being dead,
> your words alone of them all
> rang unutterably true,
> you meant what you said.

This affirmation brings the second section of 'I Said' to a climax which is also the mid-point of the poem:

> anyone to-day who can contemplate
> the idea of death, abstract death,
> (romantic though he be,
> young without doubt, mad perhaps)
> anyone to-day who can die for beauty,
> (even though it be mere romance
> or a youthful geste)
> is and must be my brother.

The use of masculine pronouns here, not to speak of the expression 'my brother', is grammatical with the poem's celebration of masculine heroism, but confusing to the reader aware of its lesbian intertext, as the neutral pronouns 'I' and 'you' are not. Readers of H. D. will recall actual ungrammaticality in poems like 'Amaranth' of the same period, where names and pronouns have been changed from version to version, so that the outcome is an apparently heterosexual text, like some Latin translations of Sappho. Is the sudden presence of masculine referents in 'I Said' due to confusion of gender-identity on the poet's part, or to deliberate dissimulation? If dissimulation, is it comparable to the fugitive fictional versions of this conversation in which Bryher presents herself alternately as a young woman ('Nancy') or a young man ('Ernest'), choosing in each case names with 'queer' or Wildean overtones?[53] H. D., at the rhetorical climax of her poem, seems to be endorsing Bryher's desire to be a man, while diverting Bryher's desire for herself into a fantasy of male fellowship. This form of double-talk is marked by further ruptures in the text, in the form of two parentheses, each of which contains the uneasy conditional 'though':

> (romantic though he be
> young without doubt, mad perhaps)

and

> (even though it be mere romance
> or a youthful geste)

In effect, these lines are less an endorsement of masculine heroism than a questioning of its premises; the brackets seem to mark spaces for the speaker's doubt, while the obscure word 'geste' is disturbing in this context. In one of the typescripts of the poem, which Bryher herself preserved, it is italicized and spelt *jeste*.[54] We seem to be in the presence of one of H. D.'s inspired bilingual puns. Her posthumous male editor has opted for the single meaning that is most coherent with the rest of the text: an anglicized version of French *geste*, that is an heroic poem, but one in the Romantic rather than the Classical tradition. Yet H. D.'s original ambiguous spelling or mis-spelling catches many meanings in a knot, exemplifying Macherey's idea of the unconscious element in a literary work, and Riffaterre's notion of ungrammaticality. In English, a *jest* is something said or done for amusement, but it may also be an object of derision or a laughing-stock. In French, *geste* means gesture or movement, as well as act or deed; it can be an heroic act or a despicable deed. In either language, then, the word is a sign looking two ways, signifying approval or disapproval, acceptance or threat, joy or fear. Thus the word *jeste*, as H. D. spells it, marks the semantic insecurities of the lesbian context of 'I Said'. Hidden within it is the ambivalent position of homosexuals in a heterosexist society, and the doubly ambivalent position of homosexual women in a sexist society. This is no laughing matter, as suicides show, but a matter of life and death. Yet H. D.'s use of this odd word is playful, inviting the reader to read the text in several ways and to address the contradictions of her lover's position. By referring to 'mere romance or youthful geste' she hints at W. B.'s immaturity, while also gesturing at the doomed heroic themes of the *chansons de geste*. The poem's title may seem to refer to one side of the dialogue, but a more complex statement is made by the entire text. The reader can attend to this only by listening to what is not said, and by being alert to what Riffaterre describes as 'the transformation of texts into larger wholes'.

University of Durham

An earlier version of this article, entitled 'What is not said: Lesbian texts and contexts', was presented at the Conference of the Higher Education Teachers of English at the University of Kent in 1987. I am indebted to Kate Flint and Maggie Humm for that opportunity, and to Elaine Hobby and Chris White for subsequent discussions. I developed the article while on research leave from the University of Durham, holding the Donald C. Gallup Fellowship in American Literature at the Beinecke Library, Yale University. I want to thank Wayne Koestenbaum and other participants in the eventful Conference on Lesbian and Gay Studies held at Yale in 1989, who have informed my thinking on this otherwise unthinkable subject. Above all, I am grateful to Sandi Russell for sharing African-American literature with me, and to Joseph Bristow for his patience and encouragement.

1 Havelock Ellis, *Sexual Inversion* (Philadelphia: F. A. Davis, 1901), p. v.
2 Eve Kosofsky Sedgwick, 'Denaturalizing heterosexuality', Third Annual Conference, Lesbian and Gay Studies Center, Yale University, 1989.
3 Monique Wittig, 'Author's Note', *The Lesbian Body*, trans. David Le Vay (New York: Avon Books, 1978), p. ix. Originally published in French as *Le Corps lesbien*, 1973.
4 Adrienne Rich, 'Women and honour: some notes on lying', in *On Lies, Secrets and Silence: Selected Prose, 1966–1978* (London: Virago, 1980), p. 190.
5 Audre Lorde, 'Uses of the erotic: the erotic as power', in *Sister Outsider: Essays and Speeches* (Trumansburg, New York: The Crossing Press, 1984), p. 57. Presented to the Fourth Berkshire Conference on the History of Women, 1978.
6 *The Lesbian Body*, p. x.
7 Virginia Woolf, *A Room of One's Own* (Harmondsworth: Penguin Books, 1945), ch. 5, p. 84. Based on papers presented at Newnham and Girton Colleges, Cambridge, in 1928.
8 Adrienne Rich, 'It is the lesbian in us . . .', in *On Lies, Secrets and Silence*, p. 201. Presented at the MLA Convention, 1976.
9 Virginia Woolf, 'Reminiscences', in *Moments of Being: Unpublished Autobiographical Writings*, ed. Jeanne Schulkind (St Albans: Triad/Panther Books, 1978), pp. 41–42. Subsequent quotation from the same passage. Schulkind says that 'Reminiscences' was begun in 1907.
10 James Merrill, *The Inner Room: Poems* (New York: Alfred A. Knopf, 1988), p. 92.
11 Alice Walker, title essay, *In Search of Our Mothers' Gardens: Womanist Prose* (London: Women's Press, 1984), p. 235.
12 Ann Ferguson, 'Is there a lesbian culture?', Third Annual Conference, Lesbian and Gay Studies Center, Yale University, 1989.
13 Audre Lorde, *Zami: A New Spelling of My Name* (Trumansburg, New York: The Crossing Press, 1983), p. 179. Lorde identifies 'Zami' as 'a Carriacou name for women who work together as friends and lovers'.
14 *Zami*, p. 179.
15 *Zami*, p. 180.
16 Nella Larsen, *Quicksand & Passing*, ed. Deborah McDowell (New Brunswick, NJ: Rutgers University Press, 1986). *Passing* was originally published in 1929.

17 Audre Lorde, 'Scratching the surface: some notes on barriers to women and loving', *Sister Outsider*, p. 48. Originally published 1978.

18 See Henry Louis Gates, Jr, *The Signifying Monkey: A Theory of African-American Literary Criticism* (New York and Oxford: Oxford University Press, 1988), pp. 51–60.

19 For Jordan's poem, see *Early Ripening: American Women's Poetry Now*, ed. Marge Piercy (New York/London: Pandora, 1987), pp. 107–14.

20 *Zami*, p. 224.

21 ibid., p. 226.

22 ibid., p. 249.

23 ibid., p. 252.

24 Adrienne Rich, 'When we dead awaken: writing as re-vision', in *On Lies, Secrets and Silence*, p. 45. Presented at the MLA Convention in 1971.

25 Audre Lorde, 'The transformation of silence into language and action', in *Sister Outsider*, p. 41. Presented at the MLA Convention in 1977.

26 *Sister Outsider*, p. 40.

27 'An interview: Audre Lorde and Adrienne Rich', *Sister Outsider*, p. 98. The interview was held in 1979 and first published in 1981.

28 *Sister Outsider*, p. 99. The publisher was the Black poet Don E. Lee of the Broadside Press.

29 See Gillian Hanscombe and Virginia Smyers, 'Amy Lowell's garden', in *Writing For Their Lives: The Modernist Women, 1910–1940* (London: Women's Press, 1987), pp. 63–75; also Lillian Faderman, *Surpassing the Love of Men* (New York: William Morrow, 1981), pp. 392–9.

30 Audre Lorde, *Chosen Poems – Old and New* (New York: W. W. Norton, 1982), p. 77. First published in *New York Headshop and Museum* (Chicago: The Broadside Press, 1975).

31 Compare the spatial metaphors and bodily detail of Amy Lowell's 'In Excelsis', in *What's O'Clock* (Boston: Houghton Mifflin, 1925), pp. 54–7:

> I drink your lips,
> I eat the whiteness of your hands and feet.
> My mouth is open,
> As a new jar I am empty and open.
> Like white water are you who fill the cup of my mouth,
> Like a brook of water thronged with lilies. . . .

32 In *The Southern Review*, 18 (1982), pp. 344–7.

33 One of the typescripts of the poem is headed 'I Said/(Winter 1919)'. In a letter to John Cournos, believed to be dated November 1919, H. D. wrote of Bryher's 'suicidal madness' and her own efforts to secure medical help for her friend. She adds: 'The worst thing is that the girl is in love with me, so madly that it is terrible.' Bryn Mawr College Library; see Donna Hollenberg, 'Art and ardor in World War One: selected letters from H. D. to John Cournos', *Iowa Review*, 16, 3 (1986), pp. 145–7.

34 *Poetry*, 17, 3 (1920), pp. 136–7. The poems – 'Blue Sleep', 'Eos' and 'Wild Rose' – were reprinted in Bryher's volume *Arrow Music*, (London, J. & E. Bumpus, 1922). See my 'Images at the crossroads: the H. D. scrapbook', in Michael King (ed.), *H. D.: Woman and Poet* (Orono, Maine: National Poetry Foundation, 1986), pp. 366–7.

35 See Barbara Guest, *Herself Defined: The Poet H. D. and Her World* (New York: Doubleday, 1984), pp. 122–3; also Phyllis Grosskurth, *Havelock Ellis:*

A Biography (London: Allen Lane, 1980), p. 296–7.

36 This phrase occurs in an obituary of H. D. for the *Bryn Mawr Alumni Bulletin* (1961) by her friend Marianne Moore; summing up the earlier poetry, Moore writes: 'H. D. contrived in the short line to magnetize the reader by what is not said.' Reviewing H. D.'s *Collected Poems* (1925) for *The Dial*, Moore compared H. D. with Sappho. *The Complete Prose of Marianne Moore*, ed. Patricia Willis (New York: Viking Penguin, 1987), pp. 558, 114.

37 Pierre Macherey, 'The spoken and the unspoken', in *A Theory of Literary Production*, trans. Geoffrey Wall (London: Routledge & Kegan Paul, 1978), pp. 87, 86 respectively.

38 Michael Riffaterre, 'Conclusion', in *Semiotics of Poetry* (Bloomington: Indiana University Press, 1978), p. 164. The definition of 'intertext' is from 'The semiotic approach to literary interpretation', a paper presented to the Georgetown Conference on Literary Criticism, 1984.

39 Julia Kristeva, 'Place Names', *Desire in Language*, ed. Leon S. Roudiez (Oxford: Basil Blackwell, 1981), p. 291.

40 Catharine Stimpson, 'Zero degree deviancy: the lesbian novel in English', *Critical Inquiry*, 8, 2 (1981), p. 364. The expression 'intertexts of relation and desire' was used by Rachel Blau DuPlessis in a paper presented at the MLA Convention, 1986.

41 *Semiotics of Poetry*, pp. 164–5.

42 The correspondence between Bryher and H. D., Bryher and Ellis, and H. D. and Ellis is in the Beinecke Rare Book and Manuscript Library, Yale University. The unpublished Bryher material concerning her relationship with H. D. was, in 1986, reunited with the unpublished H. D. material in the same archive.

43 H. D., 'I Said', *Collected Poems: 1912–1944*, ed. Louis L. Martz (New York: New Directions, 1983; Manchester: Carcanet, 1984), pp. 322–5.

44 Manuscript pages preserved by Bryher and bound in H. D., 'Poems II', Beinecke Library, Yale University.

45 Adrienne Rich, Poem IX of 'Twenty-One Love Poems' in *The Dream of a Common Language* (New York: W. W. Norton, 1978), p. 30; see also her 'Vesuvius at home: the power of Emily Dickinson' (1975), in *On Lies, Secrets and Silence*, pp. 157–83.

46 H. D., 'The Master', *Collected Poems: 1912–1944*, p. 453. In Bryher's unpublished 'Notes', this fragment seems to describe H. D.: 'A volcano that had fettered its own force.' Beinecke Library, Yale University.

47 Ros Carroll, 'Flower on flower: H. D. and the Sapphic tradition', unpublished essay, University of Cambridge, 1989.

48 Bion the Smyrnean, *The Lament for Adonis*, trans. Winifred Bryher (London: A. L. Humphreys, 1918), p. 13. This may have been the book that Bryher sent H. D. before their meeting in July 1918.

49 H. D., *Notes on Thought and Vision & The Wise Sappho* (London: Peter Owen, 1988), p. 57. Originally published by City Lights Books in 1982.

50 L. R. Farnell, *The Cults of the Greek States* (Oxford: The Clarendon Press, 1896–1909), vol. 2, p. 126. The passage is marked in H. D.'s copy of this volume, inscribed 'Mullion Cove, 1919'.

51 H. D., 'The Mysteries', *Collected Poems: 1912–1944*, p. 304.

52 H. D., *Tribute to Freud* (New York: New Directions, 1984), p. 56; during her analysis with Freud, he indicated his statuette of Nike with the words:

'She has lost her spear' (*Tribute to Freud*, p. 69). Bryher describes H. D., when they first met, as 'a spear flower if a spear could bloom', *Two Selves* (Paris: Contact Editions, 1923), pp. 124–5.

53 See my 'H. D.'s "Gift of Greek"/Bryher's "Eros of the Sea"', forthcoming in *H. D. Newsletter* (1990). I quote there the version in which Nancy (Bryher) tells Helga (H. D.) of her intention to drown herself, adding in words close to those of 'I Said': '"I know it is not Greek but then I'm not a Greek".' Bryher's prose ends more positively than H. D.'s poem, climaxing wordlessly on a kiss, to which Nancy responds: 'Because of your lips I will live.' Bryher Papers, Beinecke Library, Yale University.

54 The holograph version of 'I Said' has this variant text: 'being a girl-heart, proud of her vast gest'. H. D., 'Poems II', Beinecke Library.

ALAN SINFIELD

Who was afraid of Joe Orton?

Oscar Wilde: [Secrecy] seems to be the one thing that can make modern life mysterious or marvellous to us. The commonest thing is delightful if one only hides it.[1]

Joe Orton: The whole trouble with Western Society today is the lack of anything worth concealing.[2]

Joe Orton went to study at the Royal Academy for Dramatic Art in 1951, in the heyday of Terence Rattigan, Whitehall farces, religious verse-drama and Agatha Christie. The Wolfenden Report on homosexuality was still six years away, and the film *Victim* ten. Theatre was often 'queer', but it was always discreet. In the late 1950s, Orton showed no interest in the socially and politically aware plays of Osborne, Delaney, and Wesker, though they accompanied and contributed to a great increase in public discussion of homosexuality – by 1958 the Lord Chamberlain, the Crown official whose task it was to censor stage plays, was obliged to allow serious treatment of the topic. Orton and his lover Kenneth Halliwell were conducting a more distinctive and anarchic cultural critique by redesigning the covers of library books.[3]

However, in 1963, with the mysterious menace of Pinter's plays in the ascendancy, Orton wrote *Entertaining Mr Sloane*. In 1966 *Loot* was successfully produced – London was swinging and 'permissive' and Orton was asked to write a film script for the Beatles. He died in 1967, the year when male homosexual acts were made legal (provided there were only two people, in private, over twenty-one, and not in the armed services, the merchant navy, the prisons, Northern Ireland or Scotland). In 1968 stage censorship ended, and explicit gay plays – *Spitting Image*, *Fortune and Men's Eyes*, *Total Eclipse* – were produced in London. Plays in the London theatre in 1969 besides Orton's *What the Butler Saw* included *Boys in the Band*, *Oh, Calcutta!* and *Hair*; it was the year when the unprecedented resistance of gays to police harassment at the Stonewall Inn in New York's Christopher Street led to the formation of the Gay Liberation Front. So Orton's involvement in theatre spans the crucial period when the scope for homosexuals, both in British society and in the theatre, was sharply contested. This was the period when Gay Liberation became conceivable.

This article explores how Orton's plays effected quite specific negotiations of these changing opportunities for theatre and male homosexuals (in this paper I discuss men in Britain; the histories of lesbians generally and of men in other countries, though partly similar, are distinct). Orton exploited and contributed to the process through which homosexuality gradually became publicly speakable, and, as theatre audiences split and reformed, he was a focus of ideological conflict. Yet, I will argue, the terms of that conflict finally trapped Orton and limited his audience and his sexual politics, particularly in the play critics have most praised, *What the Butler Saw*. I invoke another gay play as a possible model for a gay cultural politics.

SILENCE AND THE CLOSET

Typically, from Ibsen to Christie and Rattigan, naturalistic plays disclose a danger to the social order. Often it takes the form of a socially unacceptable character – an outlaw-intruder who threatens the security of the characters and, by inference, the audience. Usually the problem is satisfactorily contained at the final curtain, though dissident authors might suggest that the disruptive intruder or misfit manifests in some ways a superior ethic or wisdom.[4] Pinter's plays reorganized this pattern. In them the sense of mysterious, ominous presence is often embodied in an intruder, though now its focus is not social propriety but an unstable compound of metaphysical vacuity and sexual challenge. Its ultimate residence may be the psyche of the threatened character. Notoriously, the danger hovers also in silences in the dialogue, pregnant now not with class disapproval but with a loosely 'existential' anxiety about emptiness and disintegration.

The outlaw-intruder pattern had obvious resonances for male homosexuals, especially of the middle and upper classes. They felt obliged to 'pass' as heterosexual, and thus themselves effected the intrusion of an 'undesirable' element into good society. They might fear the irruption of knowledge about homosexuality and hence their own exposure; further, they might themselves introduce the threatening lower-class person to whom they might be attracted (this was a common pattern and constituted the dominant concept of the homosexual liaison).[5] J. R. Ackerley remarked, almost in passing, how he and his friends were 'outcasts and criminals in the sight of the impertinent English laws'; Peter Wildeblood said in 1955 that he 'would be the first homosexual to tell what it felt like to be an exile in one's own country'.[6] Homosexuality hovered upon the edge of public visibility, defining normality against a deviation so horrific that its occurrence could scarcely be admitted.

Pinter's version of the outlaw-intruder was apposite to homosexuality at this time: both were imagined as mysterious and violent, lying in wait in the silences, explicitly nowhere but, by so much, potentially everywhere. Homosexuality might manifest itself as an over-emphatic and hence potentially violent inflection in a relationship. It might even be lurking, scarcely recognized, in the psyches of 'normal' people. Most of

Pinter's early plays have a homosexual inflection. There are intense male relationships in *The Birthday Party* (Goldberg and McCann; 1958), *The Dwarfs* (1960), *The Caretaker* (1960) and *The Dumb Waiter* (1960). In *The Birthday Party* Stanley resists Lulu's advances and is 'mothered' by Meg; in *The Homecoming* (1965) Lenny boasts of violent relations with women but is easily disconcerted by Ruth. It is not that these plays are 'really', 'underneath', about homosexuals; to say that would be to override the ambiguity which at the time was crucial. During those decades of discretion we should not imagine homosexuality as *there*, fully formed like a statue shrouded under a sheet until ready for exhibition. The closet (as discreet homosexuality was named when it came under scrutiny in the 1960s) did not obscure homosexuality – it created it. Freud makes a similar point when he disputes that one should expect to find 'the essence of dreams in their latent content': the important thing is the dream-*work* which produces such images.[7] Similarly, oblique homosexual representation should be studied for the *process* that constitutes it so, and for the social reasons that demand such a process.

As censorship gradually relaxed, Pinter wrote *The Collection* (1961). There is tension in the (evidently) homosexual relationship of Harry and Bill and in the marriage of Stella and James because, it emerges, there is a question whether sexual congress has occurred between Stella and Bill. Homosexuality is to be inferred from the usual stereotypical cues – the 'artistic' menage of Harry and Bill, the fact that Bill is a dress designer, and the domineering attitude of the wealthier and older Harry. Martin Esslin deduces that Bill may have wanted to sleep with Stella because he 'may have been made into a homosexual by an older man who offered him social advancement, a good job, life in a middle-class milieu'.[8] We never find out what 'actually happened', of course. The need to infer the sexuality of Harry and Bill produces an additional layer of obscurity. Customary discreet indirection about homosexuality feeds neatly into Pinter's blend of mystery and menace.

While the Chamberlain's power persisted, Pinteresque mystery was a convenient mode for handling homosexuality on the stage. In *The Trigon*, by James Broom Lynne (produced at the Arts theatre in 1963), Arthur and Basil are presented through manifest homosexual hints – as the play opens, Arthur is wearing Boy Scout uniform and playing a record of 'Dance of the Sugar-Plum Fairy'. Their intentions towards their friend Mabel are evidently half-hearted (compare Stanley and Lulu in *The Birthday Party*) – it is said that if they both addressed her 'She wouldn't know which way to turn.'[9] But there is no indication of sexual feeling, as such, between the two men. The intruder, Charles, is also mysterious – though compatible with the stereotypical notion that homosexuals gain satisfaction from breaking up other people's relationships. He expels Basil and Arthur from their flat, but it is suggested that they will be better for the self-knowledge he has produced: 'It's no good either of us thinking of Mabel. Or any other woman for that matter. We'll make plans for each other. No third party' (p. 152).

This conclusion ought to mean that Arthur and Basil come to terms with their sexual relationship, but that cannot be shown. Inexplicitness makes *The Trigon* unactable outside its time. Of course Basil and Arthur are discreet about homosexuality (if wearing Boy Scout uniform and playing 'The Sugar-Plum Fairy' is discreet). And they may delude themselves about the chances of making it with Mabel. But there is no dramatic reason for them to be discreet when they are alone together. The reason is extra-dramatic: they are being overheard by the audience, and this makes their privacy public and subject to censorship. To the reviewer of *Theatre World* (July 1964) the characters were 'inexplicably bound together emotionally'. The mystery in this play has nothing to do with the absurdist project usually attributed to Pinter, it is simply the limits of what James Broom Lynne was allowed to say.

ENTERTAINING HOMOSEXUALITY

Entertaining Mr Sloane followed *The Trigon* into the Arts theatre in 1964 and was published in the same volume of *Penguin Modern Plays*. The whole manner was in the air, provoked by the demands of speaking the unspeakable in the conditions of that moment. However, Orton's use of 'Pinteresque' indirect dialogue and the mysteriously powerful intruder is cunning and distinctive. He incorporates them into the action, making them required by the concerns of the characters. We understand the middle-aged Eddie to be homosexual because it is the only way of making sense of his toleration of Sloane, his interest in Sloane's physique and sex life, and his horror of heterosexuality. Eddie is indirect in his approach to Sloane because he assumes he must be cautious. Sloane evidently reads this indirection: he suggests that Eddie is 'sensitive'. But Eddie denies it, insisting, 'I seen birds all shapes and sizes and I'm most certainly not . . . um . . . sensitive' (p. 204). Sloane carefully plays Eddie along because, as Orton explained, Sloane knows the score but 'isn't going to give in until he has to'.[10]

In *Sloane* obscurity and indirection make sense *within* the action as the inhibitions of discretion. The play makes apparent the operations of the closet; it comments on the discretion of the censor and polite society, as well as being subject to it. Orton also makes sense of 'Pinteresque menace'. The attractive youth, Sloane, has killed a man who wanted to photograph him, and this danger is not merely arbitrary, metaphysical, or paranoid, but part of that experienced all the time by homosexuals. In *Serious Charge* by Philip King (1955) and *The Children's Hour* by Lillian Hellman (1934; produced at club theatres in 1950 and 1956) an attractive, dishonest and violent young person tries to ruin a plausibly homosexual adult by accusing him/her of homosexuality (the accusations are false, but suspicion is allowed to remain, humouring conventional notions about artistic, bachelor vicars and intense, unmarried lady schoolteachers). In actual life, often, homosexuals are subject to violent assault and murder. By the end of the play Sloane has killed two men, and

Kath and Eddie are rash to assume that he won't kill again.

The changed use of obliquity and innuendo in Orton's plays was possible partly because, by the mid-1960s, understanding was no longer the special secret of a few. A perverse benefit from the witch-hunt against homosexual men in the early 1950s was enhanced visibility and a great increase in public discussion – provoked also by the Kinsey Report (1948). In the United States, where persecution was even more vigorous, John D'Emilio observes that 'attacks on gay men and women hastened the articulation of a homosexual identity and spread the knowledge that they existed in large numbers'.[11] Commentators have often observed that in the 1950s homosexuality came to be considered less an evil or a sin, and more a medical or psychological condition. That is true, but also, increasingly, it was discussed as *a problem*. A Church of England pamphlet was called *The Problem of Homosexuality* (1954). This was the era of the problem (juvenile delinquency, unmarried mothers, the colour bar, latch-key children . . .); and it involved an expectation that the state would encourage public discussion and then pass laws to improve matters. The Wolfenden Committee on homosexual offences (and prostitution) was set up in 1954 after a minister for home affairs declared: 'Quite clearly, this is a problem which calls for very careful consideration on the part of those responsible for the welfare of the nation.' By the end of the decade Gordon Westwood believed that his 1952 objective, of bringing 'the problem of homosexuality . . . out into the open where it can be discussed and reconsidered', had been achieved.[12] Homosexuality was no longer unspoken. When *The Killing of Sister George* by Frank Marcus was playing at Wimbledon in 1967, Orton prophesied: 'I don't suppose they'll understand what the play is about.' 'Don't you believe it,' Halliwell replied, 'They'll know very well what it's about.' Orton acknowledges: 'He was right. It became clear, from the opening scenes, that they understood and weren't amused.'[13]

They could have found out from BBC radio comedy. In 1960 Peter Burton experienced the homosexual slang 'Polari' as 'our own camp secret language with which we could confound and confuse the *naffs* (straights)'.[14] But from 1964 Polari expressions such as 'bona' (attractive), 'varda' (look at), 'omee' (man) and 'polonee' (woman) featured regularly in the dialogue of two very camp men in the Light Programme comedy series *Round the Horne*, with Orton's friend Kenneth Williams as Julian (Jules) and Hugh Paddick as Sandy. Here is a typical instance from March 1967, with the couple as journalists:

PADDICK Can we have five minutes of your time?
HORNE It depends what you want to do with them.
WILLIAMS Well, our editor said, Why don't you troll off to Mr Horne's lattie. . .
HORNE Flat or home – translator's note.
WILLIAMS And have a palare with him. . .[15]

For regular listers, as well as for gays, the 'translation' would be unnecessary. Its offer was part of the joke, signifying that the private was in the process of becoming public. In 1967–8 the laws on homosexuality and stage censorship were changed. By 1969 Lou Reed was a cult hero, and by 1972 Alice Cooper and David Bowie took gender-bending into the pop charts. Unevenly, in diverse institutions, homosexuality was becoming less secret.

HE DO THE POLICE

In the heyday of Noël Coward, audiences divided according to whether they would pick up hints of homosexuality. From the mid-1960s the split was hardly over decoding competence, but around a contest as to what could be said in public. Homosexual nuances in Coward's plays either were not heard, or they were rendered tolerable by the acknowledgement (in their indirection) that such matters should not be allowed into public discourse. As homosexuality became more audible, it became the subject of explicit contest.

Some people were certainly upset. When *Sloane* was considered for television the company's legal officer thought it disgusting: 'Perfectly horrible and filthy. I don't know why we want to consider such a play.'[16] She had understood what it was about. Outside London, *Loot* provoked walk-outs – 'Bournemouth Old Ladies Shocked', reported *The Times*.[17] But the shockable audience understood that homosexuality (and other such causes) were at issue. Furthermore, it was confronted by another audience, associated typically with the Royal Court theatre, that wanted to see progressive plays. In the subsidized sector of theatre especially, the left-liberal intelligentsia was winning space for its kinds of representation – to the extent that a 'taboo' subject like homosexuality was hardly challenging to the people likely to attend a production known to feature it. This audience had come to indulge what was being called 'permissive-ness', and felt confirmed in their progressive stance. In 1966 Frank Parkin found between 75 and 94 per cent (depending on social class) of CND supporters agreeing that laws against homosexual acts by consenting adults should be repealed.[18] While *Sloane* was running, establishment West End producers complained fiercely about 'dirty plays' – particularly at the subsidized Royal Shakespeare Company. Their objections were used to advertise *Sloane* – so far from being a disadvantage, the scandal was played up.[19] Compare what happened when Wilde was arrested: *An Ideal Husband* and *The Importance of Being Earnest* had been attracting large audiences, but Wilde's name was taken off the hoardings and the plays soon closed.[20]

However, *Entertaining Mr Sloane* does contain a challenge for a progressive audience (this was my experience). It resides not in the homosexuality, but in the lack of interpersonal feeling which, in the character of Sloane, produces psychopathic violence. This disappoints a left-liberal pleasure in Sloane's initially relaxed attitude to homosexuality, and frustrates a wish to see diverse kinds of sexuality justified by the affective quality of the relationship. Further, progressive plays generally presented the young person as a victim of the grown-ups (for instance, *A Taste of Honey* by Shelagh Delaney, *Five Finger Exercise* by Peter Shaffer, *Roots* and *Chips with Everything* by Arnold Wesker). In part Sloane is such a victim – at the end Kath and Eddie are able to force him into their 'family'.[21] But he is also the unsocialized hooligan whom conservatives were invoking as grounds for clamping down on all youthful self-expression. He is set up in some ways as the attractive character among the four, but kicking old men to death is carrying intergenerational conflict a bit too far.

Loot was better attuned to the liberal-progressive audience (I went with a group of fellow students – it was someone's birthday). The play is on the side of the boys, Hal and Dennis, and attacks officialdom and traditional moral atttitudes. Some of the dialogue is in a discreet manner, but deployed so as to challenge hypocrisy and bogus formality ('And even the sex you were born into isn't safe from your marauding').[22] Above all, *Loot* excited the youthful left-liberal intelligentsia by its treatment of the police and the law. During the relative social harmony of the 1950s, unusually, the image of the friendly 'bobby' was relatively unchallenged (though homosexuals always had reason to distrust it). But repressive attitudes to political demonstrations from around 1960, and then to drugs, gradually shifted left-liberal opinion. In 1965, while Orton was writing *Loot*, the case of Detective Sergeant Harold Challenor came to prominence. He had arrested, beaten, and planted a brick and an iron bar on people demonstrating against the Greek monarchy (because it sponsored the fascist dictatorship in Greece). Orton, says Kenneth Williams, became 'obsessed with Challenor', and as the play was reworked the part of Inspector Truscott was developed.[23]

It is not usually stressed that Orton's critique of police malpractice goes far beyond anything previously seen in the theatre, or indeed other media.

TRUSCOTT (*shouting, knocking HAL to the floor*). Under any other political system I'd have you on the floor in tears!
HAL (*crying*). You've got me on the floor in tears.

* * *

TRUSCOTT   And you complain you were beaten?
DENNIS   Yes.
TRUSCOTT   Did you tell anyone?
DENNIS   Yes.
TRUSCOTT   Who?
DENNIS   The officer in charge.
TRUSCOTT   What did he say?
DENNIS   Nothing.
TRUSCOTT   Why not?
DENNIS   He was out of breath with kicking.[24]

To have such things said in public, I recall, was as exciting as the relaxed attitudes to homosexuality attributed to Hal and Dennis. In the closing moments McLeavy tells Truscott 'You're mad!' The response recalled the Challenor case: 'Nonsense, I had a check-up only yesterday' (p. 274). Orton even worked into the text Challenor's actual words, reported in court: 'You're fucking nicked, my old beauty.'[25] Hilariously, the Lord Chamberlain would not allow 'fucking'. With the repressive state apparatus starkly displayed, he was still chasing after naughty words.

Introducing *Loot*, Simon Trussler said it outrages 'every expectation of a *morally* appropriate outcome'. However, in an article Trussler remarked the difference between '*kinds* of audiences': one kind 'may understand *Loot* because they share its moral assumptions', the other will prefer Whitehall farces and 'either ignore *Loot* or hate it'.[26] For left-liberals its critique was exhilarating. McLeavy's fate does not trouble us much, for he has foolishly worshipped the authority that victimizes him. The ending of *Loot* is triumphant because it displays most completely, in Truscott's behaviour, the corruption of established power and authority. (The effect is similar in the last moments of at least two other early-1960s new-wave plays, Wesker's *Chips with Everything* and Giles Cooper's *Everything in the Garden*.) Further, the final lines propose that Hal, Dennis, and Fay should all live together. This arrangement offers to resolve unconventionally but pleasantly a tension among the three most likeable characters. In fact it is exactly the happy ending of Noël Coward's *Design for Living* (1932). But times have changed and in *Loot* the idea can no longer be welcomed innocently – 'People would talk. We must keep up appearances' (p. 275). In so far as this does not repudiate the *menage à trois* as such, it is pleasing to left-liberals and, in so far as it exposes the hypocrisy of 'people' once more, it is a final blow against convention.

After difficulties in the provinces, *Loot* was a hit in London. Its success could be partly because traditionally-minded people enjoyed feeling indignant – Hal says of his father, 'His generation takes a delight in being outraged.'[27] But mainly it was because younger people were excited by it.

THE MOMENT OF ORTON

The 1960s intensified both libertarian and reactionary attitudes and their conflict was staged in the theatre. These were the circumstances that permitted Orton's notoriety. Earlier, he would not have been tolerated; later he would not be so significant (though he would be the subject of determined recuperation). We might call it the moment of Orton. The plays' prominence depended on the social atmosphere of the 1950s – which produced and talked anxiously about, but did not enact, Wolfenden. They were written to scandalize the Aunt Ednas (and remember, this 'middlebrow' follower of theatre was invented by Rattigan). But the condition of their presentation and success was the fact that discretion and the audience that assumed it were already under pressure. By making visible the structure of the closet, the plays helped to make its dismantling possible. The 1960s liberalization that helped make Orton a celebrity, therefore, also set a limit to his moment.

Orton (like most people) had difficulty seeing himself as part of a trend. He enjoyed watching audiences upset by *Loot*, and believed his 'authentic voice' was 'vulgar and offensive in the extreme to middle-class susceptibilities'.[28] He scarcely realized that they were already on the run and that there was enthusiastic support for the critique he was mounting. This is partly because he had few links with the student culture of the subsidized theatre audience and distrusted its earnestness. He had studied at the Royal Academy of Dramatic Art in the early 1950s, well before the student radicalism of the CND generation, and his attitudes to homosexuality and theatre tended to assume the milieu of Coward or Rattigan. (Osborne partly shared Orton's background, and this helps to explain his poor fit with the progressive movement he initiated. He edged back to the discreet, upper-class theatrical world of Rattigan in *Hotel in Amsterdam* (1968) and *West of Suez* (1971).) Orton wanted commercial managements to present his plays. He thought Kenneth Tynan wouldn't dare include 'Until She Screams', the sketch he submitted for *Oh, Calcutta!* in 1967; but this piece had basically been written in 1960. As Simon Shepherd remarks, Orton 'had a rather inflated idea of his own shockingness: they did dare do his sketch. Orton's underestimate of the sexual "liberation" of others is a mark not just of his vanity but of his isolation.'[29]

The confusions of the moment of Orton were manifested institutionally. So vigorous was the left-liberal theatre audience that it encroached on the West End, partly through the efforts of progressive impresarios to make a distinctive space for themselves. Michael Codron and Donald Albery were looking for 'disturbing' plays, and hence keen to produce *Sloane*; Codron thought it 'might turn out to have the most exciting commercial possibilities since *The Caretaker*'.[30] By the mid-1960s the boundary between West End and subsidized theatre was blurred, and Orton was unclear about where he belonged. His *Ruffian on the Stair* and *The Erpingham Camp* were presented by the Royal Court (in 1967), and when *Loot* wasn't going well Orton doubted whether it was right for commercial theatre and thought of putting it into the Royal Court or the National.[31]

More damagingly, Orton's commercial success kept him among the older type of discreet theatre homosexual, who identified with a privileged, leisure-class outlook in which conservative attitudes to homosexuality and theatre went together and constituted an inevitable and largely desirable state of affairs.[32] They believed – rightly – that more openness would spoil their kind of accommodation to homosexuality (even as it spoiled the Orton moment). In his diaries Orton shows virtually no interest in other gay plays, or in the new 'fringe' companies, or in moves to abolish stage censorship, or even in the legalization of male homosexuality. Rattigan commented: 'Orton thought it very funny that I, of all people, should have thought his play so good.'[33] Actually, they were not so far apart, for Orton's satire depended on Rattigan's world.

What the Butler Saw includes powerful satire against the oppressive constructions of medicine and psychiatry, and creates continuous gender confusion, with cross-dressing and 'inappropriate' sexual advances. But it was not too disturbing for Orton's discreet friends. They were very enthusiastic about it[34] and encouraged him to have it produced by Binkie Beaumont and Tennents, with Ralph Richardson, at the Haymarket – in other words, in the heart of traditional West End theatre. Evidently Orton thought he was setting a trap: he wanted a conventionally 'lovely' set so that 'When the curtain goes up one should feel that we're right back in the old theatre of reassurance.'[35] But Orton doesn't consider why Beaumont should want to do the play; it is he, Orton, who was trapped. Commentators agree that the text was played without flair – it wasn't the censor (by then defunct) who would not allow Churchill's 'missing part' to be produced on stage, but Richardson, the Beaumont star.[36] The production pleased neither of the divergent audiences who were striving to claim theatre for their point of view.

Nevertheless, *What the Butler Saw* has been praised by the best commentators on Orton. Albert Hunt suggests that it 'would, presumably, have been revised and tightened had he lived', but still admires the way it destroys 'the sexual stability on which the mechanics of bedroom farce depend'.[37] Hunt adduces the description by Dr Prentice of his wife:

> My wife is a nymphomaniac. Consequently, like the Holy Grail, she's ardently sought after by young men. I married her for her money and, upon discovering her to be penniless, I attempted to throttle her. She escaped my murderous fury and I've had to live with her malice ever since.[38]

It had been complained that if Mrs Prentice is indeed so liberal about sex then the principal motive of the action becomes absurd – namely her husband trying to keep from her his attempt to seduce his secretary. This is the point, says Hunt: the logic of farce collapses.[39] But that logic requires the assumptions of a 1950s farce audience. By 1969 very many people no longer believed that it is important to conceal adultery, that Christian imagery is sacrosanct, even that female sexual desire is shocking and/or funny. Brian Rix, sponsor of the Whitehall farces, had remarked in 1966: 'with the more tolerant climate there now is, we could put on a farce about adultery and our audience wouldn't bat an eyelid.' And he attributed 'the more liberal attitude' partly to Royal Court plays. Orton was not unaware of the issue. In the same article he is quoted as complaining: 'A lot of farces today are still based on the preconceptions of a century ago, particularly the preoccupations about sex. But we must now accept that, for instance, people *do* have sexual relations outside marriage.'[40] Things were moving faster than he realized. Back in 1962, Giles Cooper's *Everything in the Garden* was powerful when it showed conventional middle-class people finding themselves involved in prostitution and murder and getting used to the idea. In 1969, for many people, the concern in *Butler* with adultery and nakedness was merely quaint – and the speech about Mrs Prentice's 'nymphomania' sounded like it was straining to shock (and nothing is done with Prentice's 'murderous fury'). Progressive audiences would be disappointed at the failure to develop the homosexual theme after the initial interview between Prentice and Nick.

Simon Shepherd observes that instead of a return to order at the end of *What the Butler Saw*, incestuous desire is revealed. He believes the audience, 'like any comedy audience ... *sees* itself to be like the characters in expecting an ending to disorder; but discovers that ending to be alien and uncomfortable. Thus trapped the audience is driven wild. The first performances succeeded: people stormed out or barracked the players.'[41] But suppose one did not find incest between consenting adults so very terrible? To be sure, the play upset some of Richardson's older admirers in the preliminary week in Brighton (I saw it there). And it was booed and jeered on the opening night in London, though this was not a naïve response but an organized campaign by the group of gallery first-nighters, followers of traditional theatre, that had already disrupted Colin Spencer's *Spitting Image* a few months previously.[42] But – my title question – who was afraid of Joe Orton? Was it important to taunt those people in 1969, especially at the price of framing *Butler* in terms they would react against? The play's title, which refers to ancient seaside machines showing 'sexy' pictures of women's knickers and suspenders for a penny, was of course meant to be ironic, but it holds Orton bound to the framework of attitudes that he wants to oppose. Furthermore, he could affront the Aunt Ednas only by failing to engage with other audiences. A different kind of farce, plucking at the susceptibilities of a sophisticated liberal audience, was just ahead in the work of Alan Acykbourn and Michael Frayn. And plays on explicit gay themes – *The Killing of Sister George, When Did You Last See My Mother?, Staircase, Spitting Image, Fortune and Men's Eyes, The Madness of Lady Bright, Total Eclipse* – had been produced in London (most of these began in 'alternative' venues; all but the last two transferred to the West End).

Jonathan Dollimore has also praised *Butler*: he calls it 'black camp', and remarks the irony, parody and pastiche, held together by 'a stylistic *blankness*'. He argues that the play insinuates 'the arbitrariness and narrowness of gender roles, and that they are socially ascribed rather than naturally given'.[43] The play is thus in the mode of Wilde who, Dollimore shows, validates the artificial, the non-natural, the insincere. Wilde thus subverts the demand for depth – for authenticity, sincerity and the natural; and these are 'dominant categories of subjectivity which keep desire in subjection'.[44] So we may see that sexual relations are not essentially thus or thus, but are based on manners, convention, custom, ideology, power. This is indeed what *Butler* does some of the time. It 'becomes a kind of orgy of cross-dressing, gender confusion and hierarchical inversion', and the dialogue calls into question the 'natural' – in circumstances where the speaker is in fact mistaken, because of cross-dressing, about the 'naturalness' of the very example he is using.[45] But even so, much of the comedy depends on believing that such attitudes are outrageous, and that, whatever their clothes, Nick is really a boy and Geraldine really a girl. I am inclined to see Orton's refusal of depth as indicating weakness rather than strength. This is not the assured position, perhaps the arrogance, of Wilde; it is looking over its shoulder to see how Aunt Edna is responding.

There is an alternative strategy to Wilde's cultivation of artificiality, as Dollimore shows. It appropriates parts of the dominant discourse, asserting the naturalness of gay relations and seeking to use sincerity and authenticity against their usual implication. This strategy was cultivated by Radclyffe Hall and André Gide. Of course, it may be no more than a pathetic plea to be allowed to share the power of the oppressor. But, alternatively, it may seize the ideology of depth and authenticate the unorthodox. And hence it may contribute to the development of what Foucault calls 'a reverse discourse', whereby 'homosexuality begins to speak on its own behalf, to forge its own identity and culture, *often in the self-same categories by which it has been produced and marginalised*, and eventually challenges the very power structures responsible for its "creation".'[46]

This latter was in fact the main strategy of the 1960s homosexual law reform capaign[47] and, shortly after Orton's death, of Gay Liberation – to produce and believe in positive representations of homosexuality ('gay is good'; the validation of surface over depth was slightly later, stimulated by such diverse concepts as the pink economy, poststructuralism, and high-energy disco-dancing). Orton was out of step with that reforming tendency; he refused nature, depth, and sincerity at least partly because, although he felt an intuitive opposition to the prevailing sexual ideology, he had difficulty conceiving a positive view of the homosexual.[48] He was stuck, in other words, in the Orton moment.

To be sure, Orton shows an untroubled practice of homosexuality in some characters – Sloane, Hal and Dennis, perhaps Nick. But none of them is apparently *a homosexual*. The instance of that is the older, closeted Eddie in *Sloane*, and his devious exercise of power makes him unattractive. This is reminiscent of Coward who, I have argued elsewhere, validates deviant sexuality when it is part of a general bohemianism but makes his specifically homosexual characters unappealing.[49] Orton was very concerned that there should be nothing 'queer or camp or odd' about Hal and Dennis – 'They must be perfectly ordinary boys who happen to be fucking each other. Nothing could be more natural.' He also objected to Eddie appearing camp.[50] This seems radical; it is against stereotypes and appropriates nature. On the other hand, 'we're all bisexual really' is the commonest evasion. Hal and Dennis are said to be indifferent to the gender of their partners ('You scatter your seed along the pavements without regard to age or sex').[51] That was an unusual and disconcerting thought; it takes the implications of cross-dressing and superficiality quite literally; it could be utopian. But it also keeps a distance from very many actual homosexuals; it was not how Orton lived, or others that he knew. At this time male homosexuals were struggling to be gay, not to be indifferent to sexual orientation. Of course, we all think we want to get away from stereotypes. However, these are not arbitrary external impositions, but are implicated in the whole construction of sexuality in the modern world; they figure, positively and negatively, in gay self-understanding. You challenge them not by jumping clear but by engaging with them.

'SPITTING IMAGE'

It may be that Dollimore's two strategies can be combined – so that the strategy of superficiality deconstructs normative assumptions about patriarchy, heterosexuality and the family, and then the strategy of sincerity asserts the claims of unorthodox sexuality. I would suggest that Caryl Churchill's *Cloud Nine* (1979) does this. So does *Spitting Image* by Colin Spencer. This was produced in 1968, when the abolition of the Lord Chamberlain's censorship function made it suddenly possible to present plays that would make sense to and for a gay audience. To be sure, homosexuals had frequented discreet plays, even regarding theatre as a specially homosexual medium, but that discretion enshrined heterosexist assumptions. *Spitting Image* is written to make best sense to a gay audience eager for its own theatre. It opened at the Hampstead Theatre Club, a suitable location for a progressive audience, and proved strong enough to gain a brief West End transfer to the Duke of York's. There, *The Times* reported, it received 'loud boos from the gallery and sustained applause from the stalls': it upset the old-fashioned moralists and energized gays and radicals.[52]

To general astonishment and fear, one partner in a male homosexual couple, Gary and Tom, conceives and bears a child (who calls them Daddy One and Daddy Two). Familiar structures are shifted onto this strange situation.

DOCTOR   Yes, yes, any other symptoms, Mr Dart?
TOM   Oh, just the normal ones, you know.
DOCTOR   Normal?
TOM   I mean, well, morning sickness in the first two months and then . . .[53]

Normality disintegrates in such a bizarre application. The relation of mother and infant is one of the strongest sites for the ideology of sincerity, nature, and depth, but its images scatter. 'It's so difficult to adjust to . . . one gets so used to the idea of mother, like you know, on those TV commercials' (p. 33). The play misses no opportunity to get the language of patriarchy, family, and heterosexuality to entangle itself. When a girl friend tries to kiss him Gary retreats: 'It's wrong. I'm a mother . . . I can't go around kissing girls' (p. 37). The authorities want to get hold of the parent and child, and decide that their tactic should be to 'break up the family unit' (p. 35): they use the term 'family' even as they plot against Gary and Tom because they are not a family.

But also, as they struggle against hostile officials and stereotypes, the gay couple appropriate the genuine and human. A psychiatrist asks: 'and would you say that you are the active partner of this relationship?' Tom replies: 'Eh? No, not really. I mean, it comes and goes. Sometimes one thing, sometimes another' (p. 28). I recall people in the audience applauding at this repudiation – in public – of one of the heterosexual myths that aspire to organize gay sexuality. Gary and Tom are not sentimentalized – most of the time they are bickering because of the strain of the situation ('Doctor Spock says that parents often find it difficult to adjust' (p. 33)). John Russell Taylor found them 'an entirely believable married couple, living and growing together and apart. Few heterosexual plays have done this so well.'[54]

Of course, gay men were to repudiate the manoeuvre that 'tolerates' us so long as we appear to approximate to supposed heterosexual norms (though in 1968 this was a provocative claim). However, *Spitting Image* never allows the heterosexist values that it is appropriating to settle down. It both subverts the ideology of depth *and* claims it for gays. It would be difficult to say which is happening when Gary, disappointed at Tom's lesser commitment, makes an emotive speech about parenthood:

> You're all surface aren't you mate? All you think about is the kind of place we live in, your pay packet, the films, plays, dinner-parties we used to go to. That was all your whole bloody life. Haven't you ever stopped for one minute and thought that we've created a new human being, a tiny creature who looks for us for love, guidance and security, who trusts both of us absolutely? (p. 36)

It is an appeal to depth, embedded in a situation where it must be absurd. Spencer said he wanted to present both the reality of a love relationship and the responsibility of having a child, and a farcical attack on bureaucracy: 'The whole play's style had to change gear constantly.'[55]

The civil service and government assume that such offspring must be studied, hidden, and prevented:

> The confusion would be unimaginable, it would distort the whole legal system. Think of the manpower lost in the professions and industries if these damned pansies are always prancing off becoming mothers. . . . Homosexuals of all races, colours and creeds would suddenly be given the hope of creating offspring. And what is more likely than that the offspring themselves will have the same sexual abnormalities. The whole world would be overrun – ugh! (pp. 33–4)

This homophobic utterance deconstructs itself by invoking the potential of what was soon to be called gay power. Indeed, it transpires, in the play, that many such children are being conceived. Daddy One responds by organizing a national movement (though Daddy Two is initially apathetic). The tactics are specifically reminiscent of the Suffragettes but also, in a stroke of inspiration, they anticipate the mass solidarity of Gay Liberation.

> But don't you see? Before we were alone, utterly alone, a freakish development. Now we are stronger. . . . At first we're bound to be a deprived minority. The Government will be trying to hush the whole thing up. Well I'm not going to let it. . . . (p. 40)

Spitting Image is organized around a biological impossibility – that is the repudiation of the conventional ideology of depth. But the ending is gloriously triumphant. Gary and Tom's offspring is not only unusually strong, intelligent and humane (he worries dreadfully about the Vietnam War), he is also able to infiltrate Downing Street at night and affect the Prime Minister's mind by auto-suggestion. As a result the law is changed, producing 'happy homosexuals' (p. 45). Daddy Two conceives. Nor is the effect limited to gays: Tom's mother is converted ('Well if the papers say it's all right, I suppose it is', p. 45), and the Prime Minister repudiates militarism. Gay Liberation correlates with peace and love generally; indeed, the genuine freeing of a major oppressed group, if it occurred, would perhaps amount to that.

Of course, the triumphant ending is even more of a fantasy than the rest – 'Funny how people's attitudes have changed' (p. 45). But fantasies are important: they mark the boundaries of the plausible, and may help us to see that plausibility is a powerful social construction – dominated, of course, by patriarchy, heterosexuality, and the family. Nancy K. Miller has noted the way women writers are frequently accused of falling prey to implausibilities in their fiction. They are said to manifest sensibility, sensitivity, extravagence – 'code words for feminine in our culture' – at the expense of verisimilitude. But such 'improbable' plots may be read as comments on the prevailing stories of women's lives – they manifest 'the extravagant wish for a *story* that would turn out differently'.[56] That is, the wish of women for power over their lives cannot be expressed plausibly within dominant discourses, only as fantasy. The improbability in *Spitting Image* is utopian, but it also alludes to that fact, and to the scale of social change that would have to occur for gays to become acceptably empowered.

Colin Spencer's play has continuing resonances for gay culture. The obvious analogue for its main situation now is the oppression of lesbian mothers, whose children are taken from them in the way that is attempted in *Spitting Image*. And the government decision to place the gay parents compulsorily in an 'enclosed colony', telling them they have 'a rare disease' (p. 39), is all too like modes of control that have been proposed for people with AIDS.

Gay men have found support in the notion that homosexuals have been creators of Art (well, it's got to be better than disc jockeys and royalty). To be sure, we can and should uncover the underlying gay significance in such work. But that very act tends to reinforce a notion that gay creativity must be covert. Decoding the work of closeted homosexual artists ought to produce a recognition of oppression, rather than a cause for celebration. Theatre has long been a site of homosexual culture, but it had always to be glimpsed through ostensibly heterosexual texts and institutions. *Spitting Image* represents a new break, because although in a public mode and a public venue, it is written not for the Aunt Ednas, but for gays. It appropriates theatre for an explicit gay culture, anticipating the Gay Sweatshop company. Other audiences are invited, but they will have the perhaps disconcerting experience – which gays have all the time – of sitting in on someone else's culture. *Spitting Image* signals the possibility of a non-closeted gay subculture.

It is through involvement in a subculture that one discovers an identity in relation to others and perhaps a basis for political commitment. A subculture creates a distinctive circle of reality, partly alternative to the dominant. There you can feel that Black is beautiful, gay is good. Such a sense of shared identity and purpose is necessary for self-preservation. However, subcultures may also return to trouble the dominant. They are formed partly by and partly in reaction to it – they redeploy its cherished values, downgrading, inverting or reapplying them, and thereby demonstrate their incoherence. Their outlaw status may exert a fascination for the dominant, focusing fantasies of freedom, vitality, even squalor. So they form points from which its repressions may become apparent, its silences audible.

University of Sussex

NOTES

1 Oscar Wilde, *The Picture of Dorian Gray* (Harmondsworth: Penguin Books, 1949), p. 10.
2 Joe Orton, *The Orton Diaries*, ed. John Lahr (London: Methuen, 1986), p. 219.
3 In 1962 Orton and Halliwell were sent to prison for stealing and damaging library books: they made cover pictures bizarre and typed in false blurbs. See John Lahr, *Prick Up Your Ears* (Harmondworth: Penguin Books, 1980), pp. 93–105; Simon Shepherd, *Because We're Queers* (London: GMP, 1989), pp. 13–14.
4 See Alan Sinfield, 'Theatre and politics', in Malcolm Kelsall, Martin Coyle, Peter Garside and John Peck (eds), *Literature and Criticism* (London: Routledge, forthcoming); Alan Sinfield, 'Closet dramas: homosexual representation in postwar British theatre', forthcoming.
5 On the cross-class liaison, see Jeffrey Weeks, 'Discourse, desire and sexual deviance: some problems in a history of homosexuality', in Kenneth Plummer (ed.), *The Making of the Modern Homosexual* (London: Hutchinson, 1981), pp. 76–111, p. 105; Jeffrey Weeks, *Sex, Politics and Society* (London and New York: Longman, 1981), pp. 108–17; Alan Sinfield, *Literature, Politics and Culture in Postwar Britain* (Oxford: Basil Blackwell, 1989; Berkeley: California University Press, 1989), ch. 5; Sinfield, 'Closet dramas'; Sinfield, 'Private lives/public theatres: Noël Coward and the politics of homosexual representation', forthcoming.

6 J. R. Ackerley, *My Father and Myself* (London: Bodley Head, 1968), p. 120; Peter Wildeblood, *Against the Law* (London: Weidenfeld, 1955), p. 55. On the marginal, scarcely audible status of homosexuality, see Eve Kosofsky Sedgwick, 'Epistemology of the closet (I)', *Raritan*, 7 (1988), pp. 39–69; Jonathan Dollimore, 'Homophobia and sexual difference', in *Sexual Difference*, ed. Robert Young (special issue of *Oxford Literary Review*, 8, nos. 1–2; 1986), pp. 5–12; Jonathan Dollimore, 'The dominant and the deviant: a violent dialectic', *Critical Quarterly*, 28, nos. 1–2 (1986), pp. 179–92.

7 Sigmund Freud, *The Interpretation of Dreams*, trans. James Strachey (New York: Avon Books, 1970), p. 545.

8 Martin Esslin, *The Peopled Wound* (London: Methuen, 1970), p. 129. John Marshall shows the persistence into the 1960s of the distinction between inverts (effeminate, anomalies in nature) and perverts (wilfuly debauched); see Marshall, 'Pansies, perverts and macho men: changing conceptions of male homosexuality', in Plummer, *The Making of the Modern Homosexual*, pp. 145–50.

9 James Broom Lynne, *The Trigon*, in John Russell Taylor (ed.), *New English Dramatists 8* (Harmondsworth: Penguin Books, 1965), p. 106. *The Creeper*, by Pauline McCauley (1964), was another 'Pinteresque'/homosexual play: as in *The Servant*, for which Pinter wrote the screenplay, a leisure-class man employs a mysteriously menacing, lower-class companion (*The Creeper* also resembles *The Green Bay Tree* by Mordaunt Shairp, on which see Sinfield, 'Private lives/public theatres').

10 Lahr, *Prick Up Your Ears*, p. 178; for Sloane's awareness, see Joe Orton, *The Complete Plays* (London: Eyre Methuen, 1976), pp. 125, 135.

11 John D'Emilio, *Sexual Politics, Sexual Communities* (Chicago and London: University of Chicago Press, 1983), p. 52. On the situation in the US theatre see Kaier Curtin, *We Can Always Call Them Bulgarians* (Boston: Alyson Publications, 1987).

12 H. Montgomery Hyde, *The Other Love* (1970); (London: Mayflower, 1972), p. 238; Gordon Westwood, *A Minority* (London: Longman, 1960), p. 93, referring back to Westwood's *Society and the Homosexual* (London: Gollancz, 1952). See D. J. West, *Homosexuality*, revised edn (Harmondsworth: Penguin Books, 1960), pp. 11, 71; Jeffrey Weeks, *Coming Out: Homosexual Politics in Britain, from the Nineteenth Century to the Present* (London: Quartet, 1977), ch. 14. Plays that figured in this process included *The Green Bay Tree* by Mordaunt Shairp (1933, revived in London in 1950); *Third Person* by Andrew Rosenthal (1951); *The Immoralist* by Ruth and Augustus Goetz (1954); *South* by Julien Green (1954); *Serious Charge* by Philip King (1955); *The Prisoners of War* by J. R. Ackerley (1925, revived in 1955); *The Children's Hour* by Lillian Hellman (1934, produced in London in 1956); *The Lonesome Road* by Philip King and Robin Maugham (1957); *The Balcony* by Jean Genet (1957); *The Catalyst* by Ronald Duncan (1958); *Quaint Honour* by Roger Gellert (1958); *The Hostage* by Brendan Behan (1958), *Five Finger Exercise* by Peter Shaffer (1958). Some of these evaded censorship by being produced at the 'private' Arts theatre club (see Sinfield, 'Closet dramas').

13 Orton, *Diaries*, p. 127.

14 Peter Burton, *Parallel Lives* (London: GMP, 1985), p. 42 and pp. 38–42; Weeks, *Coming Out*, pp. 41–2.

15 Barry Took, *Laughter in the Air* (London: Robson Books, 1981), pp. 153 and 146–55.

16 Orton, *Diaries*, pp. 78–9. On decoding and Coward, see Sinfield, 'Private lives'.

17 Lahr, *Prick Up Your Ears*, pp. 250–1; see Orton, *Diaries*, p. 112.

18 Frank Parkin, *Middle Class Radicalism* (Manchester: Manchester University Press, 1968), p. 43. The figures were 94 per cent in social classes 1–2, 87 per cent in classes 3–4 and 75 per cent in classes 5–7. See Alan Sinfield, 'The theatre and its audiences', in Sinfield (ed.), *Society and Literature 1945–1970* (London: Methuen, 1983).

19 Lahr, *Prick Up Your Ears*, pp. 206–7; Shepherd, *Because We're Queers*, pp. 119–20.

20 Richard Ellmann, *Oscar Wilde* (London: Hamish Hamilton, 1987), p. 430.

21 See Shepherd, *Because We're Queers*, pp. 74–7, and his comments on the cult of The Boy, the fantasy answer to so many tensions of that time (pp. 60–4); this too was affronted by the character of Sloane. The US director had difficulty with Sloane's capricious murder of Kemp (Lahr, *Prick Up Your Ears*, p. 215).

22 Orton, *Complete Plays*, p. 200.

23 Lahr, *Prick Up Your Ears*, pp. 236–8, 255–6. Also it had been revealed shortly before that rhino whips were in use in a Sheffield police station. For another appreciation of the play from this point of view, see Albert Hunt, 'What Joe Orton saw', *New Society*, 17 April 1975, pp. 148–50.

24 Orton, *Complete Plays*, pp. 245–6; and see pp. 248, 255, 266, 271–5.

25 Orton, *Complete Plays*, p. 273; for the Lord Chamberlain's changes see Simon Trussler (ed.), *New English Dramatists 13* (Harmondsworth: Penguin Books, 1968), p. 84.

26 Trussler, introduction to *Loot*, in *New English Dramatists 13*, p. 11; Trussler, 'Farce', *Plays and Players* (June 1966), p. 72.

27 Orton, *Complete Plays*, p. 262.

28 Lahr, *Prick Up Your Ears*, p. 249; see also p. 227, and Orton, *Diaries*, pp. 75–6, 150.

29 Orton, *Diaries*, p. 91; Shepherd, *Because We're Queers*, p. 126.

30 Lahr, *Prick Up Your Ears*, p. 175.

31 Lahr, *Prick Up Your Ears*, pp. 247, 258.

32 This account is indebted to Simon Shepherd's *Because We're Queers*, especially pp. 26–8, 31, 56–8, 89, 97–8, 111. Shepherd calls the standard view of Orton as hampered and ruined by Halliwell 'The Revenge of the Closet Queens' (p. 26). I have benefited also from William A. Cohen, 'Joe Orton and the politics of subversion' (unpublished paper, University of California, Berkeley, 1989), and from the comments of Joseph Bristow, Peter Burton, William A. Cohen, Jonathan Dollimore, and Simon Shepherd.

33 Lahr, *Prick Up Your Ears*, p. 204. Rattigan put money into *Sloane* – he thought it was about a society diminished by watching television (Lahr, *Prick Up Your Ears*, p. 184). Like Rattigan, Orton was not straightforward about himself in interviews (Lahr, *Prick Up Your Ears*, p. 180; Shepherd, *Because We're Queers*, p. 86).

34 Orton, *Diaries*, pp. 249–50.

35 Orton, *Diaries*, p. 256. *Butler* was produced by Beaumont and Oscar Lewenstein at the Queen's Theatre in 1969.

36 Orton, *Diaries*, p. 256; Lahr, *Prick Up Your Ears*, pp. 330–3.

37 Hunt, 'What Joe Orton saw', p. 149.

38 Orton, *Complete Plays*, p. 368.

39 Hunt, 'What Joe Orton saw', p. 150.
40 Simon Trussler, 'Farce', *Plays and Players* (June 1966), pp. 58, 72. Orton also said: 'There's supposed to be a healthy shock, for instance, at those moments in *Loot* when an audience suddenly *stops* laughing. So if *Loot* is played as no more than farcical, it won't work' (p. 72). Orton seems to have abandoned this idea in *Butler*.
41 Shepherd, *Because We're Queers*, p. 96.
42 Orton, *Diaries*, pp. 256–7. Stanley Baxter is quoted there saying that the barracking started ten minutes after the start of the second act. I'm grateful here for a personal communication from Colin Spencer, author of *Spitting Image* (on which see below).
43 Dollimore, 'The dominant and the deviant', p. 189; and Dollimore, 'The challenge of sexuality', in Sinfield (ed.), *Society and Literature*, p. 78.
44 Jonathan Dollimore, 'Different desires: subjectivity and transgression in Wilde and Gide', *Textual Practice*, 1, 1 (1987), p. 59; see also Dollimore's *Sexuality, Transgression and Subcultures*, forthcoming.
45 Dollimore, 'The dominant and the deviant', p. 189; Orton, *Complete Plays*, p. 416.
46 Dollimore, 'The dominant and the deviant', pp. 180, 182; see also Dollimore, 'Homophobia and sexual difference', p. 8.
47 Weeks, *Coming Out*, chs. 14, 15.
48 So Shepherd, *Because We're Queers*, p. 111.
49 Sinfield, 'Private lives'.
50 Lahr, *Prick Up Your Ears*, pp. 248, pp. 187, 189.
51 Orton, *Complete Plays*, p. 244.
52 Michael Billington, *Times*, 25 October 1968, p. 8. *Spitting Image* was favourably reviewed there and by Philip French in the *New Statesman* and Hilary Spurling in the *Spectator*. But Milton Shulman's review in the *Evening Standard* was headed 'Ugh!'
53 Colin Spencer, *Spitting Image*, printed in *Plays and Players*, 16 (November, 1968), p. 28.
54 John Russell Taylor, review of *Spitting Image* in *Plays and Players*, 16 (November, 1968), p. 64.
55 Colin Spencer, interview with Peter Burton, *Transatlantic Review*, 35 (Spring 1970), p. 63. Spencer was moved partly by the attempt to gain access to his son, which was being opposed on the grounds of his homosexuality (personal communication).
56 Nancy K. Miller, 'Emphasis added: plots and plausibilities', in Elaine Showalter (ed.), *The New Feminist Criticism* (London: Virago, 1986), pp. 357, 352. See Sinfield, *Literature, Politics and Culture*, pp. 25, 225–6, 300–4.

REVIEWS

JOSEPH BRISTOW

- Celia Kitzinger, *The Social Construction of Lesbianism*, Inquiries in Social Construction Series (London: Sage Publications, 1987), 198 pp., £8.95

- Lynda Nead, *Myths of Sexuality: Representations of Women in Victorian Britain* (Oxford: Basil Blackwell, 1988), 212 pp., £19.50

- Graham McCann, *Marilyn Monroe* (Oxford: Polity Press, 1988), 219 pp., £25.00 (hardback), £8.95 (paperback)

- Rowena Chapman and Jonathan Rutherford (eds), *Male Order: Unwrapping Masculinity* (London: Lawrence & Wishart, 1988), 329 pp., £7.95

I

Although the point may seem far-fetched (and potentially very irresponsible), it needs to be borne in mind that during the first half of 1988 Britain witnessed the most iniquitous attack on the civil rights of lesbians and gay men since the brutalities of the Third Reich. Throughout a period of six months, the streets of London and many regional cities filled with demonstrations to 'Stop the Clause' – the now notorious Clause (later Section) 28 of the Local Government Bill, a piece of legislation that was raced through the parliamentary machinery. Eventually recognized as a largely unworkable law, this section prohibits the loosely formulated 'promotion' of homosexuality by local authorities. Its entry into the wide-ranging provisions of this act (covering dog licences as well as sexual deviants) was, in many respects, a reflex action against the increased visibility of gay men in relation to AIDS. It was also, of course, part of a wider programme designed to consolidate conservative myths of the family at a time when such a naturalized unit was, in all its bourgeois self-sufficiency, becoming increasingly remote from many people's lives. What is particularly significant in the context of this review is that among the key proponents of Clause 28 were two Tory women: Jill Knight and Margaret Thatcher. In an epoch when feminism has radically altered both perceptions of women (acknowledgements of sexism, for example) and how, indeed, the 'political' is defined ('the personal is political'), Margaret Thatcher, who is located in opposition to feminism, holds sway over an electorate which, to a great (if grudging) extent, consents to her politics. Unswerving and authoritarian, Thatcher presents the image of a woman who must be obeyed.

Campaigns to 'Stop the Clause' brought about a fierce resistance not only from well-organized groups of (and alliances between) lesbians and gay men but also from various trustees of the arts. It was the arts that captured most media attention in the defence of homosexuality, and the theatre in particular loudly voiced concerns about censorship. What about those scenes from Shakespeare? And what of Oscar Wilde? (Librarians rightly shared many of these anxieties.) These phenomena bore out one conspicuous point – that it was not just socialism and feminism that were alien to Thatcher; artistic life was also her enemy. All of a sudden, defenders of 'great' literature found themselves realigned on the left. And there was – more visibly perhaps than ever before – public recognition that much 'great art' had been produced by gay men. (Lesbian culture had, once more, to exist in the shadows of this public debate.)

One document from this brief period of agitation was by the painter, David Hockney, a producer of 'great' rather than popular art. He wrote in *The Sunday Times* of his hatred for 'Nanny England'. His nanny is, by implication, Thatcher. Hockney claimed that he was an exile from Britain because of its narrow-mindedness. In this censorious culture, it seems he could only be treated like a naughty boy. Imaged in this way, such resentment of his nanny's authority carries with it a fear of Thatcher's femininity, and is resonant with the misogyny that shapes much male behaviour under Thatcher. (Conservative politicians have taken up Hockney's metaphor and remodelled it to their own ends, as an attack on welfarism – the dreaded 'nanny state'. Yet, again, the fear of the powerful woman remains.)

Jacqueline Rose has opened up the discussion of Thatcher's ambiguously revered and despised femininity by examining 'what it might be about a woman in power that brings us up against the furthest and most perverse extremities of society itself.'[1] To put it bluntly, whatever political position one takes up, Thatcher's image brings out the worst in people. And this perversion is necessarily tied up with the impossibility of femininity itself – a point repeatedly returned to whenever feminism addresses psychoanalysis, a theoretical dialogue in which Rose's work is central. The argument put forward in what follows examines several issues that keep the problematic of femininity in play in studies that obey divergent methodologies. It is all too obvious (but vital) to observe that the 'problem' of femininity is inextricable from the (no quotation marks) problem of *men*. In this connection, one point taken up here concerns the recent interest in masculinity (particularly by self-identified radical men) and its intervention in current debates within sexual politics. The role of men (like me) writing in and around (but not presumptuously on behalf of) feminism will be examined because such work can appear to re-enact a familiar sexist scene of seduction.

II

Section 28 presents the first legal recognition of lesbianism on the statute books. (The previous interference in lesbian lives has most frequently been around custody cases – which have almost invariably meant the removal of children to their fathers.) The lesbian counts among the most demonized of women, as the actions of the lawcourts all too clearly demonstrate. In the popular imaginary, myths of lesbianism circulate in violently contradictory ways. Men have been known to phone up lesbian lines to make contact with prostitutes – a strange but telling equation between altogether different kinds of deviant femininity. More commonly, the lesbian is conceived of either as a man-hater or man in a woman's body: the archetypal 'invert'. In either respect, lesbianism is defined against the idea of women who have problems with men, or women who overidentify with men. That men might not figure in definitions of lesbianism is rarely taken into account. Celia Kitzinger's book inquires into lesbian self-perceptions by inviting a sample of women to go through questionnaires structured around a mathematical point system ('Q' methodology). Mechanical it may be, but it produces a diverse range of results which shows plainly that there cannot be a lesbian stereotype.

Kitzinger's study has one overarching point to make. At one time, social science dutifully pathologized the lesbian. She was a subject for corrective treatment. Then, with the advances of liberal humanism, the lesbian was accommodated by a normative model of happy and healthy individualism. Unfortunately, instead of being this time someone who was diseased, she had to come to terms with one thing still retarding her: her political disposition – either her separatism or radical feminism (the two are not the same). Kitzinger cites a number of appalling articles which set out to hierarchize the stages of so-called 'lesbian development' where the triumphant point of 'maturity' is reached when the lesbian ditches her feminism (or, worse, separatism) and is finally integrated into an accepting and cosily free-to-choose society. Sifting through her results, Kitzinger states:

> I do not glorify [what I consider to be] the best lesbian identity account by designating it as the most 'well adjusted', or placing it at the apex of some developmental hierarchy, with all other identity accounts trailing behind, indicative of psychological immaturity, but instead argue for my value claims explicitly, and from an overtly political perspective. (p. 93)

Kitzinger writes as a radical feminist, and she remarks upon her standpoint frequently (as here) to indicate how her work is explicitly informed by her politics. Throughout, Kitzinger is precise about the sample of women she has interviewed, and she brings into the foreground women who – for clearly stated reasons – have refused to co-operate with her. (A letter from a Black lesbian is cited: 'I do not want my black experience filtered through your white academic language, the rage and passion edited out, explained away' (p. 88)). Out of all of these findings, very different lesbianisms emerge – political, self-oppressed, individualistic, fulfilled, and so on.

This book has already generated a great deal of discussion in the feminist press where debates about the politics of lesbianism and lesbian desire have often appeared fraught.[2] Although I am not on the inside of these debates, it strikes me that the polarization within lesbianism (with sado-masochist dykes at one end of this culture and political lesbians at the other) points up the fundamental incoherence of what we now call 'sexual politics'. The politicization of sex and the sexualization of politics are the distinct but allied achievements of this term. In sexual politics, political agency and sexual desire are fused in a contradiction between acting and wanting, particularly when it must be admitted that declarations of specific kinds of sexual identity clearly cannot represent the heterogeneity of desire itself. (Issues similar to these have recently been discussed by Eve Kosofsky Sedgwick in an essay from her ongoing project, *Epistemology of the Closet*.)[3] One question that arises from this debate concerns the tension between what is thought to be politically right-on and what is sexually right-off. (Sado-masochism – the most controversial of sexual practices between consenting adults – frequently takes centre stage here.) Are we to police our desires to control ourselves or are our desires to be liberated from such mechanisms of social control? Lesbians and gay men have, usually in separate contexts, been examining this question with greater intensity than anyone else.

The libertarian side of this question – the need to unfetter ourselves from our persistent Victorianism – was brought into prominence by Foucault's brief and confusing Introduction to *The History of Sexuality* (1977), from which Lynda Nead's study takes its cue. Her work modifies and focuses more clearly Foucault's hypothesis about the production of sexuality via public discourses. Nead's topic is the representation of women in Victorian visual culture. (Black women and white women in the colonies do not form part of this project. It is something of a loss that Black women are not represented here since the regulation of Asian and African female sexualities says much about British self-perceptions of gender.)[4] Chapters examine in turn the wife, the adulteress, the fallen woman, the prostitute, and the female philanthropist. *Myths of Sexuality* is a pre-eminent example of the New Art History which differs sharply from the connoisseurship still present within the discipline. Visual representations are contextualized within a broader field of social concerns, and so a new art history emerges from an analysis of public discourses on femininity, the family, and the home. Nead's opening paragraphs outline two main areas of imprecision in Foucault's Introduction: first, his vague use of the term 'discourse', and second, his insensitivity to gender in the shaping of sexuality. There are further points about the Introduction worth contesting, as many of Foucault's readers have indicated. His free-floating conception of power – born of resistance as well as dominance, which is productive as well as coercive – loses sight of human agency. Power is conflated into 'discourse' and 'discourse' is then left to be the sole arbiter of history. The key problem here is that power becomes relativized, so much so that it almost disappears. Foucault does not attribute power to specific formations of class, gender, or nation but to institutional discourses – medicine, education and so on – that supposedly saturate the culture. The political investments in the public institutions of power are practically obscured from view.

Nead alerts us to these methodological stumbling-blocks. But there still remains a procedural difficulty in her prioritization of 'public' discourses (such as William Acton's influential *Prostitution* (1850)) over 'private' ones (letters, diaries, and so on), especially when the pictures she analyses put on public display images pertaining to the realm of privacy consolidated in the Victorian period. In a telling footnote, Nead glances at Peter Gay's *Education of the Senses* (1984), a compendious piece of psycho-history that examines nineteenth-century bourgeois sexuality by way of private documents:

> Gay treats these texts [diaries and other intimate correspondences] as meta-discourses; as authentic and expressive documents which reveal the 'real' attitudes of bourgeois women behind the public façade of respectability. There are a number of problems with Gay's approach. Obviously, it is impossible to assess how representative these diaries are and to what extent they may be said to illustrate 'general' attitudes and experiences among Victorian women. (p. 87)

There is the underlying assumption here that 'public' discourses are somehow more *representative* of cultural values than 'private' ones. Is Nead implying that 'public' discourses are more significant because they are more 'powerful'? It seems to be the case. This question of representativeness, therefore, is working on a model of the 'general' (the 'public') and the 'specific' (the 'private'), which is entirely common-sensical but which is none the less problematical given the content of many of the visual works under consideration. These are, to reiterate, works that often usher the realm of the private into public spaces. It is obvious that the 'public' will necessarily inform bourgeois 'privacy', and vice versa, through a number of complex transactions between both domains. Yet the transactions between one and the other are not entirely apparent in Nead's study. It is as if the powerful public realm is the only arena of discourse for comprehending bourgeois private life.

A number of questions, therefore, are posed by this discussion. When, where, and how do 'public' and 'private' become distinct from one another in these pictures? How might a knowledge of 'intimate' representations contradict or conform with 'official' discourses? Such inquiries are sometimes made in Nead's exceptionally clear and engaging readings of these representations of women. Yet, to give one example, this exclusive emphasis on the 'public' looks peculiarly imbalanced in her treatment of Augustus Leopold Egg's *Past and Present* (1858). Nead relates this serial painting to the moral panic focused on the mutiny at

Lucknow in 1857 which crystallized extraordinary fears around not only the Empire but also sexual relations, of which the Matrimonial Causes Act (1857) was one part. Nead makes startling connections between visual significations and cultural anxieties. But the direction she takes runs completely away from those private discourses that might inform the woman's 'fall'. The reason for the woman's 'fall' puzzled critics in 1858. Nead is willing to identify the male construction of female sexuality in Victorian criticism of the painting but is reluctant to investigate those private desires that fatally exile the woman from her home. The emphasis on official discourse has, then, rendered the figures in the painting silent, and so it is possible to overlook the significance of the letter read by the husband in the first frame that reveals his wife's infidelity. Is the debate around the Matrimonial Causes Bill to articulate more about this picture than the types of private writing Gay is dealing with?

Graham McCann's study of Marilyn Monroe attempts to make audible the film star's private voice – a voice pornographically silenced by biographers such as Norman Mailer. *Marilyn Monroe* is a repetitious book that tries to let Monroe speak on her own terms – or, to be more precise, McCann's '*empathic projection*' (p. 202) of what *he* considers to be *her* terms. His sorrowful concluding chapter focuses on his 'emotional involvement' (p. 206) with Monroe as it has arisen in his critical reappraisal of her biographically abused career. Putatively averse to the misogyny of so many of Monroe's male commentators, McCann seeks out a radical male position from which to justify his fascination with her:

> As women work to redefine the site of sexuality, I try to learn from them: this learning I work with a mixture of anxiety, pleasure and resistance. What I have attempted to do with the myth of Monroe is to cancel out the other male texts to consciously counteract the distortions fostered by men's uncritical styles. Monroe, for these men, is a mystery to be 'looked into' by the inquisitive male investigator: he wants to get things straight, to know who she is and who they are not. At the same time as men write Monroe's womanhood, they also write their manhood. The sense that all one really knows is one's own experience should be admitted when speaking of any experience so intimate as the sense of their own sex. (p. 214)

These are troubling sentences. They imply that McCann has transformed Monroe from an object of pornographic delectation into a vehicle to interrogate the questions about masculinity arising out of his self-conscious male spectatorship. In other words, he is using Monroe to speak about his own anxieties about speaking about Monroe. Consequently he – not Monroe – turns out to be the tragic subject of his study: 'Throughout this book,' he writes, 'I have experienced the fascination, the frustration, the feeling that just as my montage of images is set to capture the spirit of Monroe, she somehow eludes me' (p. 204). There follow a number of agonized sentences describing the painful paradoxes confronting the man who wishes to participate in feminist debate. 'Men *can* do something to help, contribute and criticize, but they must resist the temptation to assume women's space' (p. 213). Such remarks are by now familiar from the multi-cross-referenced essays to be found in *Men in Feminism* (1987), a rather wearisome enterprise where most of the (straight) male contributors draw attention to their ostentatiously impossible relationships with the women's movement.[5]

Dean MacCannell's briefer (and altogether sharper) analysis of the spate of Monroe biographies has a title that stands as a corrective to McCann's indulgences: 'Marilyn Monroe was not a man'. MacCannell's search into twentieth-century sexual history interprets Monroe's iconography as part of a distinctly modern heterosexuality:

> Marilyn's demand that we look at her backside is her naive, literalistic version of the intersubjectivity of history's first heterosexual couple – with an emphasis all the way across HETEROSEXUAL – in which both the male and female are facing in the same direction, or have adopted the same perspective on history.[6]

These remarks glance at one exceptionally large part of our sexual lives that, in spite of the immense number of 'how-to' books on the topic, has yet to be adequately theorized – that is, the history of heterosexuality. (The term itself came into being after homosexuality was named in the late nineteenth century.) MacCannell argues that 'Marilyn's representation of the attractive single woman as something airily light, friendly, openly sexual, trusting, fun, competent, and interesting, is sheer cultural terrorism' (p. 126). 'Terrorism' is not exactly apposite here but the endurance of Monroe's myth says much about something that changed in relations between American men and women in the 1950s. But what exactly was it? What might be that 'perspective on history'? What power was heterosexuality perceiving about itself in relation to increasingly visible homosexualities? And how did the advance of what has been named in the 1980s as 'heterosexism' gain ascendancy along with other social prejudices around class, age, and race?

Part of the answer relates to the intensification of the male pornographic gaze, identified by many radical feminists (especially Andrea Dworkin and Susan Griffin) as the look of death.[7] And this look emerges in a supposedly redefined form in McCann's extended musing on the photograph of Monroe by Bert Stern that graces the cover of his book:

> This singular image of Monroe caught my attention when I began writing this book and has remained in my mind. When I try to describe this feeling I court controversy: feminists have often pointed out that the veneration of physical characteristics is always a kind of objectification – yet as I try to pinpoint the essence of the image, this is what happens. This Monroe *holds* me, though I cannot say why or *where*: is it the heavy eyelids, the smoothly curved neck, the soft-lit skin, the position of the hands, the shape of the shoulders? (p. 203)

Or is it – more to the point – the way in which McCann is dramatizing this scenario? It is *how* he looks rather than *what* he is looking at that he disingenuously avoids confronting. This discomfiting book presents itself as the product of a 'sensitive' New Man investigating his masculinity with what might be described as authentic male hysteria – an uncontrollable pseudo-femininity that can only express what it 'cannot say'.

Male Order – which counts among the best of many recent studies of masculinity – analyses the male look from several perspectives: feminist, Blackgay, and radical male. The impressive Blackgay dossier on 'Race, sexuality and black masculinity' by Kobena Mercer and Isaac Julien is the most significant of the many adventurous contributions because it shifts the masculinity debate onto a different terrain, beyond the all too gender-bound sexual politics that has, until recently, remained imperialistically white. The other essays make points that are altogether more familiar to white readers on the left, if without (in the case of the men's contributions) the soul-searching that vitiated aspects of earlier collections on masculinity such as Martin Humphries and Andy Metcalf's *The Sexuality of Men* (1985). This book – in part, the outcome of debates generated by *Marxism Today* – is to be wholeheartedly welcomed since it helps to extend the terms to analyse how our sexually oppressive lives are lived, and how and why in Britain at the end of a decade of Thatcherism a new language for 'sexual politics' must be found. Otherwise, those of us involved in resisting the violation of civil rights will inadvertently participate in perpetuating what are oppressive sexual myths – like that of 'Nanny England'.

Sheffield City Polytechnic

NOTES

1 Jacqueline Rose, 'Getting away with murder', *New Statesman and Society*, 22 July 1988, p. 35. This essay has been reprinted in greatly extended form as 'Margaret Thatcher and Ruth Ellis', *New Formations*, 6 (1988), pp. 3–29.
2 Divisions within lesbianism are focused in a number of contributions to Gail Chester and Julienne Dickey (eds), *Feminism and Censorship: The Current Debate* (Bridport, Dorset: Prism Press, 1988).
3 Eve Kosofsky Sedgwick, 'Epistemology of the closet (I)', *Raritan*, 7, 4 (1988), pp. 39–69.
4 On Black female sexuality in the Victorian period, see Sander L. Gilman, 'Black bodies, white bodies: Toward an iconography of female sexuality in late nineteenth century art, medicine and literature', *Critical Inquiry*, 12 (1985), pp. 204–42, reprinted in Henry Louis Gates Jr, *'Race', Writing and Difference* (Chicago: University of Chicago Press, 1986).
5 On Alice Jardine and Paul Smith (eds), *Men in Feminism* (London: Methuen, 1987) and several other recent studies of masculinity, see Joseph Bristow, 'How men are: Speaking of masculinity', *New Formations*, 6 (1988), pp. 119–31.
6 Dean MacCannell, 'Marilyn Monroe was not a man', *Diacritics*, 17:2 (1987), p. 117.

7 For a challenging counter-statement to Dworkin's account of male necrophiliac desire, see Mary Merck, 'Bedroom horror: The fatal attraction of *Intercourse*', *Feminist Review*, 30 (1988), pp. 89–103.

MARY HAMER

- Marleen S. Barr, *Alien to Femininity: Speculative Fiction and Feminist Theory* (New York: Greenwood Press, 1987), 189 pp., £30.75

When Patrick Parrinder's *Science Fiction, its Criticism and Teaching* came out in 1980 it addressed a body of writing not then much taught in British universities. He was constructing both a history and a methodology. Founding fathers were prominent. The part played by Wells, Dostoevsky, Kingsley Amis, J. B. S. Haldane, J. D. Bernal and others received judicious consideration. The merits of teaching the genre either as a branch of American writing or as a genuinely comparative topic in world literature were discussed. Politics, perhaps not surprisingly in this pioneering study, were more or less submerged: the implications of Haldane and Bernal, themselves scientists, preaching that the scientific worker was essential to human progress were not explored. Sexual politics too were overlooked or denied. Women in Parrinder play little part either as writers or readers.

It is clear though, from the vantage point of the present, that women's contribution to the genre was not to be confined to production of the exceptional text, such as *Frankenstein*. Since the mid-1970s, when the first body of work in science fiction criticism coincided with a phase of energy and optimism in the women's movement, North American women have been producing some of the most interesting and innovative work in science fiction.

Traditionally, science fiction had privileged the 'hard' sciences: women like Marge Piercy, Joanna Russ and Tanith Lee moved in to fantasize on the basis of other kinds of knowledge, the 'soft' sciences such as anthropology, sociology, and psychology. Received patterns of relationship, sexuality, reproduction, the construction of the public and the private, work and leisure were challenged in an attempt to rethink and restructure the forms of social organization. Instead of seeking to ignore or transcend the bounding realities of the body, by means of mechanical inventiveness, their fictions worked over alternative possibilities for ways of living in community.

Not all women writing science fiction, however, have abandoned the conventional masculinist model, which has itself continued to develop. Rockets are now found only in 'space opera'. It is images from information technology and the language of computer jargon that go to create 'cyberpunk'. Here the body is once more revamped or mastered. Bodily integrity is out, prosthetics are in: implants are available for extra strength, mind implants for access to multiple artificial intelligence. But the fictions that are the subject of Barr's study have little in common with this world.

Barr describes herself as a feminist scholar of speculative fiction, a term she prefers to the narrower implication of the more familiar label, because it emphasizes the use made of fantasy by feminist writers to experiment with social and gender relations. As a student of science fiction, Barr has two aims. First, she is setting out to secure serious critical attention for the work of feminist women writers in the genre. She is one of the earliest to produce a book-length study – another is Sarah Lefanu whose engaging work, *In the Chinks of the World Machine*, came out from Women's Press last year. Barr's book, however, is firmly transatlantic in focus and the texts she discusses in detail, with the exception of Zoe Fairbairns's *Benefits*, all received their first publication in the States.

Interest in women's writing in this area is developing fast among both readers and critics in Britain: in 1985 The Women's Press launched a separate sci-fi list. Feminist science fiction was featured in the ICA series 'From my Guy to Sci-Fi', now published in book form under the same title by Pandora, and earned a chapter in *Sweet Dreams: Sexuality, Gender and Popular Fiction* (London: Lawrence & Wishart, 1988). This is no accident, for this writing poses the problem of value in acute contemporary form. It circulates as popular culture, its appeal is to pleasure and fantasy at the same time it is unambiguously political.

Formulating the critical appeal of the genre in this way, though, is no preparation for discussing Barr's work. Her interest in these narratives is of a different kind, one very much formed by the concerns of a particular sort of transatlantic feminism. Her title indicates that she set out to read a number of narratives from her chosen field in the light of feminist theory, with the clearly specified intention of getting male readers and critics of science fiction to reassess their reading practice: she hopes 'male speculative fiction critics will move beyond the belligerence of their opposition to thoroughly familiarising themselves with feminist theory and female speculative fiction'. The same simplicity characterises her approach to the reading of narrative and its discussion.

Her plan is to take a number of different theoretical texts per chapter and juxtapose them with selected science fiction narratives. The sort of theory Barr is using, however, is not exclusively literary theory. She includes Auerbach on communities of women but she is just as likely to quote Chodorow's work on mothering or essays on the technology of reproduction. Disconcertingly, she is also liable to give other fiction the status of 'theory' on occasion. The reader quickly becomes confused about what kind of enterprise is under way. How is the 'theory' supposed to react with the text? Is this an exercise in developing readings, and if not, what is going on? The uncertainty is only clarified by a study of the bibliography in which 'theoretical' sources are listed. Here, the presence of single works or essays by Victor Turner, Jane Gallop, Donald Winnicott and Xavière Gauthier make one suspect that attempts were made to get Barr to open up a rather closed world of uncompromisingly feminist interests by considering a variety of perspectives.

The purpose of bringing 'fiction' and 'theory' together appears to be mutual confirmation. Barr identifies themes in her chosen fantasy narratives – the dream of female communities, the possibility of female heroism and the conflicts around sexuality and reproduction – and wishes to establish that they are reflected in non-fictional texts. This, it is then argued, shows that we should realize that feminist science fiction reflects real problems in ordinary women's experience in the contemporary world. And shape up.

It is probably not too soon to admit that Barr's critical practice does not give much help with the puzzles that her chosen texts can offer. Fantasy reworkings of gender difference, for instance, though they may be politically desirable, produce, if we are honest, as much queasiness as deliverance. Stories about males giving suck, for instance, or union with gentle many-limbed aliens who perish at orgasm, pose problems at the least of readerly response. Their very imaginative freedom can mean that these stories are not easy reads or can only remain easy reads by acts of suppression or omission.

There is interesting work to be done on such problems: what kinds of failure are inevitable in trying to transform in fantasy the present grounds of gender relations? (It is a question raised by Lisa Moore with reference to Manet's Olympia, in a recent issue of this journal.) Suzette Haden Elgin's novel, *Native Tongue* (London: The Women's Press, 1985), offers an interesting example from within science fiction itself. Inspired in some features it is also deeply unsatisfactory. Elgin, herself a linguist, takes the principle that social relations are formed in language and tells the story of a society in which a women's language, which she calls Láadan, is created. The women believe its use, merely among themselves, will bring revolutionary change, as form is given to their previously muffled perceptions. By the end of the novel women and girls are speaking it. The changes it brings are these. The men notice the women are less easily upset and more placid. Finding this uncongenial, the men decide they will be more comfortable if the women live apart from them in a separate community. The promise of the novel's initial proposition is never honoured: readers are fobbed off with a retreat into a revived nineteenth-century female world of love and ritual, baking and quilting.

Even as I write Barr's book off as disappointing, I realize that in itself it simply reiterates the problem of the evaluation of popular culture. Barr's work, though caparisoned with the trappings of the academy – a Fulbright, footnotes, a clearly defined methodology and an extensive bibliography – is effectively addressed to a community that is not academic, not even feminist academic but feminist, in a quite specific way, *tout court*. It is itself the product of a certain sort of popular culture. Its sense of community is strong and it is a local community, of the writer's friends, colleagues, and fellow enthusiasts. The book may even be in the business of creating a readership – hailing readers where their passion for SF, gender justice and recorded precedent overlap. I can only report that its greeting fell on deaf ears here.

University of Cambridge

ROBERT HOLUB

- Jonathan Arac (ed.), *Postmodernism and Politics*, Theory and History of Literature 28 (Manchester: Manchester University Press, 1986), xiii & 171 pp., £8.95

I

Two events during the late 1980s have thrust the topic of the connection between politics and theory more urgently into the limelight than has usually been the case in the post-war era. The first of these was the revelation that Paul de Man, one of the most respected critics in American letters during the past three decades, contributed articles to newspapers, *Le Soir* and *Het Vlaamsche Land*, which harboured pro-Nazi sympathies. Even his strongest defenders do not pretend that these articles do not contain repugnant passages which implicate him in a discourse of racist and nationalist stereotypes. Since he composed them as a young man in Belgium during the early 1940s, however, there are not many serious critics who would claim that theoretical pronouncements he made after the completion of his graduate studies in the early 1950s are necessarily tainted by fascism or racism. Those who, for example, would simplistically view deconstruction, the philosophical persuasion de Man embraced towards the end of his life, as a late mutation of National Socialist ideology are wholly ignorant of both the philosophical diversity and complexity of the deconstructive enterprise and the historical forms in which German fascism proliferated. Anyone with even a cursory knowledge of philosophy under National Socialism knows that the relationship between this discipline and the state was rarely direct and unproblematic; only the most crude philosophical hacks were open propagandists for the fascist cause. Even the worst of de Man's early essays do not fall into this category.

Still there are several troubling aspects to de Man's recently discovered political activities. First and foremost among these is his total silence about any involvement with politics during these crucial years. From all the public testimony which has emerged thus far it seems that he was not candid with even his closest friends, and certainly this behaviour must strike those of us who are not quite beyond good and evil as morally reprehensible. But these articles also cast a shadow on his later theoretical work, and critics will undoubtedly read him now somewhat differently than they have in the past. Of central concern should be what topics he favoured, which subjects he eschewed, and above all how he intervened or failed to intervene politically in his writing and as a scholar/teacher at various points in his career. This sort of debate was inaugurated already in the earliest essays of de Man's supporters. They admit the undeniable fact that de Man wrote indefensible passages about the Jews in the early 1940s, although an effort is usually made to minimize his involvement with actual fascist propaganda or the most virulent forms of antisemitic prejudices. More important for the business of theory, however, is the fact that a consistent line emerged on how deconstruction fits into a possible de Man biography. Instead of entertaining the possibility that deconstruction may be an approach with some connection to de Man's own conduct, that is, an attempt to cover the past rather than to face it and admit error, de Man's later work has been seen as an attempt to deal theoretically with the very mistakes he committed in his youth. In an essay in the *London Review of Books*, for example, Christopher Norris argues in general that the thrust of de Man's critical work after he reached the United States can be understood as an implicit rejection of the very type of essentialist philosophical stance associated with both Heidegger and with the political position de Man himself formerly advocated in print.[1] In this line of argument Heidegger becomes the heavy, and Norris's playing off of de Man against the German philosopher of Dasein makes the former a champion of philosophical progressiveness and an enemy of all retrograde theoretical undertakings. Geoffrey Hartman takes a similar approach in his essay in *The New Republic*.[2] When de Man speaks of 'killing the original' and of 'essential failure', Hartman maintains, he is referring to 'the mediated and compromised idiom of his early, journalistic writings' (p. 30). Indeed, Werner Hamacher is even so bold as to assert that de Man's writings are an immense 'work of mourning' (*Trauerarbeit*), a term reserved almost exclusively in the German context for coming to terms with the National Socialist past.[3]

Despite the insistence of these various advocates and their exegetical manoeuvres, such a defence simply will not do. Norris's notion that de Man's highly sympathetic readings of Heidegger contain the seed of a political opposition is at best an odd interpretation of these texts. If de Man had really been so concerned about Heidegger's association with National Socialism – as he indeed should have been – a much more likely step for him would have been simply to write about it. But de Man avoided this topic, just as he shunned almost all overtly political topics as a professor of literature. Let me cite only one illustration of how obdurately he avoids political discourse. I take this example purposely from his later work, since all recent defenders of de Man appear convinced that his deconstructive efforts shortly before his death were deeply political. De Man had just delivered the last of six Messenger Lectures at Cornell in March of 1983 on Benjamin's essay 'The task of the translator'. The audience then engaged him in discussion, and we are fortunate enough to possess the transcript of this exchange.[4] Of particular interest is the question posed by Dominick LaCapra, who sees Benjamin as a thinker combining the subtlety of contemporary French criticism with a 'political dimension that's very much identified with messianic hope and utopianism' (p. 102). But de Man swerves away from this potential political issue and pushes Benjamin into a less dangerous Nietzschean camp, even though he is compelled to admit that Benjamin admired the leftist philosopher Ernst Bloch. His answer here, as in his discussion of Benjamin in his introduction to a collection by Hans Robert Jauss,[5] has the effect of severing Benjamin from Marxism, Brecht, and perhaps most importantly, from Benjamin's opposition to and fate at the hands of fascism. That Hartman can perversely evaluate this subversion of the hope that was so central for Benjamin's revolutionary politics as de Man's confrontation with his own past shows precisely to what lengths critics are going to suppress the simple fact that de Man went out of his way to avoid political topics in many of his later essays. It is therefore hard to believe, as Norris claims, that de Man envisioned a thorough-going investigation of Marx, Adorno, Althusser, and other Marxist thinkers – except perhaps to undermine their political value – and equally difficult to fathom how Norris can maintain that 'on the basis of those writings we do possess it is clear that his work had long been directed towards problems in exactly this area' (p. 10).[6] As strange as these claims may appear, they are relatively inoffensive when compared with Hartman's transparent excuses for his former colleague. The defence of de Man reached an apologetic low point when he accounted for racist remarks by asserting that in the early 1940s de Man 'had been trapped by an effect of language' (p. 31).[7] Since plans are well under way to make de Man's politics a discourse event – a rather apposite fate for the writings of someone who valorized rhetoric over logic – we will no doubt be treated to similar apologies in the not-too-distant future.[8]

The other event which has revived a discussion of politics and theory is the publication in France of Victor Farias's *Heidegger et le nazisme*.[9] This book, which caused such a stir in French intellectual circles, contains nothing startlingly new about Heidegger's relationship with National

Socialism, but it does demonstrate that his involvement was more sustained and more enthusiastic than had previously been thought. Heidegger's case, of course, is slightly different from de Man's. There has never been any dispute that he was a member of the party, that he lent his considerable prestige to the fascist cause when he became rector of the University of Freiburg in 1933, that he supported various principles of Nazi ideology in public speeches, and that he praised the 'Führer' as the 'Existenzprinzip' and as the highest law. That the French were so shocked by this information, all of which had been documented and discussed for decades, shows perhaps the political oblivion and the ideological naïveté in which supposedly sophisticated avant-garde theory has thrived for the past two and a half decades. Where de Man and Heidegger were most similar, besides (apparently) in their basic political views for a time, was in their inability or unwillingness to come to terms with their rather dubious past activities. De Man, as we have learned, went out of his way to conceal his past. Heidegger, for whom concealment was no longer a possibility, simply ignored the topic completely. His only sustained discussion of these controversial issues came in an interview that he gave on the condition it be published posthumously. In it he is obviously defensive and prevaricating.[10] These are neither the actions nor the words of a man with a clear conscience.

Heidegger, like de Man, avoided overtly political topics in his published works after the war. He exhibited no feelings of remorse or guilt for personal actions and, like most German intellectuals – Karl Jaspers is the great exception here – he evidently did not feel the least bit compelled to account for the horrific occurrences on the battlefield or in the concentration camps in terms of philosophical reflection. One of the few documents we possess which gives an indication of his views on undoubtedly the most shocking aspect of National Socialist barbarity – the endeavour to annihilate European Jewry – is the correspondence with Herbert Marcuse in 1947 and 1948. Actually we have only two letters, both written by Marcuse, but from them one can easily infer Heidegger's attitudes. Marcuse had met and spoken with Heidegger in Todtnauberg after the war, and in the first letter, dated 28 August 1947, he mentions issues that still trouble him from his visit. Specifically he expressed his disappointment and distress because his former teacher has never publicly disavowed his earlier ties to National Socialism. Heidegger evidently replied late in January of 1948. He appealed apparently to the difficulty of discussing these matters with those who themselves did not remain in Germany and experience National Socialism at first hand, but Marcuse correctly counters that the difficulty lies less in a possible incongruity of experience than in the Nazis' perversion of language and feelings, and the ready acceptance of this perversion by large sectors of the German population. What is most offensive and revealing about Heidegger's response, however, is his equation of the mass murder of the Jews with the Allied policy towards Germans in Eastern countries, the so-called

'Ostdeutsche'. With some justification Marcuse is enraged by Heidegger's disingenuous line of argument:

> With this proposition [equating the Holocaust to the treatment of the Eastern Germans] do you not stand outside of the dimension in which a discussion can still be conducted between human beings – outside of the logos? For only completely outside this 'logical' dimension is it possible to explain, to excuse, to comprehend a crime by insisting others would have also done the same thing. Moreover, how is it possible to place the torture, maiming, and annihilation of millions of human beings on the same level with the forced relocation of groups when none of these horrible deeds occurred? Today's world is such that the difference between inhumanity and humanity lies precisely in the difference between Nazi concentration camps and the deportations and internment camps of the post-war period.[11]

Heidegger's arguments quite obviously follow an apologetic conservative line, and until recently, when an equally pernicious variation was picked up by Ernst Nolte, Andreas Hillgruber, and other conservatives in the 'Historikerstreit', such an apology for the attempted annihilation of the Jews was considered illicit in the public sphere.[12] What Marcuse's letters tell us therefore is that the man many tout as the foremost philosopher of the twentieth century was unable to cope with the most elementary ethical distinctions, and that at least with regard to Germany and the Second World War he himself was an illustration as well as an advocate of anti-Enlightenment thought and values.

As in the case of de Man, the central question here is what effect, if any, did Heidegger's politics have on his philosophy. The issue is perhaps a bit more complicated and momentous for two reasons. First, unlike de Man, whose life can be divided into a period of youthful mistakes and mature theoretical pronouncements, Heidegger held repugnant political views at a time when he was in his philosophical prime. Second, despite the wide respect de Man enjoyed in critical circles in the United States, his influence is in no way comparable to Heidegger's. Indeed, it is fair to say that French philosophy from the middle of the twentieth century – and by extension recent developments in Western theory that include de Man's work – is unthinkable without him. Thus if Heidegger's work is somehow politically implicated in conservative or even fascist ideological movements, we might feel compelled to re-examine a good deal of what has been written under his considerable influence. In my view this may not be a bad suggestion for contemporary theorists, and I will suggest a theoretical framework within which this may be carried out in a moment. For now, however, it is germane to remark that the political implications of Heidegger's philosophy, including its possible connection with National Socialism, have been dealt with in some detail by Theodor Adorno, Robert Minder, and more recently Jürgen Habermas.[13] Even if Farias had not provided additional evidence for his proximity to fascism, it would behoove us to renew our interest in these studies and in general to take more seriously the ramifications of the seemingly abstract turn to ontology and the search for a realm of more fundamental being. Heidegger's apologists and disciples, of whom there are many, have generally avoided such 'non-philosophical' topics, but perhaps the trend towards repoliticizing theory will prompt others to take a more critical approach to these matters as well.

II

The volume under review might not seem to relate directly to the ongoing controversies around de Man and Heidegger. First of all the essays included in this collection were all written at a much earlier date; in their original form they appeared in a double issue of *boundary 2* in 1982–3 – although just selected essays from this issue are reprinted here. Only the introduction by Jonathan Arac is of more recent vintage. But more importantly the title of this book promises to draw connections between politics and post*modernism*, not politics and post*structuralism*, a topic which would relate more naturally to de Man and Heidegger. For the connection between poststructuralism, deconstruction, or any of the other various offshoots of Heideggerian criticism, and the general cultural trend labelled postmodernism is not at all certain. In fact Andreas Huyssen, in his recent volume *After the Great Divide* (1986), has argued convincingly that 'poststructuralism is primarily a discourse of and about modernism',[14] and that postmodernism has quite different concerns and a somewhat distinct trajectory. Unfortunately, however, these issues are never seriously considered by most of the contributors. Outside of Arac's introductory piece, which is highly informative and endeavours to outline and draw connections among a variety of contemporary issues, no one seems to have made anything more than a polite gesture to the postmodern. Indeed, the word itself appears in only three of the essays. Thus the title is slightly misleading, since many of the contributions make no attempt to focus our attention on what is ostensibly the theme of the volume.

This does not mean, of course, that the various essays are uninteresting or without political implications. Paul A. Bové's 'The ineluctability of difference', for example, urges critics to follow the example of Stanley Aronowitz and rethink the function of the intellectual in modern society. Although I find it difficult to agree with the postmodern label he puts on his suggestions, his call for an engaged critic who addresses 'the politics of the moment' (p. 22) is surely welcome. Mary Louise Pratt's critique of reader-response criticism in 'Interpretive strategies/Strategic interpretations' is similarly commendable although unrelated to anything recognizable as postmodernism. Treating the theoretical works of Gerald Prince, Jonathan Culler, and Stanley Fish, Pratt shows how each partakes of a perhaps unwitting conservative strategy. Prince is taken to task for maintaining artificial distinctions among the text, the reader, and the narrator; Culler's hypothesis of 'literary competence' is found 'to naturalize and legitimize the set of practices summed up under interpretive criticism, not to undermine them' (p. 44); and Fish's model of interpretive communities is attacked for ignoring the power relations which always inform them. Dana B. Polan's ' "Above all else to make you see" ' makes a greater gesture to the postmodern in analysing spectacle in film as a device which jettisons narrative myths while self-reflexively pointing to the fictionality of fictions. John Higgin's short contribution on Raymond Williams simply calls attention to his views on ideology, particularly as they differ from those of Althusser, but again the postmodern connection is missing. And Bruce Robbin's observations on John Berger's *Pig Earth* examine an exemplary case of a writer's 'engagement with our impalpable postmodernity'. Although there may not be much that one would like to label postmodern in Berger's works, they do raise one of the most important questions for western political thought: namely, how to satisfy 'the need to replace a humanist vocabulary that has been discredited along with the parties that have used it, and the equal need for a theoretical clarity that in interpreting the world would not renounce the drive to change it' (p. 149).

Those who associate politics and poststructuralism claim that French theory satisfies both of these needs, but the contributions which employ a poststructuralist methodology would seem to belie this claim. Most troubling in this regard is the essay by Andrew Parker on Ezra Pound's antisemitism. Parker undertakes an analysis which seeks to uncover a more profound explanation for Pound's racist attitudes. Via a consideration of Aristotle's *Politics* and its notion of usury, Parker arrives at the conclusion that excess is 'the most significant of the "Jewish elements" that Pound would purge' (p. 79). As anyone familiar with the French scene knows, however, excess is also a quality associated with writing (*écriture*), particularly among deconstructionists. Equating both excesses, Parker can then posit 'Pound's irreducible Jewishness' (p. 85), thus interpreting his antisemitism as an aspect of the aporia of writing against writing. In typical poststructuralist fashion, and parallel to Hartman's apology for de Man, this analysis therefore trivializes the political by making it a function of linguistic games. Pound's statements about Jews are ripped out of their historical context and placed instead in an abstract philosophical realm which encompasses everything from Aristotle to Derrida. Rather than using logical connections, Parker employs the more questionable, but unfortunately popular, device of analogy. Without explaining why, Parker assumes that the mere appearance of 'excess' in both discourses can replace an argument that would link them causally or logically. Indeed, the very uncertainty of Parker's entire undertaking can be seen in his repeated use of conditional sentences at key points in his essay:

> If this excess by which writing is characterized can be understood (provisionally) as 'an experience of the infinitely other' ... we might then infer that Judaism conveys a rhetorically similar experience, for it forms an analogous, unassimilable 'excess' on the margins of the dominant Western culture. (p. 80)

> If ... both Jews and money can function as alternate figures for 'writing', each term will maintain with the other a 'relationship of reciprocal metaphoricity in which the Jews represent money and money represents them'. [?] (p. 81)

> If, then, it were admitted that usury and rhetoric share an identical structure of 'excess', it would not be unreasonable to expect that Pound will fulminate against rhetoric and writing in the same ways that he attacks usury and Judaism. (p. 81)

> Since, in Derrida's words, 'writing will appear to us more and more as another name for this structure of supplementarity' – and since we previously discovered [!] that 'usury', 'rhetoric', and 'Judaism' may figure as alternate names for this structure as well – we then may infer that this supplementary logic would equally subvert all the dichotomies on which Pound's writings are founded ... (p. 85)

The problem here is that the dependent clauses are all so hypothetical that we should avoid drawing any conclusions from them at all. It is worth noting as well that in the first two sentences the conclusions do not follow even if we admit the condition. But the poststructuralist argument is apparently undaunted by such minor matters as logic and consistency. It is more persuasive – since rhetoric is more essential than logic anyway – to invoke Derrida, to work with vague and imprecise associations as if they were proven connections, and to build arguments progressively on any piece of speculation that strikes one's fancy. Since much of poststructuralist theory appears to be written for the initiated anyway, no one has to fear being called to account for his/her reasoning. In an essay about a novel or some obscure metaphysical point such a tactic might be merely the occasion for a good laugh. But when the politics of antisemitism are treated with the same type of 'logical' rigour that legitimated the mass murder of European Jewry, the matter is rather more pernicious in its ramifications.

Rainer Nägele's essay, 'The scene of the other', draws connections between the Negative Dialectic of Theodor W. Adorno and various aspects of poststructuralism. Unlike Parker, therefore, who applies a poststructuralist approach to a political issue, Nägele relates poststructuralism and politics by means of a third party. His analysis, similar to sections in Michael Ryan's *Marxism and Deconstruction*, relies on the political credentials of the Frankfurt School to demonstrate the oppositional valence of modern French theory. Because he takes up a limited (although hardly simple) task, this essay is one of the most successful in the volume. Especially in their opposition to a unified subject and to thinking in systemic totalities, Adorno parallels poststructuralist thought very closely. What would have to be examined more closely, of course, is whether these points of similarity are themselves political and how they relate to both the political context of their own times and ours. Nägele seems to assume that the critique of subjectivity, as undertaken by Adorno and Derrida/Lacan, is a political act, but he does not endeavour to connect this primarily epistemological concern with ethics or action. Ultimately he too, therefore, falls back on rhetoric to persuade the reader of the progressive nature of his enterprise. Near the beginning of his essay he ridicules the anxiety in the American academy which reveals itself 'in the name of humanistic scholarship and scientific objectivity' (p. 93). The real radicals, Nägele would have us believe, are those who adhere, as he does, to post-Freudian – that is, Lacanian and Derridean – modes of reading. While I would admit that such an anxiety perhaps exists among some more conservative scholars, the more disturbing tendency, I would submit, is another type of anxiety. It is most manifest among young critics and students who fear appearing positive or naïve, and who find that in the current academic climate, particularly among theorists, it is not chic to embrace any principles except those that maintain the inevitability of aporia, contradiction, and nihilism. This is a much more troubling anxiety for me because it is so widespread and because it has most often served to inhibit, rather than enhance, discussion of real political issues. It is also an anxiety that this collection will encourage rather than deter, although one might hope that the most recent shock waves from Belgium and France will restore a more differentiated political outlook.

III

Before we turn to the final essay in this volume, I would like to take a closer look at anxiety, politics, and the way to overcome the former without sacrificing the latter. Let me begin by pointing to one other instance of a somewhat too hasty affirmation of what we might call the anxiety of appearing naïve. In connection with his postulate of a humanistic anxiety, Nägele mentions in a dismissive fashion Georg Lukács' *The Destruction of Reason* (1954), a work meant to trace the ideological history of German fascism. It is probably not coincidental that Andreas Huyssen, whom I mentioned above, alludes to Lukács in a similar context, revealing I think the precise complex to which I have made reference. Defending his own critical, but largely affirmative, views on contemporary culture, Huyssen speaks of the fear of becoming the Lukács of the postmodern. He is referring, of course, to Lukács' attacks on expressionism and other modernist forms in the 1930s and is observing as a truism that we would not want to place ourselves in an analagous position *vis-à-vis* postmodernism. What is interesting in this implied admonition is Huyssen's phrasing. It suggests that we, as critics or theorists, in order not to appear naïve or dogmatic, must validate what is new, current, and 'in', and implies that there is some necessary or natural connection between the theoretical or artistic avant-garde and the political avant-garde. The problem with this stance, however, is that it departs from the very political perspective Huyssen otherwise embraces. For one thing it treats Lukács' views on modernism too simplistically. The real problem with Lukács' perspective was its dogmatic adherence to an epistemological and aesthetic prejudice, not his opposition to certain tendencies in modernism. In positing cognition and clarity as the chief features of our literary interaction with texts, he is compelled to adopt a formalist valorization of realism. For all his railing against formalism, Lukács is the most dogmatic formalist of all. From our perspective it should therefore be evident that it is the foundation of Lukács' critique of modernism which is faulty, not or not exclusively its political objectives. What would have been needed – and what is needed today for postmodernism, poststructuralism, and any of the other various 'post's flourishing in contemporary culture – is a differentiation based on political categories. Modernism as such is neither reactionary nor progressive, although certain types of modernism may fit either label very well. Brecht and T. S. Eliot, both well known modernists, cannot be lumped together politically; they are similar only by dint of formal and aesthetic, not political distinctions.

The real question, of course, is how to develop or locate these political categories. My suggestion is the following. In contrast to the poststructuralist prejudice for valorizing language and text over action and effect, I would insist that these categories, if they are to be truly political, must be derived from praxis. Politics, whether it is conceived as the interpretation of a literary text or the struggle for a specific cause, is a fundamentally ethical proposition. And since I would like to avoid recourse to propositions such as the cynical, orthodox Marxist proposition that we derive our morality from the class struggle – since this has more often than not been the pretext for the abuse of ethics – I would suggest, with Jürgen Habermas, that we take a closer look at the values propagated by the European Enlightenment. Nothing, of course, has been more disdained than the Enlightenment by avant-garde theorists since the Second World War. From Adorno and Horkheimer's violent attack in *Dialectic of Enlightenment* to the more recent work of Derrida and Foucault, the ideals of the Enlightenment, particularly reason, have been constantly besieged by theories which claim to know better. The works of Heidegger and de Man are heavily indebted to this tradition as well, and part of the politicized re-examination of them that I suggested above might also involve the implications of their rejection of Enlightenment thought. One book which has suggested a clear and comprehensible approach to this entire question is Jürgen Habermas's recent *Philosophical Discourse of Modernity*.[15] In this work Habermas champions Enlightenment and shows that the bold claims of writers from Heidegger to Derrida to escape its reach are never actually achieved. Theory remains trapped in a modern problematic which is first enunciated by Hegel and which Habermas calls 'the philosophy of the subject'. Indeed, the strength of Habermas's own project, which he posits as an alternative to this tradition, is that it is not an attempt to overcome the Enlightenment, but rather to rethink its premises from an intersubjective, communicative perspective.

Although Cornel West in his observations on Jameson's Marxism (pp. 123–44) does not rely specifically on the notion of Enlightenment, I do not think that my suggestion is incompatible with his critique. His main point is that Jameson assumes a homology between epistemology and ethics and thus too readily accepts poststructuralist methods as politically relevant. I believe that West is also correct in reproaching Jameson – and by extension others who too readily apply poststructuralism to politics – for not examining deconstructionist strategies themselves as modes of ideological activity. Poststructuralism, West argues, lives in a symbiotic relationship with the very philosophical tradition it purports to subvert. The question he poses is therefore not how to integrate poststructuralism into political theory; rather, he favours historicizing the poststructuralist enterprise itself:

> The Marxist lesson here is that only if one has taken metaphysics, epistemology, and ethics seriously will one be attracted by Heideggerian rhetoric about going beyond metaphysics or Nietzschean rhetoric about going beyond good and evil. If one instead takes history seriously – as do Marx and after 1844 American pragmatism at its best – then metaphysics, epistemology, and ethics are not formidable foes against which to fight nor are the Ali-like shuffles of the deconstructions that 'destroy' them impressive performances. On this view, deconstructionists become critically ingenious yet politically deluded ideologues, who rightly attack bourgeois humanism, yet who also become the ideological adornments of late-monopoly-capitalist academies. (p. 138)

Although West polemicizes heavily here against ethics, he does not mean to exclude this realm from a politicized theory. Rather, he criticizes Jameson's work precisely for leaving 'little or no space for either highlighting issues of political praxis within its theoretical framework or addressing modes of political praxis in its own academic setting' (p. 140). The task West envisions is thus not to go beyond existing discourses or to integrate them into a Marxist framework, but rather to transform 'present practices . . . against the backdrop of previous discursive and political practices, against the "dead" past'.

The reason that I feel this task still involves the Enlightenment is because only when we adhere to Enlightenment principles do we actually make connections with the most important political movements of our own time. For Enlightenment, conceived in its widest sense, entails emancipation from imposed hegemony, whether this hegemony appears in the form of a church, a state, linguistic structuration, or discourse. Furthermore, although a good deal has been made of the fiction of the autonomous subject and of the necessity for anti-humanism as political prerequisites in the postmodern age, there is no evidence that these notions appear either desirable or progressive to anyone except those inside a small circle of academicians, chiefly in humanities departments in the most advanced western nations. The women's and civil rights movement, as well as gay and lesbian rights movements, would appear to be extremely old-fashioned, perhaps even reactionary to most avant-garde theorists, since they demand the very kind of individual autonomy and validation of subjectivity that is currently declared a metaphysical delusion. The blacks in South Africa, the Palestinians in the Middle East, and the Sandanistas in Nicaragua would similarly be retrograde – or at least theoretically naïve – by the postmodernist yardstick for their struggle for peace, freedom, and democracy, without outside interference or intervention. Indeed, if we observe the key goals and demands from the most concrete political movements in this country and throughout the world – demands for which many have sacrificed their lives – it will not be difficult to find an almost exclusive adherence to notions propagated by the Enlightenment. I am not suggesting that we have nothing to learn from contemporary directions in theory. Foucault's notion of power, Derrida's deconstructive readings of western philosophy, Lacan's reconception of the unconscious, to name only three illustrations, are undoubtedly important contributions to our understanding of our history, our present, and ourselves. It would be foolish to think that these theories cannot be useful inside the framework of a larger strategy for change. But it seems to me that if theory in the humanities is going to contribute politically, it must concern itself less with radical gesturing, which is frequently allied with a nihilistic denial of our ability to control our own destiny through reason, co-operation, and mutual respect, and more with an alliance with those forces seeking the realization of the uncompleted task of the Enlightenment.

University of California, Berkeley

NOTES

1 Christopher Norris, 'Paul de Man's past', *London Review of Books*, 10, 3 (4 February 1988), pp. 7–11.
2 Geoffrey Hartmann, 'Paul de Man, fascism, and deconstruction: Blindness and insight', *The New Republic* (7 March 1988), pp. 27–31.
3 Werner Hamacher, 'Fortgesetzte Trauerarbeit: Paul de Mans komplizierte Strategie: Eine Erwiderung', *Frankfurter Allgemeine Zeitung* (24 February 1988). Indeed, the controversy about de Man in Germany has been more strident than one would expect, considering the meagre reception of deconstruction in literature and philosophy departments in the Federal Republic. The German interest in this matter seems to stem as much from their own recent controversies about the past, the so-called 'historians' debate' (*Historikerstreit*), as from an independent interest in de Man and deconstruction.
4 Printed in Paul de Man, *The Resistance to Theory* (Minneapolis: University of Minnesota Press, 1986), pp. 73–105.
5 Paul de Man, 'Introduction' to Hans Robert Jauss, *Toward an Aesthetic of Reception* (Minneapolis: University of Minnesota Press, 1982), pp. vii–xxv.
6 A quick perusal of three recently published volumes of de Man's work turns up only a handful of passing references to Marx, Adorno, and Althusser, and although I am obviously not as acquainted with de Man's work as Norris is, I fail to remember any of his later published essays that took up issues of

ideology or politics in any but an oblique fashion.

7 The absolute determinism Hartman offers as apology here shows exactly how questionable deconstructionist politics can be. Such a view is also philosophically unfounded, as Manfred Frank, perhaps the most astute German observer of recent theory, has shown in numerous works, the most recent of which is *Die Unhintergehbarkeit von Individualität* (Frankfurt: Suhrkamp, 1986).

8 Since I wrote this review in the Spring of 1988, scores of essays from various perspectives have appeared about de Man. The 'discourse event' to which I refer has also taken place in the form of two volumes edited by Werner Hamacher, Neil Hertz and Thomas Keenan, *Paul de Man, Wartime Journalism* and *Responses: On Paul de Man's Wartime Journalism* (both Lincoln: University of Nebraska Press, 1988 and 1989 respectively).

9 Victor Farias, *Heidegger et le nazisme* (Paris: Lagrasse, 1987).

10 Martin Heidegger, ' "Nur noch ein Gott kann uns retten": Spiegel-Gespräch mit Martin Heidegger am 23 September 1966', *Der Spiegel*, 30 (31 May 1976), pp. 193–219.

11 Herbert Marcuse, 'Gegen die Aufrechnung des Leidens' (letters to Martin Heidegger from 28 August 1947 and 13 May 1948), *Pflasterstrand*, 209 (4–17 May 1985), pp. 43–4.

12 See *Historikerstreit: Die Dokumentation der Kontroverse um die Einzigartigkeit der nationalsozialistischen Judenvernichtung* (Munich: Piper, 1987).

13 Theodor W. Adorno, *The Jargon of Authenticity*, trans. Knut Tarnowski and Frederic Will (Evanston, Ill.: Northwestern University Press, 1973); Robert Minder, 'Heidegger und Hebel oder die Sprache von Meßkirch', in *Hölderlin unter den Deutschen und andere Aufsätze zur deutschen Literatur* (Frankfurt: Suhrkamp, 1968), pp. 86–153; Jürgen Habermas, *The Philosophical Discourse of Modernity*, trans. Frederick G. Lawrence (Cambridge, Mass.: MIT Press, 1987).

14 Andreas Huyssen, *After the Great Divide: Modernism, Mass Culture, Postmodernism* (Bloomington: Indiana University Press), p. 207.

15 See note 12.

SHARON LARISCH

- Tzvetan Todorov, *Literature and its Theorists: A Personal View of Twentieth-Century Criticism*, translated by Catherine Porter (London: Routledge, 1988), vii + 203 pp., £25.00

In his influential book *The Conquest of America*, Todorov approached the problem of otherness and difference by narrating the discovery and conquest of America as an exemplary story: a story that would be 'as true as possible' but told with an eye to what biblical exegesis used to call tropological or ethical meaning. Both his 'true' history of the conquest and his meditation on the proper treatment of the other (the ethical meaning of the conquest) were based on Todorov's readings of sixteenth- and seventeenth-century Spanish chronicles. He argued that the conflation of descriptive and normative modes in those histories relegated otherness to an inferior position or erased difference all together. No chronicler, however well disposed, was able to grant difference an equal status or engage the other in dialogue. Todorov's own exemplary story, by its very nature, was informed by a similar conflation of the descriptive (the 'true' story of the conquest and the chronicles) and the normative or ethical (the equitable treatment of difference and otherness), but he did not subject the ethical implications of his own practice and of exemplary story-telling in general to scrutiny.

In his most recent exemplary narrative, *Literature and its Theorists*, however, Todorov cannot avoid examining his own position. His narrative is again both descriptive – a study of 'how people have thought about literature and criticism in the twentieth century' – and normative – a search for a type of truth, for the 'possibility of opposing nihilism without ceasing to be an atheist' (p. 2), as well as a continued investigation of otherness – in this case, the otherness of different authors, texts, and topics in literary criticism. Todorov sets himself in opposition to a 'Romantic ideology' whose cornerstone is a belief in the immanence and autotelism of the text. The immanent critic, he argues, is necessarily nihilistic and relativistic since he cannot 'ask "Does the text speak rightly?" but only "What exactly is it saying?"' (p. 7). Meaning is thus severed from truth or judgment and the possibility of any community based on a common understanding or a 'general human truth' must be abandoned. Todorov does not advocate a return to a sort of classical dogmatism – his example here is patristics – which applies a previous truth to a text. He seeks, rather, to mediate between dogmatism and nihilism. Since *Literature and its Theorists* is itself a book of criticism the exemplariness of the narrative must apply not simply to the subject of otherness and the critics in question but to Todorov's treatment of others and otherness as well. Therefore, he must avoid implying that he possesses an established truth and at the same time counter the nihilism and relativism of his age by including ethical and moral judgments. Todorov chooses the novel as his model, as he did in *The Conquest of America*; his book, he says, is 'nothing but a Bildungsroman, a novel of apprenticeship – and moreover one that remains unfinished' (p. 9). The truth is not present at the beginning of the 'novel' nor is it fully revealed at the end, although some progress towards truth is expected.

Literature and its Theorists does at times seem to trace a sort of education. The first four essays detail how a number of critics glimpse a way out of the Romantic bind while remaining mired in certain precepts of the Romantic ideology: the definition of poetic language (the formalists), the intransitivity of art (Barthes, Sartre, Blanchot), radical historicism (formalists, Sartre), a radical antihistoricism that privileges the present (Blanchot), paradox, undecidability (Blanchot, Barthes). After these opening essays, however, Todorov begins his discussion of Bakhtin, and we arrive at a crucial point in the *Bildung*. If we were to read *Literature and its Theorists* as a novel, as Todorov suggests, we would surely note that structurally and thematically the chapter on Bakhtin is the hinge of the book. It is the fifth of nine chapters, and Bakhtin's dialogic criticism is touted as a way to escape the nihilism and relativism of the modern age without falling back into dogmatism. This chapter thus serves as a critical analogue to a conversion scene. Further, we could not help but notice that Bakhtin's conversion from a type of formalist criticism to a consideration of otherness and dialogue anticipates the evolution of Todorov's own work from early formalist studies to books on alterity and, finally, ethics and morality. Bakhtin appears here as a harbinger of a new dialogic criticism:

> To reduce the other (here, the author studied) to an object is to fail to recognize this principal characteristic, namely, that he is a subject, that is, someone who speaks – exactly as I do in commenting upon him. But how can we give him back his discourse? By recognizing the kinship of our discourses, by seeing in their juxtaposition not that of meta-language and object-language, but the example of a much more familiar discursive form: dialogue. Now if I accept the view that our discourses are in a dialogic relation, I also agree to raise once again the question of truth. This does not mean returning to the situation that existed prior to Spinoza, when the Church Fathers could openly refer to truth because they believed they possessed it. Here one is aspiring to seek the truth rather than considering it as a given in advance: the truth is an ultimate horizon and a ruling idea. . . . For dialogic criticism, truth exists but we do not possess it. (p. 87)

Todorov admits that Bakhtin's practice of dialogic criticism may disappoint, and, indeed, Bakhtin's criticism often remains so firmly fixated on the formal elements of texts (the oppositions of high and low, life and death; the complex cataloguing of relationships among voices in a work; the analyses of genre) that his own voice as critic seems to go unnoticed and unexamined. But Todorov wants to *practice* dialogue in criticism rather than examine dialogue in particular works. Sartre, he claims, treated Flaubert, Baudelaire and Genet as objects, but a dialogic critic can – and should – eschew meta- or object language and the inequality between writer and critic (or, in this case, critic and critic) that such language inevitably creates.

Literature and its Theorists, then, becomes a sort of test of the possibility of passing from dialogism as an object of formalist study to dialogue and a recognition of otherness in criticism. This is the ultimate trial of the *Bildung*, and the chapters that follow Todorov's discussion of Bakhtin should best exemplify this possibility of transcending descriptive and formal criticism and acceding to intersubjectivity and a normative, common truth. At first glance it looks promising. Following the pattern of the first part of the book, Todorov exposes certain elements of the Romantic ideology in Northrop Frye's criticism, but his commentary seems to be more on a level with Frye's own discourse and he ends by praising Frye's humanness:

> The context recreated by Frye's works is that of a dialogue, not that of an impersonal study. . . . And although after finishing one of Frye's books the reader may not always have the impression of having learned a great deal, one nonetheless feels that one has been in contact for a time with a mind endowed with the rare quality of nobility. (p. 105)

The two chapters that follow his essay on Frye are, at least in their formal aspects, dialogues: an epistolary exchange with Ian Watt and a 'conversation' with Paul Benichou. In the final chapter Todorov again chooses himself as an example, recounting how his own views have changed through encounters with others, and reiterating his vision of dialogic criticism.

But the impression of dialogism and equality is, I believe, deceptive and created by Todorov's choice of interlocutors whose views closely parallel his own. If, as Todorov claims, there can be no dialogue with complete agreement, one wonders what degree of deviation from total accord can really constitute dialogue. In the case of his 'dialogues' with Watt and Benichou, Todorov summarizes his views of their work and the critics respond with slight modifications, but there is little if any progress over the course of the exchange and no significant challenge to either party's opinions. Could Todorov practice dialogic criticism if a critic's stance were very different from his own, very 'other'? The tone of the second appendix to the English edition in which Todorov surveys recent American criticism suggests that he could not, and leads us to question the status of truth in Todorov's notion of dialogism and of exemplarity in *Literature and its Theorists* and *The Conquest of America*.

Literature, Todorov argues, has truth as its object: 'literature has to do with human existence, it is a discourse oriented toward – let us not be intimidated by the ponderous words – truth and morality. . . . Literature would be nothing at all if it did not allow us to reach a better understanding of life' (p. 164). Hence, Todorov claims, criticism also must be oriented towards truth and morality, and it is here that modern criticism goes astray. But how does one define this truth? Todorov first explains his idea when commenting on a passage in A. Böckh's 1886 encyclopedia of philosophy concerning Scriptural interpretation. Noting that Böckh has passed from the affirmation that 'prior knowledge of the truth of a text cannot be used as a means for interpreting it' to 'a declaration that any question having to do with the truth of the text is irrelevant', Todorov claims that by 'truth' 'we are expected to understand not factual adequacy, which would be in any event impossible to establish in the case of the Bible, but general human truth, justice, and wisdom' (p. 7). 'General' is the key word here, and Todorov constantly appeals to a notion of universality and communality:

> Without turning one's back definitively upon universal values, one may posit them as a possible area of agreement with the other rather than as an a priori certainty. . . . The truth may be a common horizon, a set of directions for the journey, rather than a point of departure. Instead of abandoning the idea of truth, one may change its status or function, making it into a regulatory principle behind the exchange with the other, rather than the content of the program. (p. 160)

Todorov's dialogues with Watt and Benichou seem to work, then, because this universal and regulatory notion of truth is assumed before the dialogue begins. But a dialogue with critics who historicize truth or question the notion of universality – Marxists, deconstructionists, New Historicists – seems impossible. Such critics apparently have lost any claim not only to truth, but to basic human values and ethics – and, presumably, the right to engage in dialogue. Todorov's *practice* suggests that they become proper objects of criticism not potential interlocutors. They do not speak in *Literature and its Theorists* (for the most part, Todorov is content to let Robert Scholes's negative assessment represent them), and although Todorov criticizes Blanchot's criticism for leaving authors 'pathetically undifferentiated', he does not hesitate to lump infidels under one banner:

> Is it appropriate to bring these two critical tendencies [deconstruction and 'pragmatic' criticism as represented by Stanley Fish] together under a common label ('post-structuralism'), despite their theoretical and rhetorical divergencies? I think it is. They have common roots in Nietzschean philosophy. They have common enemies: on the one hand, universal values, justice, ethics; on the other, truth, knowledge, science. And they have shared affinities: the one revealed by the more or less explicit praise of force (hence the proximity with Harold Bloom, another militant Nietzschean), the other with subjective idealism (the world does not exist in itself, but only in my perception). (p. 188)

Leaving aside questions of accuracy in Todorov's assessment (one wonders especially how deconstructionists can emerge as supporters of subjective idealism), it is obvious that Todorov's truth reduces to a *belief* in a universal and general truth. If this is missing, no other common or provisional truth can exist and no dialogue can occur. In such a case, it is legitimate to abandon the notion of equality of discourse and treat the other as an object.

That Todorov drops his exemplary dialogic stance in favour of forcing his discourse on to the ideas of an absent other is unsettling, but not at all surprising. His actions are in a way determined by a previous conflation of relativism and dogmatism in terms of their use of force, a view he may have inherited from Plato. In the absence of any belief in a universal truth, he argues, force is the only means of imposing one's views. Therefore, even Stanley Fish's rather benign interpretative communities are, at best, special interest lobbies and, at worst, equal to the Party which 'decides on the meaning and nature of past events by constantly rewriting history' (p. 188). Todorov's *practice* implies that one must fight force with force and abandon dialogue in the name of truth and morality, and here, again, he seems to be following Plato who also found it necessary at times to tell (undialogic) stories as 'proofs' to counter the beliefs of his uncooperative interlocutors.

We are led to wonder, then, if Todorov's 'exemplary narratives' can be open-ended and dialogic, and if his practice can be seen as an exemplary application in criticism of Bakhtin's discussion of otherness. The problem lies with the status of an example. As Wittgenstein's discussion of 'sample' suggests, no work or author is inherently an example of anything. The form of the whole must be previously established in order for us to see each piece – be it a coloured scrap of paper, a literary work or an author – as an example of a particular thing. Similarly, each element of a *Bildung* can only be understood by appealing to the final shape of that education. His exemplary narratives may indeed be engaging and intended to shape the horizon of the dialogue, but they cannot by their very nature treat their subject dialogically nor remain incomplete.

The test of dialogue must take place in a far more open arena and among participants with more good will and fewer aspirations to power than Todorov seems willing to grant many critics. Bakhtin ultimately chose not to follow his subject outside the text or the enclosed space/time of carnival. Todorov's excursion into modern criticism leaves us thinking that this omission was not simply fortuitous but, rather, a conscious choice and a recognition of the incompatibility of criticism and dialogue.

Reed College, Portland, Oregon

LAWRENCE VENUTI

- Robert D'Amico, *Historicism and Knowledge* (London: Routledge, 1989), 174 pp., £35.00 (hardback), £9.95 (paperback)

'Historicism', the view that culture is always constituted by its relation to a specific historical moment, received its first decisive statements with Vico and Herder and then in diverse formulations – metaphysical, naturalistic, and aesthetic – it came to dominate the full range of the human sciences in nineteenth-century Germany.[1] In a steady stream of

Continental philosophers from Hegel to Nietzsche to Croce to Mann-heim, historicism has been advocated as a world view which appeared at a crucial moment to valorize historical change and dislodge earlier, static views of human life, like medieval providentialism and enlightenment mechanism. The term 'historicism' began appearing in Anglo-American philosophy only during the twentieth century, in the late 1930s and 1940s; and since this philosophical tradition had already been decisively shaped by forms of logical analysis, realism, and naturalism associated with the natural sciences, historicism underwent a telling transformation from which we are only now beginning to recover: it became an intellectual bugbear in the philosophies of history and science, with a revised meaning that more than a little reflected its critics' social situation by expressing fears of totalitarian government. No longer a general vision of human experience, historicism was reduced to a wrong-headed methodological belief in the social sciences: it was said to vitiate efforts to explain and evaluate past events by assuming a linear, evolutionary process of historical development which prompted 'scientific' prediction and social planning. In the 1940s and 1950s, this anti-historicist view was trumpeted forth in Karl Popper's attack on Marxist and other varieties of historicist thinking because they aspired to a totalizing control over social phenomena instead of the more 'open' form of 'piecemeal social engineering' which he preferred.[2] Perhaps the continuing strain of anti-historicism in contemporary analytic and poststructuralist philosophy should likewise be associated with a residual Cold War loathing for the philosophical tradition in which Marxism emerged.

Robert D'Amico's suggestive little book, however, sets aside all such historical (or historicist?) explanations of philosophical problems. With a masterful command of the literature, D'Amico shows that historicism resurfaced with a vengeance during the period after the Second World War, but he restricts his investigation to philosophy, particularly the history and philosophy of science and the epistemological questions with which poststructuralism has confronted the analytic tradition. He is out to make a case for a special, contemporary brand of historicism. He proceeds indirectly at first, through a shrewd deconstruction of Popper's anti-historicist commentary on Marx (it turns out to possess historicist assumptions), and then more explicitly, through several carefully argued critiques of philosophers and theorists from different disciplines and traditions, including Imre Lakatos and Michel Foucault, Donald Davidson and Jürgen Habermas. In having 'taken the concept as a thread running through what may seem at first a strangely diverse group of philosophers' (p. xi), D'Amico has in fact written a comprehensive history of historicism in its latest, post-war manifestations. Although he prefers to organize his chapters according to 'specific issues such as rational reconstruction, theory of interpretation, relativism, and objective know-ledge' (p. xiii), he implicitly presents a chronological alignment of texts from the 1940s to the 1980s across varied fields of philosophical inquiry. Yet his account, though it can be called historical, is not historicist in his own terms: for while he asserts that 'historicism treats its own reflections as bounded by interests, assumptions, and context' (p. xi), the only context he reconstructs is the philosophical one of conceptual issues; as a result, his consideration of the 'interests' which bound his history is extremely limited. There is a gesture toward 'recent trends in literary criticism, historiography, and the continuing debate about the role of classic texts in the educational curriculum' (p. x), but D'Amico does not link his advocacy of historicism with such a larger context in any detailed way. Inevitably, his book raises questions about its own conditions of possibility, which are left to the reader to answer.

The absence of a more sustained self-reflection seems to issue from D'Amico's particular treatment of historicism: he rejects Popper's idea that it involves a totalizing, teleological system, and instead defines it as an ultimate kind of epistemological scepticism. 'Historicism abandons efforts to prove the validity or "rightness" of concepts', argues D'Amico, 'rather it treats concepts, standards, and presuppositions as part of historical traditions which constitute objectivity' (p. xi). D'Amico explores philosophy of science from James Conant to Thomas Kuhn to Paul Feyerabend to clarify these 'historical traditions', construing them as conceptual schemes which make possible cognitive acts, but which constitute the world, not merely represent it: 'The existing facts only emerge because the categorical scheme accommodates them' (p. 51). D'Amico's critical exposition of this basic historicist premise works by assembling philosophers who share it, analytic as well as poststructuralist. Thus, Kuhn's history of science as a discontinuous series of 'paradigms' underlying research programmes is compared both to W. v. O. Quine's notion of human experience as a system of 'cultural posits' and Foucault's histories of discursive formations governed by different 'epistemes'. D'Amico's most incisive pages are devoted to untangling historicist assumptions from philosophers who won't accept the relativism entailed by their admission of the historicity of knowledge, and who therefore resort to various argumentative moves which are shown to be ineffectual. 'While Lakatos explores the internal rationality of tradition through its historical reconstruction, he also holds to certain normative standards that would make such a reconstruction unnecessary' (p. 73); 'Foucault's investigations are meant to reconstruct these perspectives.... But Foucault also, inconsistently I believe, treats his own reconstructions as beyond perspectivism and relativism because they are written at the "right" historical moment, the moment in which a past episteme is crumbling and a new arrangement has yet to solidify' (p. 95). D'Amico's solution to the antinomies he finds in both critiques and advocacies of historicism is to admit fully its sceptical consequences, but to regard them as a form of cognitive therapy:

The prejudice or presuppositional framework which constitutes the world as the object of diverse manifestations cannot and does not attempt to prove the truth of those assumptions. It simply makes its case against the possibility of an innocent or neutral reading presented as a viable alternative to this indeterminancy. Kant called the sceptic 'a species of nomads, despising all settled modes of life'. But Kant concluded ,nat the sceptic is a 'benefactor of human reason in so far as he compels us ... to keep watch, lest we consider as well-earned possession what we perhaps obtain only illegitimately'. I have considered a way to 'keep watch' over knowledge and 'without sneers' treat this constant proliferation of systems of knowledge, so much a part of the modernist experience, as finally disruptive of those familiar 'settled modes of life'. (p. 149)

This, D'Amico's concluding passage, suggests the limitations of his reconstruction of historicism. Since the mode of life he studies most is an academic specialization, philosophy, his historicist scepticism would seem to make possible no more than a philosophical pluralism: if rational reconstructions of events are underwritten by different conceptual schemes which make all reference mediated, all truth relative, then there will be constant misunderstanding – but also the constant need for clarification and debate supported by historical commentary and reconstruction. D'Amico's historicism 'does not require that argument, reasoning, and reflection be abandoned. It does require that appeals to such terms as self-evidence, common sense, demonstrative, pure, and a priori be reconstructed' (p. 146). And of course the reconstruction of these terms will be – and can only be, in D'Amico's argument – determined by a contemporaneous episteme. Yet the concept of rationality he assumes, as the above terms indicate, is relative to current philosophical discourse and a specific position within it: an epistem-ological scepticism, quite close to poststructuralism, which distrusts any master narrative, or indeed any linearity of argument, and so projects familiar deconstructive methods of reading philosophical texts. D'Amico's introductory remark that 'My inquiry is guided not by any specific philosophical "style" as much as the versions of these debates that seem to me direct and challenging' (pp. xiii–xiv) comes to appear deeply disingenuous at the end, after his repeated insistence on the inevitability of such a "style". He finally fesses up, although in a characteristically tight-lipped admission: 'I have followed the heuristic rule of suspicion; whenever a debate can be neatly classified, resist the temptation to analyze it that way' (p. 145). Chapter after chapter shows that D'Amico is in fact a superb symptomatic reader, adept at seeking out the logical discontinuities in philosophical texts – but consistently from the standpoint of a historicist scepticism.

Unfortunately, the political consequences of this view would not seem to bear out Kant's (and D'Amico's) sense of its unsettling impact on 'modes of life'. It is worth recalling how earlier, specifically philosophical forms of scepticism understood their relationship to the world. The most radical of the Greek sceptical movements, Pyrrhonism, which survives in the writings of Sextus Empiricus (d. *c*.200 AD), sought to undermine assertions of absolute truth by developing argumentative tropes, including what D'Amico would call a historicist reconstruction of the philosophical and social context of such assertions. Pyrrhonism involved a general refusal of dogmatism, but also a conservative politics: in Sextus's words, 'we follow a line of reasoning which, in accordance with appearances, points us to a life conformable to the customs of our country and its laws and institutions, and to our instinctive feelings.'[3] This distinction between social situation and 'feelings' (or between the Roman empire and the Pyrrhonists) raises intriguing problems concerning the possibilities of political opposition and resistence in philosophical inquiry, but Sextus doesn't pursue them. Pyrrhonism was a eudaemonistic philosophy, aiming to provide freedom from mental disturbance (*ataraxia*) through a suspension of judgment on metaphysical questions. From its origins with the legendary Greek philosopher Pyrrho (d. *c.*270 BC), it was really seen as a way to *abandon* resistance, even in the form of debate. Pyrrho himself left no philosophical writings; and after travelling in the court of Alexander the Great whom he eulogized in a poem, he retired to the Peloponnesian city of Elis, where he was 'so respected' by the municipal government that he was made a high priest and all philosophers were exempted from paying taxes.[4] Sextus gave Pyrrhonism a certain philosophical rigour: in fourteen books, he codified and applied the sceptical tropes to refute a broad range of dogmatic thinkers – from logicians, physicists, and ethicists to grammarians, astronomers, and musicians. Despite this prodigious achievement, however, Sextus had no impact on Roman culture and society: he left no followers, and Pyrrhonism seems to have lain dormant until its rediscovery in the sixteenth century. What the history of Pyrrhonism shows is that scepticism becomes radical in a sense that is not strictly philosophical only when it is joined to other discourses. Thus, 'one of the main avenues through which the sceptical views of antiquity entered late Renaissance thought was a central quarrel of the Reformation, the dispute over the proper standard of religious knowledge, or what was called "the rule of faith".'[5] And since theological assumptions legitimized the authority of social and political institutions during this period, philosophical strategies designed to evoke doubt concerning standards of knowledge could acquire a socially subversive function, truly disruptive of settled modes of life.

D'Amico seems to be recommending a sceptical vigilance similar to Pyrrhonism in its classical guise, and with a similar social quietism. In his case, the institution is the academic study of philosophy, and his brand of scepticism means business as usual in the philosophy business, not so much a defamiliarization as a continuation of debates familiar to those apprised of current philosophical problems. In other words, D'Amico's specifically philosophical account of historicism recommends a sceptical attitude which reflects, but does not seem able to change, current debates within philosophy. On the contrary, his conclusion seems to be a celebration of philosophical 'diversity', thereby risking a reduction of historicism to what Fredric Jameson has recently called its 'bad sense': 'an omnipresent and indiscriminate appetite for dead styles and fashions, indeed for all the styles and fashions of a dead past'.[6] The past remains 'dead' in D'Amico's historicist scepticism in so far as reconstructions of the *philosophical* conditions of knowledge will not sufficiently challenge the present institution of philosophy where such reconstructions have already gained a foothold: they are usually called 'deconstructions'.

There are, happily, glimpses of another, different kind of argument in D'Amico's book. This is an argument concerning historicist methodology, a theme he explicitly excludes at the outset: 'I have not gone on to outline how historicist research into knowledge systems would be done but some hints may be there in the critical debate' (pp. xii–xiii). The 'hints' would in fact force him to qualify his historicism by broadening his consideration of the social and political role played by the institutions in which conceptual schemes operate. D'Amico mentions, but drops, Kuhn's argument 'that the study of scientific revolutions should include investigations of such factors as calendar reform, theological debates, and political and economic changes in society' (p. 55), in favour of an approach which follows thinkers like Popper, Foucault, Larry Laudan, and others by treating intellectual history as a self-contained process. In Lakatos's words, 'internal history is self-sufficient for the presentation of the history of disembodied science, including degenerating problem-shifts'.[7] Hence D'Amico's restriction of his own account to the conceptual issues of philosophical debates. Assuming a principle of internal development is important for his historicist scepticism because he can cut knowledge off from any metaphysical foundations in subjectivity or independently existing objects, seeing it instead as a succession of theories transforming other theories. At one point, however, D'Amico incon-sistently faults Foucault for assuming precisely this idea; the problem is that it limits attention to 'external' determinants:

> In dismissing the role of interests and practical reason behind the constitution of subjectivity, Foucault thinks he has resolved the threat of relativism and historicism – but he has done so at the cost of making his very project unintelligible. Without the subjectivity knowledge ceases to have the pedagogical, institutional, or practical functions Foucault emphasizes. (p. 106)

In such statements, D'Amico suggests that more is at stake in historicism than philosophical debate, that conceptual schemes are affiliated with centres of power in any social formation, and that historicist reconstruc-tions must theorize and assess their own social effects, their own 'interests'. His concluding image of historicist studies – 'an account of how human schemes of representation can be fruitful, symbolic, useful, and even pure' (p. 148) – would seem to require a triple historicization: (1) a reconstruction of representational schemes in the context of intellectual history, (2) a reconstruction of their functioning in specific social formations, and (3) an autocritical reflection on the conceptual and social determinants of these reconstructions.

But already I am taking D'Amico's book much further than he does. My point is that a theorization of his methodological 'hints' would require him to choose and apply a specific conceptual scheme, one with a rather complicated theory of overdetermination; and if he were to apply it with as much rigour as his book now has, his discourse would assume a level of referentiality and a political project. His historicism implicitly recognizes the institution of philosophy as a field for social action in which it is necessary to take a stand made possible by the institution, but already initiating its redefinition because of the multiplicity and inherent discontinuity of conceptual schemes. 'There must be at least two discourses for there to be a breakthrough. Theory is in part the criticism of predecessors: a textual and historical treatment. One theorizes *against* other texts, other theories, other explanations, other representations – never against the blank, given world' (p. 51; my emphasis). Without standing on a scheme, historicist reconstructions don't get produced, and 'conceptual scheme' remains a vague term, used in philosophical debates solely to provoke uncertainty about realism and reference. And if the scheme does not admit a theory of overdetermination in the study of cultural practices, it can never become an intellectual tool to force an examination of the institutional framework in which representations circulate, resulting in social effects and serving political interests. D'Amico's book demonstrates that historicism is a provocative and important vantage point from which to critique realist arguments against relativism. But his philosophical brand of scepticism makes his account frustrating because it rests too complacently within institutional limits.

Temple University, Philadelphia

NOTES

1 See Georg G. Iggers, *The German Conception of History: The National Tradition of Historical Thought from Herder to the Present*, rev. edn (Middletown, Ct.: Wesleyan University Press, 1983). Hayden White clarifies the different strands of nineteenth-century historicist thinking in 'On history and historicisms', his introduction to Carlo Antoni, *From History to Sociology: The Transition in German Historical Thinking*, trans. Hayden White (1959; Westport, Ct.: Greenwood Press, 1976), pp. xv–xxviii. The subsequent history of the topic is sketched in Maurice Mandlebaum's entry, 'Historicism', in *The Encyclopedia of Philosophy*, ed. Paul Edwards (New York: Macmillan and The Free Press, 1967), vol. 4, pp. 22–5.

2 Karl Popper, *The Open Society and Its Enemies* (1945; Princeton: Princeton University Press, 1971) and *The Poverty of Historicism* (Boston: Beacon Press, 1957).

3 Sextus Empiricus, *Outlines of Pyrrhonism*, ed. and trans. R. G. Bury (London: Heinemann, and New York: G. P. Putnam's Sons, 1933), I, 17.

4 This sentence draws on Diogenes Laertius's life of Pyrrho in *Lives of Eminent Philosophers*, ed. and trans. R. D. Hicks (London: Heinemann, and

Cambridge, Mass.: Harvard University Press, 1925), IX, 64.

5 Richard H. Popkin, *The History of Scepticism from Erasmus to Descartes*, rev. edn (New York: Harper & Row, 1968), p. 1.

6 Fredric Jameson, 'Nostalgia for the Present', *South Atlantic Quarterly*, 88 (1989), pp. 517–37.

7 Imre Lakatos, *The Methodology of Scientific Research Programmes: Philosophical Papers*, vol. I, ed. John Worral and Gregory Currie (New York: Cambridge University Press, 1978), p. 117.

MATTHEW H. KRAMER

- **Allan Hutchinson, *Dwelling on the Threshold: Critical Essays on Modern Legal Thought* (Toronto: Carswell Company/London: Sweet & Maxwell, 1988), ix + 326 pp. £32.00.**

Allan Hutchinson's book is a product of the 'critical legal studies' movement, which arose in the mid-1970s in the United States, and which has since spread to Europe and to Canada (where Hutchinson is teaching at Osgoode Law Hall). The critical legal movement is made up principally of leftist scholars dissatisfied with traditional approaches to studying and teaching law, and it has brought to bear upon legal texts the more or less systematic insights and strategies that have played a prominent role in the last two decades of literary criticism: structuralism, poststructuralism, feminism, neo-Marxism, neo-pragmatism, and so forth. Critical legal writers have also drawn extensively on the work of the Legal Realists, a group of maverick thinkers in the 1920s and 1930s who anticipated a few of the techniques and ideas favoured by more recent iconoclasts.

Most of the critical legal scholars' output has been in the form of articles in law journals, and thus *Dwelling on the Threshold* may serve with some other recent books as an opening to the broader intellectual world.[1] As a result, one feels particularly annoyed while reading Hutchinson's text. However insightful and refreshing the critical legal movement has sometimes been, it has frequently displayed serious shortcomings, and these are richly in evidence in the book under review.

Before pointing out some of the weaknesses of Hutchinson's text, I should note briefly its virtues. The book displays quite wide knowledge of the legal frameworks of three countries (Canada, the UK, and the USA), and it evinces more than passing familiarity with the law of a fourth nation (Australia). It scatters throughout its pages some of the more incisive themes of critical legal scholarship, such as the attack on public/private distinctions – though it adds little or nothing to what other critical legal theorists have argued. In a few places Hutchinson is witty, and he can sometimes nicely sustain a metaphor without falling into ludicrousness.

Dwelling on the Threshold, then, is by no means unalloyedly horrid. None the less, the book's manifest inadequacies far outweigh its merits. Most of the problems with the book can be attributed to Hutchinson's dilettantism, which his preface insouciantly acknowledges:

> In trying to resolve the mysteries of law and legal thinking, I have called in aid a whole range of different scholarly insights and disciplinary methodologies. Notwithstanding Pope's admonition that 'a little learning is a dang'rous thing,' I have preferred the risks of intoxication from 'shallow draughts' at 'the Pierian spring' to a safer, but less rewarding regimen of intellectual abstinence. (p. viii)

One should perhaps commend Hutchinson for his frankness, but one can still deplore the shallowness of his draughts. Honesty need not make for insight. When Hutchinson moves from being a law professor to being a philosopher, one can only cringe at the meagreness of his familiarity with germane writings.

Some of Hutchinson's essays are so remarkably wrong-headed that they are not worth dwelling upon here. In his treatment of Stanley Fish, for example, Hutchinson declares that 'Fish seems unable or unwilling to understand constraints as real, but tentative and as operative, but provisional: they facilitate as they foreclose meaning' (p. 157). Now, if one were hoping to summarize Fish's pragmatism, one could quite accurately maintain that Fish 'understand[s] constraints as real, but tentative and as operative, but provisional'. The neo-pragmatist version of this balancing act is both the characteristic strength and the fatal weakness of Fish's texts. (This 'fatal weakness' will be discussed at greater length presently.) One is left bemused as Hutchinson rails at Fish for not taking a position that Fish takes repeatedly. *Caveat lector.*

Other defects that may be noted in passing are Hutchinson's tendency to proclaim rather than to argue, his shaky grasp of economics, and his idealist overemphasizing of his variously articulated assumption that '[t]he world is a coral reef of the mind' (p. 181). Particularly egregious is Hutchinson's conflating of metaphysical problems and political problems – a conflation that reduces much of his book to an assemblage of wholly worthless non-sequiturs. But these and other failings will have to be put aside, as the remainder of this review concentrates on his fusing of legal theory and deconstruction.[2]

Like most legal scholars, and indeed like most literary scholars, Hutchinson has vastly oversimplified and misunderstood the tenor of deconstructive philosophy. (Not long ago on a BBC Radio Four book-review programme, a reviewer announced that a certain author had 'deconstructed childhood'. It soon became clear that what the author had done was to confirm that childhood is sometimes very unpleasant.)

Hutchinson has misconstrued Derrida's work in two main ways: as a form of scepticism or anti-foundationalism, and as a quasi-structuralist method of disclosing tensions and conflicts that pervade texts. Each type of misreading serves as a type of domestication – for each tries to reclaim coherence, though ostensibly in an ungrounded form.

(1) Hutchinson's misguided equating of deconstruction and scepticism turns up at many points, of which only a few can be remarked upon here. Hutchinson assures us that, according to deconstructive philosophy, '[no] interpretation is right or wrong,' for 'the deconstructive technique . . . is to be understood as rejecting entirely the dichotomous way of thinking about and acting in the world' (pp. 36, 37). Similarly, deconstruction 'seeks to undermine the entire literary critical project by revealing how the attempt to fix words and texts with stable meaning is a futile exercise' (p. 151). Though Hutchinson admits later that deconstruction is not nihilism – it 'does not do away with that which it deconstructs' (p. 263) – he nevertheless continues to portray it as at least a relativistic form of scepticism: '[I]t impugns the validity of all metaphysics by exposing and undermining its inescapably metaphorical roots. . . . Deconstruction is not the advance guard of nihilism, but [reveals] the fabrication of social life and thought' (pp. 263, 264). A deconstructive approach 'resists the temptation to see solid ground where there is only sea and sky' (p. 264).

Here, in short, is a picture of deconstruction as neo-pragmatism – i.e., as a relativist doctrine that stresses the contingency of the status quo by depicting the 'real world' as an interpreted construct. Alas, a little learning has indeed shown itself to be a dangerous thing; were Hutchinson to improve his shallow familiarity with Derrida's work, he might then realize that deconstruction brings out the inconceivability of a neo-pragmatist viewpoint. That inconceivability can become apparent through a direct critique of neo-pragmatism (which I shall undertake in this section) or through the fleshing out of deconstructionist insights (which I elaborate in the next section).

The paradoxes of neo-pragmatism will turn out to be subtle, and will *not* stem flagrantly from what might be called the 'self-refuting dynamic' of nihilistic versions of scepticism. Some critics have maintained, rather sophomorically, that the basic message of neo-pragmatism is as inimical to itself as to the philosophies it impugns: if all truths are indeed relative, then so too must be the claim that 'all truths are relative'. This attack can be met with ease, for relativism is not nihilism. Nihilism, which seeks to have us renounce truth altogether, leads straightaway to a conspicuously self-referential mode of unravelling. Its trueness will make it false. But relativist views will not succumb quite as blatantly, and will therefore have to be approached far more subtly. For the relativist, truth always or almost always has meaning, though each meaning will be specific to a person or context. A simplistic turning of relativist doctrines against themselves will uphold the significance of those doctrines by describing their truth in starkly relativist terms. To agree that relativist statements do not have to be true for every person is to abide by relativistic standards of truth.

Of interest here is a somewhat different problem, a problem both of continuity and of genesis. To see this problem, we must turn pragmatist theses against themselves, albeit more subtly than in the 'self-refuting dynamic' argument. Reality, so the neo-pragmatist thinks, can be regarded most usefully as a changing function of the discursive networks and hermeneutic devices that come to be in place at a given time. This position (or non-position) has left out an essential query: what is the status of the discursive networks and the interpretive devices through which we grasp reality? How are they themselves grasped? Both the starting and the continuation of an interpretative group will have hinged on the ability of its members to hold a common set of beliefs. But how does someone 'hold a set of beliefs'? If such beliefs arise only in a framework of antecedent beliefs, then pragmatists will be hurling toward an infinite regress, in which the moment of interpretation cannot arrive. Every clump of beliefs will have depended fully on a preceding clump of beliefs, *ad infinitum*. If, on the other hand, one's interpretive assumptions are deemed to be apprehended *outside* other beliefs, we shall be thrown back upon the unthinkability (of pre-interpreted knowledge) that had made pragmatism so tempting in the first place. Pragmatism leads inexorably into what it rules out, because it can supply the conditions of interpretation – which, in myriad forms, are held to make *all* knowledge interpretive – only by imputing to *them* the outlawed status of pre-interpreted knowledge. The start of interpretation will have to be its deferral, a deferral both originary and continuous.

Thus, for example, every member of one of Stanley Fish's 'interpretive communities' will be shaped and maintained *as such* by the texts she reads (and by the people to whom she talks). Apart from some miraculous inspiration, she has no other way of belonging to a hermeneutic community. At every point in time she must begin or renew contact with her assumptions, from an outlook that cannot presuppose those very assumptions – for if it does presuppose them, it cannot be used to establish them. If it incorporates them already, then *ipso facto* it will be emerging too late to *introduce* them (and to *reintroduce* them at each moment). To acknowledge this point, however, and to avert an infinite regress, Fish will have to renounce his primary insight that 'strategies exist prior to the act of reading and therefore determine the shape of what is read rather than, as is usually assumed, the other way around.'[3] Here, as elsewhere, the interpretive strategies cannot provide their own portal or their own grounding; they can never already be established before they have been established. Thus, every apparent 'ground' of contextualization will itself need to be 'grounded', and will *ergo* involve an endless vortex of ungraspable hermeneutic assumptions, or will require an acontextual stopping point – shorn of any hermeneutic assumptions – that Fish has stoutly and correctly proscribed. This blind spot will undo any pragmatist approach, for, strictly speaking, it renders pragmatism unthinkable.

(2) Hutchinson's second main *faux pas* in his fusing of deconstruction and legal theory is his assurance that deconstructive methods reveal

conflicts and trade-offs similar to those highlighted by the critical legal scholars' work. Persistently, Hutchinson advances quasi-structuralist theses which he regards as flowing from his 'deconstructive approach to social reality and thinking' (p. 292). That is, he perceives 'social reality and thinking' as structured by dichotomous sets of categories which most people view as strictly either/or choices, but which the enlightened analyst sees as intermixtures. According to Hutchinson, we should stop viewing the poles of dyads as completely external to each other, and should instead acknowledge that such poles constitute each other in part.

Numerous examples of this position could be adduced from Hutchinson's text, but, because of limited space, I furnish only two here. First, while discussing the linkages between texts and contexts, Hutchinson argues that

> although texts are produced by, and must be correlated with, [social] forces, they must not be reduced to them. To reduce text-making to the traces of historical forces is as much a distortion as it is to confine it to some ahistorically isolated cell of metaphysical activity. (p. 39)

Texts and contexts, in sum, are partially intertwined and partially independent. Hutchinson descries a similar basic blend of partial autonomy and partial dependence when he writes about the shaping of human selves: 'Our present selves are partly *being*, in the sense of what we have become, and partly *becoming*, in the sense of what we will be' (p. 281).

Hutchinson, then, has cast his lot with critical legal scholars who regard deconstruction as a method of showing that ostensibly outright contradictions are in fact involuted tangles, with sides that constitute each other in part as well as exclude each other. As he proclaims in his criticism of debates between individualists and communitarians: 'The obvious challenge is to break out of this either/or–neither/nor dialectic and to conceive of the multi-dimensional relations between subject and structure in different terms. By deconstructing the morphology of social thinking, it might be possible to reconstruct social relations' (p. 285). Alas for Hutchinson, his ferreting out of balanced mixtures has very little to do with deconstructive philosophy. Deconstruction highlights paradoxes, which is to say that it highlights the disarticulation of mixtures.

To recognize fully the extent to which Hutchinson has endeavoured to water down the boldness of deconstruction, we must look at the basic flows and counterflows in which every paradox will consist. Let us examine the most familiar – though in some ways the least important – species of paradox: i.e. that engendered by certain types of self-referentiality. If someone says that she never makes truthful statements, then her statement will have to be false if it is true, and, if she has never yet managed to tell the truth, it will have to be true if it is false. In this Liar's Paradox we have an uncanny shuttle, through which alternative evaluations (of truth or falsity) lead to their own undoing. To win is to lose and to lose is to win, for each attempt to resolve the problem will have pushed us into an opposite solution (or, rather, non-solution) and back again, *ad infinitum*. A paradox is no simple conflict, but is an ineludible course of showing that simple conflicts are turned against themselves. Paradoxes evoked by certain kinds of self-reference can display with a striking clearness the structure of dependency-cum-exclusion that every paradox will comprise. In each case, the fundamental dynamic is a whirlpool of incoherent positions that can take us out of themselves only by having doubled back on themselves. Each answer to a paradoxical problem will have gutted itself by resting on a sharply opposed answer, which always will in turn have been resting on the sharply opposed answer that has led into it. Answers undo themselves by having reversed themselves again and again. An unrestrained oscillation will have subsumed and subverted every possible standpoint; for each standpoint will have twisted itself into precisely the opposite of what it is, by virtue of being what it is.

This unthinkable movement of disruptions can never be contained by those who attempt to strike a happy balance between the poles of dichotomies. Even when the conflicting poles of an opposition are viewed not as simple exteriorities *vis-à-vis* each other but as reciprocally constitutive in part, a highlighting of paradoxes will make clear that the poles' reciprocal constitution is perforce total and therefore inconceivable (because there is no place to begin). Conflicting elements of existence are always totally present *just because* they are always totally absent, and their complete inclusion and complete exclusion will disrupt any balancing or mixing, no matter how flexible the blending may be. Differentiated poles are *completely* reliant on each other at all times (while they launch devastating pre-emptive forays against each other), and the completeness of their relationship will eventually hold sway and make itself felt. Attempts at evading this uncanny reliance, by construing it as reciprocal but partial, will thus unwittingly rive themselves in two directions at once. Splitting the difference will not fend off aporias, but will have mired itself in them with particular naïveté.

As the discipline most obviously connected to discipline, law stands to benefit greatly from critiques informed by deconstructive philosophizing. Whether one's goal be to conserve or to revolutionize existing legal arrangements, one can sharpen one's thought and one's analyses with deconstructionist insights. Had Hutchinson drunk more deeply, his book might have been powerful and refreshing. As things stand, however, he would have done well to taste not.

Darwin College, Cambridge

NOTES

1 The other texts that I have in mind are David Kairys (ed.), *The Politics of Law* (New York: Panthcon, 1982); Roberto Unger, *The Critical Legal Studies*

Movement (Cambridge, Mass.: Harvard University Press, 1986); and Mark Kelman, *A Guide to Critical Legal Studies* (Cambridge, Mass.: Harvard University Press, 1987).

2 Some of the sentences in what follows are from much longer and more self-critical arguments in my *Legal Theory, Political Theory, and Deconstruction: Against Rhadamanthus* (Bloomington: Indiana University Press, forthcoming).

3 Stanley Fish, *Is There a Text in This Class?* (Cambridge, Mass.: Harvard University Press, 1980), p. 14.

DIANA KNIGHT

- **Ann Jefferson, *Reading Realism in Stendhal* (Cambridge: Cambridge University Press, 1988), xv + 262 pp., £27.50**

When Barthes wanted to find a way to write about photography that would account for how individual photographs spoke to his soul, he did not abandon the vocabulary of *realism*. He did, however, abandon the language of semiology through which he had previously unmasked the photographic image as coded representation, suppressing, in the name of theoretical and ideological correctness, his instinct that photographs might be messages that simply didn't pass through a code. Finally careless of correct positions, he elaborated instead an intentional approach to the photographic referent through the strategic concept of the *punctum*, a marginal detail which disturbs the coded *studium* through the intensity of its appeal to the spectator. As *La Chambre claire* unfolds the *punctum* shifts in meaning from a contingent material detail (accidentally also present), to that something in a photograph which plays upon the viewer's affective reponse. This carries photography away from its role as guarantor of an historically existing reality (though it remains this as well), into the realm of desire and pity. Barthes closes the essay by declaring the two approaches (the semiological and the phenomenological) incompatible. Both, in his work, had always built in the position of the viewer or reader; only intentionality could restore the lost referent inaccessible to the Saussurian model. Had Barthes lived long enough to transpose this discussion to the reading of literary representations (he had already sent pointers in this direction in his 1978 lecture on Proust), and had the fact of his death not dominated the reception of *La Chambre claire*, I believe he might well have effected a major shift in the basic terms of the realist debate.[1]

Reading Realism in Stendhal, which cuts across all of the territory occupied in these ways by Barthes, and which attempts to mediate seemingly incompatible positions, should be acknowledged as a major contribution to setting such a shift in motion. Ann Jefferson achieves this in two crucial ways. First, by her decision to mobilize Bakhtin, to whom, in an important article, she had already had recourse to find a way out of the theoretical *impasse* of 'linguistic' versus 'realistic' perceptions of the literary referent.[2] What she called there Bakhtin's 'will to reference' already suggests the usefulness of a strategic recourse to an intentional dimension. Second, by the more basic decision to read realism in *Stendhal* rather than Balzac. For as Jefferson demonstrates, Stendhal occupies an uneasy position in most accounts of nineteenth-century French realism: acknowledged as elder brother and joint founder, yet very much the least important partner in the enterprise, a bachelor uncle with no issue. His relative failure is blamed, by both Auerbach and Lukács for example, on his ideological and aesthetic allegiance to the eighteenth century into which he was born. Jefferson takes Stendhal's straddling of centuries seriously, and uses it to problematize devaluations of his realism that operate from an exclusively nineteenth-century norm.

The importance of this move, implicit in Jefferson's argument, is spelled out more explicitly from the feminist perspective of Naomi Schor's recent attempts to unsettle the received narrative of nineteenth-century realism. In *Breaking the Chain* Schor argues that Stendhal and Balzac 'name the split within realism', and proposes that Stendhal replace Balzac as the paradigmatic realistic novelist (stressing the unlikeliness of the proposal as a measure of the critical work to be done). She sets out to show that nascent French realism depends precisely on the binding of female energy, hence Stendhal's failure to sustain the representation of a 'mobile, fully empowered female protagonist'.[3] Her attempts to uncover the gendered nature of the aesthetic value judgements which shape literary history reappear in an article on the decanonization of George Sand, where she most pertinently identifies the grip of the privileging of *Balzacian* realism from Auerbach and Lukács to Barthes and Christopher Prendergast (*The Order of Mimesis*): 'the valorization of realism – the masculine mode – remains largely unexamined in contemporary theories of representation and the canonic hierarchies they serve to secure'.[4] That Barthes's very last text should be a scintillating lecture on Stendhal's joyful, female-gendered and carnivalesque resolution of his former inability to communicate his passion for Italy, and this through the *novelistic* mediation of *La Chartreuse de Parme*, seems a happy sign that he was about to mend his ways (a posthumous sign discovered, almost comically, in Barthes's typewriter).[5] Prendergast's puzzled reaction to this 'unsatisfactory' celebration of narrative as an unblocking of desire (rather than a major cultural form of the platitude in line with *S/Z*), very much confirms Schor's important claim.[6]

Jefferson's book is organized around an exploration of Stendhal's seemingly incompatible metaphors for the novel: a mirror that 'objectively' reflects social reality, a bow that plays upon the violin of the reader's soul. She argues that it is Stendhal's adherence to eighteenth-century pragmatic aesthetics that allows him to escape the worst sins of the nineteenth-century realism to which he could not but contribute, albeit somewhat despite himself. For the imitation implied by the requirements of mimesis tended to be viewed very negatively by Stendhal. Either mimesis was feared as plagiarizing imitation of sources or the clichéd literary models of the day (his fear for himself), or as platitudinous imitation by his model-conscious readers of his characters' behaviour, or of his own aesthetic creations in an age of escalating mechanical reproduction of both the written word and the visual image. (Jefferson writes interestingly on the way mechanical reproduction impinged, and has continued to do so, on the rhetoric of representation with its clichés, stereotypes, etc.) By shaping his novelistic writing (*De l'amour* and *La Vie de Henry Brulard*, as well as *Le Rouge et le noir* and *La Chartreuse de Parme*) as a violin bow to draw out from his reader a performative response, Stendhal outplays the 'twin snares of emulation and imitation' (p. 41). For the only effective mirror is one that is also a bow: the reader is invited to validate the text as mimesis through his or her performative response to it (p. 140). Since representation for Stendhal is inseparable from response the relationship between the mirror and the bow is a symbiotic one.

Jefferson claims, therefore, that Stendhal's preoccupation with both negative and positive readers is inseparable from his basically mimetic project, both at the level of content and at the level of address. Her use of Bakhtin is very suggestive in opening up Stendhal's works as representations of conflicting discourses speaking from a whole variety of social contexts, and as the staging of an ambivalent relationship with potential readers. In the end, though, I am not sure whether Jefferson is talking about real readers, or fictionalized readers represented within the texts and crucial to their internal dynamics. Do the Happy Few live outside the text or within it? Is the violin bow destined simply for the Happy Few whose elite emotions alone might permit full validation of Stendhal's representations? Can novels work that really despise such a large proportion of their actual readership? I would personally argue that the Happy Few become enabling readers (rather than irritating, elitist readers) if they are viewed as *utopian* readers, projected into their hypothetical future from within the text, and used precisely to dialogize the mundane power struggles of the *doxa*. For in this way these supposedly petty local disputes might in their turn be allowed to dialogize the worrying elitism of the Happy Few, and even the despised readers of novels for chambermaids (or of Mme de Staël) might reclaim their political right to be heard.

For on the one hand I find the apoliticism of Jefferson's reading of Stendhal the least satisfactory aspect of the book. Jefferson appears to call up a liberal-humanist rather than materialist Bakhtin to legitimize this, with Leuwen *père* and especially Mosca adduced as wisely ironic exemplifications of the novelist's 'uncommitted representational polyphony' (p. 178). Though her comparison of the novel and the opera as polyphonic forms works rather well in her discussion of the *Chartreuse*, her equation of the general loquacity of the novels with 'a witty conversation in a salon' (p. 108), and the general emergence of 'ideological agnosticism' as an authorial ideal, seems a denial of her own more sophisticated article on Bakhtin referred to above. It is also an alarming trivialization of such morally and politically serious novels as *Lucien Leuwen* and the *Chartreuse*, which may well play off the boredom of democracies (obligation to converse with one's grocer, etc.) against the absolute-monarchy delights of the opera, but which also face up to the shadow cast by the massacre of the rue Transnonain and by Mosca's gay acceptance of his own bloody suppression of Ferrante Palla's revolution (financed by Gina's jewels). To speak in this context of the political merits of Mosca's 'disinterested pluralism' is to produce a partial reading indeed, and one surely controversial enough to require a more detailed defence than a mere footnote declaration of disagreement with H.-F. Imbert (p. 245). But, on the other hand, it is Jefferson herself who suggests ways of pushing the use of Bakhtin far enough to open up new areas of ideological ambiguity in Stendhal, for example by more attention to clashes of interest at the level of class and perhaps especially the gender of the addressed reader. All this, and especially the carnivalization so important to the *Chartreuse*, would go a long way towards dialogizing the basically conservative 'novel of worldliness' which Peter Brooks so convincingly analyses as a problematic ideal in Stendhal's novels.[7]

There is one other area in which *Reading Realism in Stendhal* does not quite strike a chord in this particular reader's soul, and that is where Jefferson seems to recommend reading parts of Stendhal's fictional universe as a rather dry allegory of the problems of literary representation as she has defined them. Thus the wonderfully passive Fabrice is endowed with a 'degree zero' character simply so that his readers won't be able to emulate him, the poetic play with omens exists merely to block a self-awareness that might create a character for Fabrice after all, while his array of masks and disguises are given a similarly 'asymbolic' reading. And, in the end, Jefferson's desire to produce an all-embracing and logical account of Stendhal's fictional practice leads her to the strange conclusion that having rethought Stendhal's realism we should not rewrite literary history and over-centralize his place in the realist tradition. For to do so would be to accuse him of having provoked imitation rather than reverie, and this would be a betrayal of the aesthetic position of blocked emulation to which he most aspired. This means that despite her another-look-at-realism framework Jefferson denies the theoretical importance of the areas opened up in this ambitious and elegantly argued book. I'm not sure if this should be attributed to authorial modesty or to the inescapable power of what Schor calls the male narrative of realism. But it seems to me important that Stendhal and this book should not be allowed to slip back into the shadow of the Balzacian model, and that Jefferson and her bachelor uncle should legitimize or at least acknowledge their literary and theoretical offspring.

University of Nottingham

NOTES

1 Roland Barthes, *La Chambre claire: note sur la photographie* (Paris: Gallimard and Seuil, 1980), and ' "Longtemps, je me suis couché de bonne heure" ', in *Le Bruissement de la langue: Essais critiques IV* (Paris: Seuil, 1984).
2 Ann Jefferson, 'Realism reconsidered: Bakhtin's dialogism and the "will to reference" ', *Australian Journal of French Studies*, 23:2 (1986), pp. 169–84.
3 Naomi Schor, *Breaking the Chain: Women, Theory and French Realist Fiction* (New York: Columbia University Press, 1985), p. 142.
4 Naomi Schor, 'Idealism in the novel: recanonizing Sand', *Yale French Studies*, 75 (1988), pp. 56–73, p. 68.
5 Roland Barthes, 'On échoue toujours à parler de ce qu'on aime', in *Le Bruissement de la langue* pp. 333–41.
6 Christopher Prendergast, *The Order of Mimesis: Balzac, Stendhal, Nerval, Flaubert* (Cambridge: Cambridge University Press, 1986), p. 145.
7 Peter Brooks, 'Stendhal and the styles of worldliness', in *The Novel of Worldliness: Crébillon, Marivaux, Laclos, Stendhal* (Princeton: Princeton University Press) pp. 219–78.

RONALD STRICKLAND

● **Paul Smith, *Discerning the Subject*, foreword by John Mowitt (Minneapolis: University of Minnesota Press, 1988, xxxix + 185 pp., $29.50 (hardback), $13.95 (paperback)**

The title of Paul Smith's book involves a pun on two obscure verbs: 'to cern', meaning 'to accept an inheritance or a patrimony'; and 'to cerne', which means 'to encircle' or 'to enclose' (p. xxx). In most recent work on the problem of subjectivity, Smith observes, the 'subject' is conceived as completely 'cerned' or dominated by forces beyond one's control – whether these forces are those of the dominant ideology (in the Marxist paradigm) or those of the textualized (and hence restricted) unconscious (in the psycholinguistic paradigm). In their emphasis on the 'subjection' of the subject, the author complains, recent theorists have left 'little room to envisage the agent of real and effective resistance' (p. 39). Against this trend, Smith's mission is to reintroduce a concept of individual agency into political and psychoanalytic theories of subjectivity.

At the outset, Smith defines a special-purpose term – the 'subject/ individual' – which is to be distinguished from the concept 'individual subject':

> The 'individual' is that which is undivided and whole, and understood to be the source and agent of conscious action or meaning which is consistent with it. The 'subject', on the other hand, is not self-contained ... but is immediately cast into a conflict with forces that dominate it. . . . The 'subject', then, is determined . . . whereas 'the individual' is assumed to be determining. (pp. xxxiii–iv)

On this account, the familiar term 'individual subject' is revealed as self-contradictory. But Smith sees this contradiction as a useful way of theorizing agency – agency can be located in the dialectical tension between the singular experience of the subject and the subject's social subjection. Or, the opposition can be thought in terms of an incompatibility between the discourses of Marxism, which 'subsume the human person under society', and those of psychoanalysis, which 'promote a view of the "subject" as a kind of "beginning and end of theory and practice"' (p. 22). Smith proposes the term 'subject/individual' as a way of recognizing that there is always some 'individual' aspect of subjectivity which falls outside the sphere of interpellation by the dominant ideology. Thus, a British subject 'is subject to particular forms of state control and hortation', but also to other, potentially conflicting discourses such as ethnic and gender status, regional identification, one's family, and 'to particular modes and languages of advertising which will place the "subject" as a consumer' (p xxxiv).

Here Smith seems to understand resistance as the product of a limited ideological conflict within a given ensemble of discourses. But at several subsequent points he abandons this strictly discursive model of subjectivity to locate resistance (and, implicitly, agency) in the singular (hence, ultimately, extra-discursive) history of the subject/individual. If it may be granted that the singular history of the subject is a source of resistance, some conscious focus of that resistance is still required for a useful concept of agency. I would argue that the point at which any subject can lay claim to a unique, singular experience is exactly the threshold of political and theoretical irrelevance. The unique experience cannot generate the power or meaning required to motivate subjects for coherent political action. Thus, in my view, Smith's identification of the subject's singular history as a 'positive' source of agency which can withstand the negative power of ideology leads no further than essentialist claims of individual autonomy. Yet, however much I disagree with his agenda and his conclusions, he provides a useful review and a series of provocative critiques of various attempts to theorize a space for agency or resistance within ideology.

Smith begins with an overview of Marxist and post-Marxist theories of ideology. Althusser's understanding of ideology as a material process is indispensable, he argues, as is the Althusserian distinction between particular forms of ideology and 'ideology-in-general'. He acknowledges the continuing usefulness of Althusser's theory that subjects are interpellated, or 'called into position by specific social discourses'. But a crucial shortcoming, as Smith points out, is that Althusser's 'individual subject' is completely overdetermined by the dominant ideology. Although Althusser distinguishes between ideology-in-general and particular ideologies, he leaves no space for ideological conflict at the level of the subject, or for individual resistance to ideological interpellation. Alluding to Althusser's familiar example of the expected baby (which is always-already an interpellated subject because it cannot escape being born into a social situation charged with overdetermining expectations), Smith points out that for Althusser, 'ideology interpellates only whole human entities' (pp. 17–18). That is, Althusser conflates the terms 'subject' and 'individual' by presuming the 'individual' to be always-already completely 'subjected' even before birth.

Some of Althusser's followers, on the other hand, have acknowledged the inevitability of contradiction or resistance in the process of interpellation. By applying Althusser's theory to the particular relationship of audience and text in the discourse of realist cinema, the work of the *Screen* group in the 1970s suggested that ideological interpellation was not monolithic: 'as soon as it is proposed that the subject is the effect of a given signifying practice, it must then be claimed that interpellation is various, a function of the almost limitless production of discourses, texts, and addresses which together constitute social life.' The virtue of 'this more sophisticated and complex view of subjectivity . . .', Smith asserts, 'is that it would be able to recognize the specificity, not only of any given signifying practice, but also of singular histories' (p. 31).

The *Screen* group, however, was not interested in pursuing singular histories – in Smith's view they were bound with a 'debilitating inflexibility' to a 'mechanistic strand' in Althusser's thought (p. 32). As Smith observes, *Screen* theory tended to posit a homology between a particular discourse (realist cinema) and its audience-as-subject, failing to consider, adequately, the subject's role as the site of discursive conflict. On this account, Smith charges the *Screen* theorists with 'a reluctance to consider the relationship between discourse and "subjects" as anything but an abstract one' (p. 32). The terms he opposes to 'abstract', however, are not terms like 'concrete', 'real', or 'actual', but terms like 'singular' and 'personal'. While acknowledging that 'subjectivity as such is always constructed within the purview of discourse', Smith insists upon the importance of individual experience: 'each of us necessarily negotiates the power of specific ideologies by means of our own personal history' (p. 37). Thus here, as throughout his book, Smith's critique of 'abstract' theories of subjectivity strives to theorize something very like a self-determined individual – a singular, unique subject that could escape the constraints of discourse.

Symptoms of this individualist agenda can be read in Smith's brief treatment of the work of the post-Althusserian philosopher of linguistics,

Michel Pecheux (pp. 32–3). In his book *Language, Semantics, and Ideology* (New York: St Martin's Press, 1982), Pecheux posits three distinct 'modalities' of the relation between the subject (the 'subject of enunciation') and its dominant ideology (the 'universal subject'). The first is 'identification', or the 'good' subject who accepts his/her place in the social order without question. The second is 'counter-identification', or the 'bad' subject who simply denies and opposes the dominant ideology on its own terms, and in so doing inadvertently reaffirms the power of the dominant ideology by accepting the 'evidentness of meaning' upon which it rests (Pecheux, pp. 156–8). The third position Pecheux calls 'disidentification': an effect which 'constitutes a working (transformation-displacement) *of the subject form and not just its abolition*' (Pecheux, p. 159; author's emphasis). In Pecheux's model, the space for resistance opened by the notion of 'disidentification' is clearly produced (and limited) by the play of conflicting discourses in a social order, rather than by the discontinuity between ideology and the subject, where Smith attempts to locate resistance and agency. But, in describing – and dismissing – Pecheux's work, Smith mentions only the concept of 'identification', omitting Pecheux's other terms. This omission, I think, is a symptom of Smith's concern to locate resistance at the level of the subject/individual rather than at the level of discourse. Pecheux's theory of disidentification is somewhat vague and undeveloped, and it allows only a fairly narrow scope of agency. Still, the concept does offer a way of theorizing conscious resistance and social change completely within the bounds of discourse. In Pecheux's theory resistance results from the conflict of interpellations (as in Smith's example of the British subject cited above); the subject's singular (and extradiscursive) experience is de-emphasized.

Smith is generally critical of theories which resist thinking of subjectivity outside of language. For example, he criticizes Derrida for trying 'to establish a kind of subjectless process which is in all essential ways given over to the force or forces of language' (p. 49). This 'subjectlessness' is identified as the source of deconstruction's apolitical tendencies, 'a patent eschewing of responsibility' (p. 50). Here Smith's notion of subjectivity (the subject/individual) depends upon a particular understanding of the unconscious as essentially extralinguistic. He elaborates this later in a reading of Lacan which yields a distinction between the 'subject' and the 'subject/individual': 'a difference ... between the actual construction of the "subject" in the realm of the symbolic and the ability of a given subject/individual to read ideological signs and messages' (p. 70). What Smith goes on to argue is that Lacan's placing of the unconscious at the mediating edge between the subject and the symbolic order effectively protects some area of subjectivity from ideological subjection. Thus, the unconscious, in Smith's understanding of Lacan, effects an 'interference ... in relation to both "subject" and Other, or to both being and meaning' (p. 74). This 'interference' is another way of expressing what Smith has elsewhere described as the gap between ideological interpellation and the subject/individual's singular history. But, at this point in the book it becomes clear that the sort of agency which can emerge from this gap between ideology and the subject is much more nebulous and negative than expected. Agency or resistance begins to look like nothing more than the 'power' of the subject/individual to be imperfectly interpellated.

Variations of this vague 'subjectivity as negativity' are located in readings of Barthes and Kristeva, but the principal showcase for Smith's notion of individual resistance is contemporary feminism. Smith finds what can only be described as a source of organic resistance in the uneasy tension between the essentialist, identitarian assumptions about subjectivity which have traditionally characterized Anglo-American feminism and the psychoanalytically informed notions of subjectivity generally associated with French feminism. He begins his chapter on feminism by criticizing Toril Moi's argument (in *Sexual/Textual Politics*, London: Methuen, 1985) that the patriarchal hegemony of language effectively forecloses any politically useful notion of feminine specificity (p. 134). For Moi this simply calls for an ideology critique of the material conditions of women's oppression. Against this strategy – which he views as too limited – Smith proposes a general and largely uncritical celebration of feminism. 'In its very constitution – as varied and variegated as that might be –', Smith writes, 'feminism can actually represent a fundamental challenge to the kinds of claims which writers such as Moi make, as well as to the more general political effects of the traditional patterns of cerning' (p. 134).

Smith might be accused, at this point, of cerning feminism himself. He joins two oppositional discourses (essentialist and poststructural feminism) under the overarching structure of what looks suspiciously like an essential contradiction. One undesirable theoretical consequence of this move, it seems to me, is to valorize humanist feminism as a serious response to discursive theories of the subject. In fact, and not altogether surprisingly, Smith's attempt to make essentialist humanism respectable under the banner of feminist dialectic quickly leads to a sort of reformist conclusion. Since women have been defined as other by the patriarchy, Smith goes on to claim, 'if women begin to speak and act from the same ground of cerned subjectivity and identity as men have traditionally enjoyed, a resistance is automatically effected, in a sense' (p. 137).

In fairness to Smith, he is quick to acknowledge that feminist subversions based on essentialist humanist assumptions have been easily recuperated by the patriarchal order. But he is not willing to give up that humanist, identitarian element of feminism. Setting aside the argument that the sort of resistance described above is clearly produced out of discursive conflict (falling neatly under Pecheux's category of disidentification), it is theoretically and politically counter-productive to hail it as a viable resistance produced out of an essentially feminine subjectivity. One can certainly concede that the growing number of women in previously exclusively male occupations represents a sort of *de facto* revolution in gender relations, but to hold this up as a model of resistance inhibits active resistance and further change while it tends to obscure the continuing oppression of women at other levels.

Responding to this essentialist strain in his foreword to Smith's book, John Mowitt observes that the argument behind Smith's proposal that feminism is an inherent site of resistance depends upon the 'sanguine' assumption that resistance 'is implicit or latent in the general dynamic of activation, what he calls negativity':

> That is, because agency is, as it were, the backdrop of subjectivity resistance will take place. Now only if one assumes that history is all but totally administered can one be so sanguine about such a state of latency, i.e., one has to assume that *anything* would be better than the present order of things to read sheer negativity as affirmable political resistance in itself. (p. xx)

This bleak, passive understanding of agency, Mowitt continues, is not really characteristic of Smith's outlook – when all is said and done, Smith 'must affirm some sort of mediation between negativity and resistance' (p. xx). 'Must affirm' may be putting it too strongly, but I agree with Mowitt that Smith is generally uncomfortable with the simple notion of agency as negativity. Surprisingly, however, Mowitt suggests that theory mediates between the two terms in Smith's thought. Perhaps. But as I read Smith, the unspoken mediator which focuses negativity into resistance is the theory-resistant individual. The importance he places on the subject/individual's singular history is only the most visible among many signs of his dissatisfaction with a discursive subject which he sees as much too tightly bound by ideology.

Illinois State University

PETER BROOKER

- Elizabeth Wright, *Postmodern Brecht. A Re-Presentation* (London and New York: Routledge, 1989), 154 pp., £8.95 (paperback)

It depends of course on what you mean by 'postmodern'. And, as it turns out, by 'deconstruction', 'poststructuralist' and 'Marxist', for Brecht is described here as all four. You read this book then wondering what its title and these assorted terms can mean together, and, inevitably, what this will mean for the flip-flopping pile of questions the words 'Brecht' and 'postmodern' trawl on to the page. What will this study say, for example, about distinctions between the avant-garde and modernism, about the shifting relations of 'art' and 'mass' culture, about critical or acquiescent tendencies in postmodernism, about Marxism and post-Marxism, about 'communist art' and the present-day crisis in communism? A tall order of course, though as Brecht said of the tasks of socialist realism, it could be made taller. (What of the influence of Brecht upon the last two decades of 'postmodern' cultural theory?) Some of these questions are touched on in these pages, but it couldn't be said that any are really fully grasped, and indeed by the end they seem to have slipped through the net as if they'd never been there.

The chapters in the book deal in turn with the critical reception, communist and bourgeois, East and West, of Brecht the man and work; with Brecht's dramatic theory; with positions in the debates on modernism and postmodernism; and with the expropriation and refunctioning of Brecht in the performance theatre of Pina Bausch and the plays of Heiner Müller. Müller is the best catch. The rest surveys the field, moving smartly from topic to topic, picking up this and that possibility, eyeing, appraising and reappraising it, only to put it down and move on. The opening chapters underline the poverty and parochialism of most English Brecht criticism and scholarship, and Wright draws intriguingly on Reiner Steinweg's research on Brecht's *Lehrstücke* (including *The Measures Taken* and *The Exception and the Rule*) to open a fresh distinction between these 'revolutionary' learning plays (which Brecht came to refer to as the drama of the future) and epic theatre which subverts bourgeois theatre from within. This and the discussion of Brecht's theory disturb the conventional chronology of youthful ideologue to great (= humanist) artist (= poet) and confirm the dialectical thrust and sources of his political aesthetic. Here Brecht is the Marxist modernist (Wright doesn't comment on distinctions or cross-over with the avant-garde, or when she does, in a summary of Peter Bürger, Brecht's '*Verfremdungeffect*' becomes a key avant-garde device).

One can think of these sections as a 're-presentation', and a valuable one, but they don't re-present Brecht as a postmodernist. How Brecht can be a Marxist and, as the 'deconstructionist' announced on page one, share Lyotard's suspicion of the 'grand narratives' of human history and emancipation, is something many would-be post-Marxists would like to know. The terms are pages apart and never properly introduced, as if in a gust of breezy 'anything goes' postmodernism (which is not I think what Wright *intends*) Brecht is caught in a pair of passing bermudas with his Doc Martens sticking out. No space is given to the argument which could be made in the name of Marxism and Brecht: that the discontinuous historical narrative of struggle and crises and of a zig-zagging dialectical drama is not the bover-booted, seven-leagued grand narrative that is thought of as Marxist. Instead we move on to the idea that epic theatre combined comic and tragic effects in a novel way (hardly again in a postmodern way since Wright feels there are the makings of a general

Marxist theory of comedy here). This is an interesting idea but again a puzzling and undeveloped one. How is this comedy related to the 'satire' that Walter Benjamin found in Brecht and in Marx,[1] and how is the specificity of Brecht's targets and his suspicion of the 'eternal comic' compatible, as Wright's argument suggests it is, with the *universal* black comedy' (my italics) Lacan finds in the play of lack and desire, across the imaginary and the symbolic? The discussion of the plays otherwise follows generally accepted lines (foregrounding the several examples of divided subjectivities), though oddly for this book the stories' moral outlines, or gestic core (Brecht's *Fabel*) are taken as given – as is, more than oddly, an invariably male spectator – and stand in for the discussion there might have been of differences in production and performance, when this arguably is the only 'reality' 'Brecht' has in the theatre.

There is, however, a business-like, and sometimes sketchy, attempt to 're-present' Brecht in these chapters. The summaries of leading positions on modernism (Brecht, Lukács, Benjamin, Adorno) and postmodernism (Habermas, Jameson and Eagleton, Lyotard) are more conventionally 'presentational'. No bad thing perhaps, except that this, if anywhere, is where the case study should have engaged with and perhaps shifted the theoretical debate. The term 'postmodernism', as others have recognized, describes a contemporary social condition and a set of positions on it. There is no sense here, in substance or in relation to how we read, re-stage, or co-opt 'Brecht', that postmodernism refers to developments in consumer or post-industrial or late capitalist society; nor is there any clear position on the politics of criticism, art, and culture in this society. Rather, beneath some broad left rhetoric the book tunnels towards the politics of no position. It would have been better to have done without the tidy summaries and to have let in more than the odd shaft of light from Lacan, Deleuze and Guattari and Lyotard – on whom the understanding of postmodernism seems most to depend. This would have opened the way, for example, for a more directed and critical discussion on Jameson on Lyotard, Eagleton on both and Linda Hutcheon, say, on all three; not because this is the route to postmodern wisdom but because there is a small intellectual narrative here, built on understandings of reactionary and left modernism, on Walter Benjamin, and on Brecht.

It might also have been worth directly juxtaposing Brecht and Lyotard: so as to re-examine Lyotard's own pretty big ideas on the structures and politics of narrative, and what it means to want to 'seize' reality, something he warns against at the close of 'What is postmodernism?'. The general, and widespread, imputation here is that those who talk of 'reality' this way have fallen for a naïve representationalism, and nurse imperialist designs upon the real, when as a 'realist' Brecht sought to intervene and help remake 'reality' in the interests of working people – on the assumption that it is an encoded set of power relations, not a ready-made totality. To put it differently, not every realist is a bourgeois realist, and not every realist in the Marxist tradition is a Lukácsian. Furthermore, it would be worth asking where Brecht fits in Lyotard's characterization of the sublime nostalgia of modernism and the double sublimity of an unrepresentable reality inscribed in the very text of the postmodern work. What does it mean to discover that the ideas and practice of a major left modernist/avant-gardist do not agree with the ideas of a major theorist of postmodernism? What does it mean to 'co-opt' the first via the second?

All of which – if I'm guessing right about Elizabeth Wright's indebtedness to Lyotard – would have amounted, as we say, to another book. Certainly it would have been a longer and more theoretically sustained and open book than the present brisk and intermittently suggestive 140-odd pages.

There is one other road not taken here which deserves mention before I turn to the postmodern Brecht who does emerge. Brecht and Benjamin were concerned with the effects and the democratic potential of new technologies and the mass production of works of art. This is one of the reasons Brecht slips set definitions of modernist against avant-garde. Benjamin's thinking on the loss of 'aura' of the traditionally unique work of art is also one of the cruxes of debate on continuities and breaks across the earlier period and postmodernism, and on the possibilities now of cultural innovation and dissent. In retrospect, one can, as it were, already see the Situationists and Andy Warhol (and Baudrillard) in this insight, as well as the sampling and scratch music, the independent video and desktop publishing packages of western culture. Wright describes Benjamin's theory in a subsection on the Brecht-Benjamin partnership, but her comment that he and Brecht were 'over-optimistic' about the political effect of modern technology (p. 87) typically pegs this issue down too smartly. Apart from anything else this verdict assumes that Brecht and Benjamin were thinking of the same thing, when their reactions to events suggest otherwise. The reasons for Benjamin's growing regret for the loss of aura were of a different kind, I would have thought, from the obstacles Nazism put in the way of Brecht's ideas for the socialization of modern media and his participation beyond *Kuhle Wampe* (1932) in any further collective film-making. That was then, perhaps, when what we're interested in is now. But as Fredric Jameson sees, while agreeing that the idea of 'refunctioning' modern technology is optimistic and 'primitive' in Benjamin and Brecht, the next move ought to be an account of our own more 'advanced' society which has made them look this way. One might then want to argue that if this 'primitive' view is rephrased in 'local', or 'community' terms, or in association with social and ethnic groups, it can again assume a new potential. Here one meets a different tradition (stretching back through the avant-garde to William Morris) and a different line of argument for a critical postmodernism; keyed, post-Benjamin, to the *control* rather than simply the supposed automatic effects of new technologies.[2]

This is one of the topics one might have expected from a book with this title. Elizabeth Wright doesn't pursue it, and it's a missed opportunity. What she does have in mind is both more surprising and more limited. She sees a 'postmodern Brecht' and 'Brechtian postmodern' in developments in the tradition of performance theatre, in those works which have probed the construction and deconstruction of subjectivity, exploring the politics of the gaze and the body. This lies behind her first, startling (and to me unconvincing) proposal that Brecht's early plays (*Baal* and *Jungle of the Cities* are the two she discusses), not the *Lehrstücke* or epic plays, are postmodern texts. Lyotard sees the postmodern as residing within the modern(ist), but it's stretching things to a paper thinness to identify the early modernist as the postmodern (in Brecht's case significantly these 'Expressionist' plays were also of course pre-Marxist).

In *Baal* and *Jungle of the Cities*, Wright finds a theatricalization of 'the spasmodic, discontinous perceptions of a reality-in-process' (p. 98). The texts are anti-narrative and decentred: a challenge to representation and to assumptions of stable identity. Baal is untrammeled desire, an experiment of the kind recommended by Deleuze and Guatarri to recover the 'deterritorialized' psychic and social zero-line of 'schizophrenic' experience; 'the only real life of the child': displaced, desiring, heterogeneous. In *Jungle of the Cities*, the apparently motiveless struggle between the timber-merchant Shlink and the young library assistant Garga is indeed motivated, not by class struggle or male competitiveness, but by a 'sheer love of fighting' which corresponds to the 'aggressivity' borne of paranoic fears of distintegration in Lacan's theory of the formation of the subject.

Wright claims that these ideas derive from the plays' 'formal characteristics' and that understood in this way they escape ideology. Neither is true, and Wright's rereadings remain ingenious despite such a claim. What is revealed, all the same, is a 'formalist' conception of postmodernism, which struggles to discover 'a political use-value' while bracketing theme and ideology, social formations and history, or more precisely capitalism and Marxism, because, one suspects, these seem to belong to an older, unreconstructed intellectual and political universe. Thus Brecht's Marxist modernism and the questions it still poses are shelved for the early pre-Marxist plays. And in these plays 'social content' and class are put to one side. Brecht described Baal as 'asocial, but in an asocial society'. The rapacious hedonism Wright describes (Baal 'uses others, particularly women, in order to gratify his needs') represents a particular social coding of the 'unformed' desiring subject. He is an alienated society's self-image, and its critique only in so far as he intensifies and so exposes its barbaric logic. These plays do not therefore *only* theatricalize the unrepresentable in their forms; the exploitation, predatoriness and aggression they also stage inescapably mirror the operations of the market, where human identities circulate in the apparent freedom and heterogeneity that goods do. To call them postmodern is thus to endorse an asocial postmodernism which assumes it can (as indeed it does) co-opt and restyle where and what it will, regardless.

From the pre-epic 'postmodern Brecht' Wright turns to a post-epic 'Brechtian postmodernism'. It is commonly thought that the central device of Brecht's epic theatre, the '*Verfremdungseffect*' ('defamiliar-ization' or 'distanciation') has gone the way of other modernist or avant-gardist effects under postmodernism: that the P-effect, as we might term it, is to absorb, annul or recycle these devices for quite different commercial and ideological ends. Wright agrees: 'in postmodernist art', she says, 'everything is subject to a V-Effect and so the concept becomes redundant' (p. 96). Everything? I can think of *The Gary Shandling Show* and *Moonlighting*, David Byrne's *True Stories* and Dennis Potter's *Singing Detective*, but soaps, news bulletins? Nor, in spite of the attraction of the 'Brechtian problematic' for post-68 British left intellectuals,[3] are V-effects everywhere in contemporary radical criticism or art, including books on Brecht and including the theatre. Most productions of Brecht don't attempt V-effects whether old or new. Wright herself contrasts a Royal Shakespeare Company production of *Mother Courage*, which signally failed to employ other than the unwanted V-effect of a delay in the performance, with the 'stunning' and 'postmodern' V-effects in a production by the Boston Shakespeare Theater Company (p. 21). Elsewhere in the course of the book the V-effect is described as 'dialectical in its very form' (p. 20), as a 'principal instrument for estranging the 'natural' (p. 51) and as a key device in 'a concerted attack on the institutionalised production and reception of art' (p. 68). None of this has become universal, and if these tasks are redundant for a radical and resistant postmodernism (the context of Elizabeth Wright's first remark above), then we are all pretty much at a loss.

Both Pina Bausch's dance theatre and Müller's work are said to be decentred and non-narrative and to explore the politics of representation and of subjectivity below the threshold of the symbolic, through sound, body, and gesture. Brecht's epic idiom and politics have therefore been restaged and re-articulated. Here the actors are engaged in real time and emotion, in a montaged discontinuous performance, which avoids firm positions on class or gender (but which for all its lack of unity is said 'to *show* people as they really are', p. 119). In Müller's work there is a more direct relation with Brechtian practice and the East German heritage which has monumentalized his drama. The play *Mauser* Wright sees as a deconstruction of Brecht's *The Measures Taken*, a debate with Brecht, but which unlike his play raises the issue of revolutionary violence. Like Bausch, Müller is said to have theatricalized the construction of language and subjectivity: 'the V-effect is at the level of the psyche' Wright says of Müller's *Hamletmaschine*.

This is where the book is most convincing on what a postmodernist, and newly sited but still 'Brechtian', political art might mean. There is a typical problem, however. This 'semiotic' theatre of experiment and deconstruction is opposed to the repressions of the symbolic order in a politically unfocused way. Wright sees the eschewal of plot and character-development in *Mauser* as 'de-historicising' the text; thus the issue of revolutionary violence becomes 'timeless and circular' (p. 127). The necessary, fuller argument appears in Andreas Huyssen and David

Bathrick's demonstration of the significantly different historical and political structures separating Brecht and Müller. Müller has accepted the post-war 'post revolutionary' East German (socialist) party as a given reality of his period, and thus in *Mauser* 'the pureness of the form – its ahistorical play quality – masks the historical reality (the party) upon which it rests'.[4] More broadly, the mystified reaction of London audiences to recent productions of Müller's work, and the *Guardian* critic Nicolas de Jongh's outright dismissal of Peter Handke's *The Long Way Round*, show at the very least an uneven development across (early communist and late capitalist) cultures, and that the gulfs and clashes between 'popular' realist conventions and avant-garde deconstructions have not been superseded so much as themselves re-staged under postmodernism.[5]

Wright says that Müller applies 'the dialectics of the past (Brecht's time) to the dialectics of the present (Müller's own time)' (p. 124). This – along with the reverse process – is a pretty good general guide for a critical postmodernism. It means that shifting social and political structures need to be read and re-presented together with artistic forms. Without this kind of 'depth', postmodernism becomes another name for the subjectivist avant-garde, and 'history' (it can do without the grandeur of Jameson's capital letter) is confirmed as it's repressed. The warning note in relation to Brecht has been sounded by Raymond Williams: 'To abstract the specific methods, or the theoretical phrases attached to them, as determining forms without reference to their very specific and limiting social situation, is to confirm the actual development of the avant-garde, culturally and politically, towards a new aestheticism.'[6]

Thames Polytechnic

NOTES

1 Walter Benjamin, *Understanding Brecht*, trans. Anna Bostock, Introduction by Stanley Mitchell (London: New Left Books, 1973), p. 84.
2 See the contributions to this debate by Dick Hebdige, 'After the masses', *Marxism Today* (January 1989), pp. 48–53; and Stuart Hall, symposium on 'The work of art in the electronic age', *Block*, 14 (Autumn 1977), pp. 11–14.
3 See Tony Pinkney, Introduction to Raymond Williams, *The Politics of Modernism* (London and New York: Verso, 1989), esp. pp. 19–21.
4 Andreas Hussyen, *After The Great Divide* (London: Macmillan, 1988), p. 90.
5 See Julia Pascal, 'Strong words, deaf ears', *Weekend Guardian*, 8–9 July 1989, pp. 19–20; Nicholas de Jongh, *Guardian*, 11 July 1989, p. 38.
6 Raymond Williams, 'Theatre as a political forum', in Edward Timms and Peter Collier (eds), *Visions and Blueprints: Avant-Garde Culture and Radical Politics in Early Twentieth-Century Europe* (Manchester: Manchester University Press, 1988), p. 317; reprinted in Raymond Williams, *The Politics of Modernism*, p. 91.

WILLY MALEY

- Antony Easthope, *British Post-Structuralism Since 1968* (London and New York: Routledge, 1988), 255 pp., £27.50

A review is often conceived of as an opportunity to take up a particular critical position against the grain of a new reading or set of readings. Reviews, then, as a sub-genre of the critical essay, do not bear any essential or necessary relation to the texts with which they purport to concern themselves. They invariably harbour traces of that other derivation of the French expression 'revoir', and present themselves as 'revues', as a series of skits on contemporary issues. A review, then, is as much a pretext for discussion as a post-text for display. This one is no exception. The following comments are intended in part as a response to Terry Eagleton's polemical review of *Post-Structuralism and the Question of History* which appeared in a recent issue of this journal, a review in which he read, for the *n*th time, the last rites to deconstruction.[1] The expiry of deconstruction, like 'the death of literature' and the demise of English, has been trumpeted to infinity by Eagleton in a series of obituary columns.[2] 'Last Post' presents itself as his final say on the matter. My own reprise in the wake of Eagleton's apocalyptic 'Last Post' is presented in the form of a review of a work which is itself a book-length review of developments in English culture and criticism over the last two decades, Antony Easthope's *British Post-Structuralism*.

In view of the extensive scope of Easthope's work and its impressionistic style – anecdotal rather than analytical – I shall concentrate specifically upon the crucial questions of Marxism, history, and nationalism raised by its title, through its critical articulation, and in its closing chapter, 'Post-structuralism and the English tradition' (pp. 191–222). 'History' is the concept around which many of the arguments between Marxism and poststructuralism have been raging, and nationalism is for Marxism the unresolved question mark over what has been optimistically referred to as 'late capitalism'.[3]

Any consideration of history and the question of poststructuralism would have to focus on the way in which certain strands of current critical theory were seen by a significant number of scholars to go beyond the limits of the structuralist project, assuming such a thing ever existed. This raises the question of poststructuralism 'itself'. Ruqaiya Hasan is almost alone in her efforts to open up poststructuralism's closure of 'structuralism', an umbrella term covering a whole series of heterogeneous texts compiled over two eventful decades. These texts, she argues, cannot be reduced to the monolith envisaged by those who claim in their own work, and whose work is claimed by others to supersede it:

As in the past, so in the present, at issue is the identity of structuralism; as in the past, so in the present, the 'post-ness' of post-structuralism is but an affix to structuralism, almost as if the very structure of the word iconically announced the impossibility of a clear break.[4]

Derrida has recently denied ever using the word 'poststructuralism', and indeed he has gone so far as to question the posteriority, or 'post-ness', of certain other expressions dear to the heart of contemporary theoretical discourse – 'post-Marxist', which he describes as 'an obscure notion', and 'late capitalism', on which he has this to say:

> each time I fall upon this expression in texts dealing with literature and philosophy, it is clear to me that a dogmatic or stereotyped statement has replaced analytical demonstration. I am still waiting for a scientific definition of what late capitalism is; I am particularly interested in this because some British Marxists (or post-Marxists) read everything in which I and some others are interested as a symptom of late capitalism, and when they cannot reduce these (recent) texts, or the texts in which these texts are interested, to previous schemes (Marxist schemes related to capitalism in its classical form – if there is such a thing), they say, 'Well, that's late capitalism.'[5]

Derrida subsequently acknowledges deconstruction's implication in contemporary politics:

> [Deconstruction is] ... already a symptom of the situation ... this change in the twentieth century in technology, in economics, in military strategies, these transformations in languages etc. I consider deconstruction to be a symptom, but at the same time, the concept of 'symptom' has to be deconstructed, has to be analysed; it's not a symptom in the sense of a sign at the surface of what is *signified* by the sign. It's a sign which *transforms* this situation, so the concept of symptom is not pertinent enough.[6]

Note that deconstruction for Derrida is not simply a by-product of capitalism, or 'late capitalism', but a force capable of effecting alterations in the social text.

Terry Eagleton appears to be much more comfortable with the expression 'late capitalism' than Derrida, since it is the main plank of his recent pronouncements on 'The end of English', a discipline whose denouement coincides rather too conveniently with 'the end of empire' and the inception of 'post-imperial, post-modern culture'.[7] 'Late capitalism' is generally associated with imperialism, and in this respect it is worth recalling that the original title of Lenin's influential pamphlet *Imperialism, the Highest Stage of Capitalism* substituted 'Latest' for 'Highest'. Ironically, the Derridean essay which provoked one of the most overtly political attacks on his work to date is entitled 'Racism's last word', but his call for an end to apartheid is arguably a much more politically forceful one than the by now jaded appeals for the end of English.[8]

Easthope elects to devote a sizeable portion of his penultimate chapter on 'Deconstruction' (pp. 161–90) to Eagleton's critique thereof (pp. 173–82), a critique which is at its most vehement when dealing with Derrida's American admirers, or 'acolytes', as they appear in Eagleton's terminology. This is not surprising, since Eagleton, we are told, is the English Marxist who has most directly confronted deconstruction, and for his troubles he has been the subject of serious criticisms from scholars eager to defend Derrida from the charges of ahistoricism levelled at him, and, by extension, at themselves.[9]

In his closing chapter, 'Post-structuralism and the English tradition', Easthope echoes Eagleton's reservations about deconstruction's ability to appeal to 'real' political struggles, and he cites as 'a more traditional Marxist argument' the nonsense that 'preoccupation with the subject is a locally Western concern rightly seen as of small importance in the jungles of Nicaragua' (p. 218). This passage bears a striking resemblance to Eagleton's own comments in the conclusion to 'Last Post', where we are favoured with some vintage Eagletonian hyperbole:

> With Derrida now ensconced in California, which can't be the best environment for his political health, and with some of his acolytes, as in this collection, still fixated on dismembering other people's teleologies, I think we now have to conclude ... that deconstruction has in fact very little to say of any relevance to the African National Congress or the Sandinistas.[10]

This final rhetorical flourish reveals Eagleton's own implication in an intellectual elitism which he would wish to confer upon deconstruction, but which in fact belongs firmly within a tradition of English radicalism which elects to speak for others rather than listening to their voices.

One might ask with some justification whether Oxford, Eagleton's permanent residence since the advent of poststructuralism, is any better for *his* political health than California is for Derrida? One might further enquire as to the relevance of Eagleton's peculiarly English brand of 'Marxism' to the national liberation movements of the developing countries? Under the guise of internationalism, a very old-fashioned English chauvinism insinuates itself here.

Easthope counters the standard argument from the Left that the foregrounding of the subject is a purely academic question with the bold assertion that it is history, and not poststructuralism, which has put the subject on the agenda. Easthope is no doubt aware of the way in which Contra propaganda relies upon a 'western' conceptualization of the subject in order to oppose a libertarian socialism with an ideology of individual liberalism. The idea that the jungles of Central America are entirely insulated from contemporary political theory is one which the most superficial acquaintance with events unfolding there would lead one vigorously to deny.

The 'conclusion' to 'Last Post' could easily have been written long before the composition of the volume it apparently refers to. Indeed, as a reasserction of Eagleton's position on deconstruction it simply reproduces the familiar criticisms contained in *Literary Theory*, written five years earlier, namely, that deconstruction is ahistorical, apolitical, and un-worldly:

> [deconstruction] ... frees you at a stroke from having to assume a position on important issues, since what you say of such things will be no more than a passing product of the signifier and so in no sense to be taken as 'true' or 'serious'.[11]

On the contrary, deconstruction forces you to do more than merely 'assume a position on important issues', it renders *movement* from one position to another possible. If this is what Easthope has in mind when he contrasts a 'determinedly American playfulness' with a 'politicised British seriousness' then his conception of gravity differs in both degree and kind from my own (p. 172). It is Eagleton who belittles 'important issues' and the value of theory in tackling them when he reduces the discourse of politics to a few gestures in the direction of 'reality'. Derrida, instead of gesturing 'outside' the academy, interrogates its own politics, its own intellectual and theoretical suppositions:

> That's why in many departments what is considered threatening is not a politically revolutionary position, if it is expressed in a coded and traditional way, rather, it is something which sometimes doesn't look political but disturbs the traditional ways of reading, understanding, discussing, writing, using rhetoric, etc. – because this undermines, or not necessarily undermines, but at least discovers, what was hidden in the institution.[12]

In his determination to be 'serious', Eagleton eagerly projects the impotence of the so-called British Left onto the critical practice that most immediately threatens its complacency. For him, the mere mention of political *realia* appears enough to constitute an intervention of great historical moment. Simply to utter the name of an ongoing political struggle is to say something *about* it, and, incredibly, to those engaged *in* it. One thinks here immediately of Shakespeare's *Henry IV, Part 1*, of Glendower's claim to be able to 'call spirits from the vasty deep', and of Hotspur's deflationary retort:

> Why, so can I, or so can any man:
> But will they come when you do call for them?
>
> (III. i. 50–2)

Eagleton is guilty beyond all reasonable doubt of the very idealism he so readily imputes to deconstruction.

It is not clear how Easthope manages to include Eagleton in 'the tradition of left deconstruction ... which prioritises the institutional practice in which texts are reproduced over any possible textual effect' (p. 220). Derrida has indicated that it is precisely those 'British Marxist' opponents of deconstruction who accuse it of apoliticism who limit themselves to 'textual effects':

> people get impatient when they see that deconstructive practices are also and first of all political and institutional practices. They get impatient when they see that these practices are perhaps more radical and certainly less stereotyped than others, less easy to decipher, less in keeping with well-used models whose wear and tear ends up by letting one see the abstraction, the conventionalism, the academism.[13]

This 'academism' is only too apparent in the writings of both Easthope and Eagleton.

Easthope maintains that 'British post-structuralism was sponsored by Marxism and shows no signs of surrendering its engagement with radical politics' (p. 219). He amplifies Eagleton's apocalyptic tone on deconstruction, deriding it in a characteristically grotesque formulation: 'The demise of deconstruction (now a dead horse?) left scorched earth which could only be occupied by one thing, Marxism' (p. 198). One wonders whether the Marxism flogged by Eagleton & Co. is a thing-in-itself or a thing-for-us, and, if the latter, of whom is this *us* comprised?

Derrida has been more reticent regarding Marxism than certain English 'Marxists' have been regarding deconstruction.[14] The famous footnote in *Writing and Difference* on the word 'propriety' in *The German Ideology* is typical of his eccentric approach to Marx. He does, however, occasionally venture a more explicit opinion, or position, on Marxism(s), and an appendix to *British Post-Structuralism* records one such position:

> Marxism, of course, is not an entity. There is not one marxism, there is not one marxist practice. . . . But I would reaffirm that there is some possible articulation between an open marxism and what I am interested in. I insist upon the *open* marxism. (p. 239)

Derrida goes on to insist upon his version of Marxism's openness and multiplicity as commensurate with its own (d)evolution:

> Marxism presents itself, has presented itself from the beginning with Marx, as an open theory which was continually to transform itself and not become fixed in dogma, in stereotypes . . . [an open Marxism] is one which does not refuse *a priori* developments of problematics which it does not believe to have itself engendered, which appear to have come from outside. (pp. 239–40)

Derrida undermines elsewhere the concept of 'a homogeneous Marxist text that would instantaneously liberate the concept of contradiction from its speculative, teleological, and eschatological horizon'.[15] He asks no more of Marxism than he claims for deconstruction: 'Deconstruction, if such a thing exists, should open up, and I have often insisted upon that point.'[16]

Here Derrida is offering an argument for a reading of 'Marx' almost identical to that which Lenin always insisted upon. Lenin wrote of being

'Marxist without words', explaining that 'Marxist words have in our days become a cover for a total renunciation of Marxism.'[17] 'Marxist without words': what are we to make of such a construction? Lenin constantly exposed those academic Marxists, First World Marxists, and, in particular, English bourgeois Marxists whom he considered to be Marxist in word but not in deed. Derridean deconstruction might 'appear to have come from outside' from the standpoint of an English 'Marxist' like Eagleton, but its concerns are quite in keeping with those which occupied Marx in his most mature writings, and which later engrossed Lenin in a thorough rereading of Marx.

Another area of concern for poststructuralism is nationalism. *British Post-Structuralism* – a title its author admits is something of a contradiction in terms, an 'oxymoron' – immediately throws up questions of national identity which are just as immediately 'answered' by way of a brief prefatorial disclaimer:

> The name 'British' is an embarassment, since it is the cover under which English imperialism imposed itself on Ireland, Wales and Scotland. This book should be called 'English post-structuralism' and this is what is meant, even though the conventional usage 'British' has been retained (p. xiv).

For a critic who has endeavoured to dismantle the 'communication model of language' the wording of this caveat seems somewhat surprising. A deconstructive reading of this passage would unpack problematic terms such as 'should be called', 'this is what is meant', and 'conventional usage'. If 'the name "British"' – only the name? – is an 'embarassment' to Easthope – and presumably this urge to blush is common to 'Left' English critics on the whole – because, we are told, it has acted as a 'cover' for 'English imperialism' – only a 'cover'? – then why was it allowed to stand as one half of the title of *British Post-Structuralism*? What could have compelled Easthope – whose very name exhibits a sense of geographic anticipation elided in his work – to decide on 'British'?

Nationalism bothers Easthope. He is clearly disturbed by the lack of text, in the narrow sense, on the subject:

> the bibliography on nationalism amounts to no more than a shelf of books, and most of them no more than a few theoretical gestures rapidly sliding into descriptive histories of particular nation-stages. (pp. 191–2)

One would have thought that 'descriptive histories of particular nation-states' was exactly what was required.[18] A few pages on, Easthope notes with approbation that 'the shelf of books on Englishness, previously and symptomatically so empty, is beginning to fill rapidly' (p. 199). This obsession with shelves of books is symptomatic of a 'British Marxism' which is in imminent danger of being left on the shelf. In any case, there is a curious shift from the earlier position on the undesirability of 'descriptive histories of particular nation-states' to an incontinent endorsement of the wealth of publications now available on the subject of 'Englishness'.[19]

British Post-Structuralism is a confusing text – part review, part preview, part mass biography, part institutional genealogy, part blurb for a disparate set of publications. Replete with potted histories of this, that, and the other, at times it degenerates into an annotated bibliography composed in an elevated journalese. It does, though, serve a need only partly satisfied by Colin MacCabe's introductory chapter in his *Theoretical Essays: Film, Linguistics, Literature.*[20] Where MacCabe confined his reflections on the French invasion of England through the 'Chunnel' of (post)structuralism to the Cantabrigian reception of Lacan and Althusser, Easthope extends the narrative to encompass Foucauldian discourse analysis and Derridean deconstruction as they manifest themselves in contemporary English academia.

The impressionistic nature of Easthope's presentation has its advantages, and as a beginner's guide to poststructuralism in an English context it certainly merits attention. At the level of theory, though, it is found wanting. The peruser of *British Post-Structuralism* is not invited to entertain a range of alternative critical positions, but is rather entreated to lie back and think of England, a thought guaranteed to deter the non-English reader from getting any further than the preface. One is tempted to conclude, after Eagleton, that British Marxism, at least as it manifests itself through the medium of (English) literary theory, has in fact very little to say of any relevance to the Irish Republican Army.

University of Strathclyde

NOTES

1 Terry Eagleton, 'Last Post', *Textual Practice*, 2, 1 (1988), pp. 105–111.

2 Terry Eagleton, 'Post-Structuralism' in *Literary Theory: An Introduction* (Oxford: Basil Blackwell, 1983), pp. 127–50. On the morbid subject of the death of English see Eagleton's 'The end of English', *Textual Practice*, 1, 1 (1987), pp. 1–9. A more temperate perspective it offered by Colin MacCabe, 'Broken English', *Critical Quarterly*, 28, 1 & 2 (1986), pp. 3–14.

3 See Derek Attridge, Geoff Bennington and Robert Young (eds), *Post-Structuralism and the Question of History*, (Cambridge: Cambridge University Press, 1987); A. Parker, ' "Taking sides" (on history): Derrida Re-Marx', *Diacritics* 11, 3 (1981), pp. 57–73; J. Culler, 'The call to history', in *Framing the Sign: Criticism and its Institutions* (Oxford: Basil Blackwell, 1988), pp. 57–68.

4 Ruqaiya Hasan, 'Directions from structuralism', in Nigel Fabb, Derek Attridge, Alan Durant, and Colin MacCabe (eds), *The Linguistics of Writing: Arguments Between Language and Literature* (Manchester: Manchester University Press, 1987), p. 104.

5 Jacques Derrida, 'Some questions and responses', in Fabb *et al.*, *The Linguistics of Writing*, p. 254.

6 ibid., p. 262.

7 See on this subject Gregory L. Ulmer, 'The object of post-criticism', in Hal

Foster (ed.), *Postmodern Culture* (London: Pluto, 1989), pp. 83–110.

8 J. Derrida, 'Racism's last word', trans. P. Kamuf, in H. L. Gates Jr (ed.), *'Race', Writing, and Difference* (Chicago: University of Chicago Press, 1986), pp. 329–38; 'But beyond ... (open letter to Anne McClintock and Rob Nixon)', trans. P. Kamuf, ibid., pp. 354–69; A. McClintock and R. Nixon, 'No names apart: the separation of word and history in Derrida's "Le Dernier Mot du Racisme"', ibid., pp. 339–53. The debate is reconstituted by D. Wood, 'Beyond deconstruction', in A. P. Griffiths (ed.), *Contemporary French Philosophy* (Cambridge: Cambridge University Press, 1987), pp. 175–94, on pp. 191–2.

9 A. Parker, '"Taking sides" (on history): Derrida Re-Marx', *Diacritics*, 11, 3 (1981), pp. 57–73; Geoff Bennington, 'Demanding history', in *Post-Structuralism and the Question of History*, pp. 15–29; J. Culler, 'The call to history', in *Framing the Sign: Criticism and its Institutions* (Oxford: Basil Blackwell, 1988), pp. 57–68.

10 'Last Post', p. 110.

11 Terry Eagleton, *Literary Theory*, p. 145.

12 Derrida, 'Some questions and responses', p. 256.

13 'But beyond', p. 367.

14 For a thoughtfully elaborate effort to realize an interchange between Derrida and Marx, see Gayatri Chakravorty Spivak, 'Speculations on reading Marx: after reading Derrida', in Attridge *et al.* (eds), *Post-Structuralism and the Question of History*, pp. 30–62. See also Michael Ryan, *Marxism and Deconstruction: A Critical Articulation* (Baltimore: Johns Hopkins University Press, 1982). A detailed critique from a Foucauldian perspective is available through Mark Poster, *Foucault, Marxism and History: Modes of Production versus Modes of Information* (Oxford: Polity Press, 1984).

15 Jacques Derrida, *Positions*, trans. and annot. Alan Bass (Chicago: University of Chicago Press, 1981), p. 75.

16 Jacques Derrida, 'Some questions and responses', p. 261.

17 V. I. Lenin, 'British pacifism and the British dislike of theory', in *Lenin on Britain* (Moscow: Progress Publishers, 1979), p. 206. For a detailed critique of what Stanley Fish has alluded to as 'Theory Fear', see Christopher Norris, 'Law, deconstruction, and the resistance to theory', *Journal of Law and Society*, 15, 2 (1988), pp. 166–87.

18 A model Marxist statement on the national question is to be found in V. I. Lenin, *The Rights of Nations to Self-Determination* (Moscow: Progress Publishers, 1979).

19 Who needs a shelf of books on Englishness? The most concise and relevant utterance on this topic I have yet encountered is located in Terence Hawkes, *That Shakespeherian Rag: Essays on a Critical Process* (London: Methuen, 1986), pp. 121–2.

20 Colin MacCabe, 'The class of '68: elements of an intellectual autobiography 1967–81', in *Theoretical Essays: Film, Linguistics, Literature* (Manchester: Manchester University Press, 1985), pp. 1–32. For a more philosophical defence of Derrida than I have been able to offer here, see Simon Critchley, 'The chiasmus: Levinas, Derrida and the ethical demand for deconstruction', *Textual Practice*, 3, 1 (1989), pp. 91–106. Critchley counters charges of hermeticism and nihilism by way of a *rapprochement* between Derrida and Levinas (pp. 97–8). One could easily construct a similar case using Marx or Lenin.

EDMOND WRIGHT and ELIZABETH WRIGHT

- Ronald Bogue, *Deleuze and Guattari* (London and New York: Routledge, 1989), 196 pp., £25.00 (hardback), £8.95 (paperback)

The way in which these two theorists are linked reflects a central feature of their argument. Deleuze and Guattari recommend the 'traversing' of definitions and systems by the questing currents of creativity, and they themselves perform this traversing. Ronald Bogue has accepted the challenging task of tracing the separate flows of their respective projects until they run into a joint texture again; he works chronologically through the works of each before drawing them together through their collective endeavours. Not only are the individual theses of the various works explained and clarified but also their continuing trajectories. Bogue charts the interconnection of new concepts without assuming previous acquaintance with the texts and their inventive vocabulary.

He starts by placing philosophy in its proper context, as part of a continuing Nietzschean critique of idealism, on the one hand levelled at a divine transcendentalism as a basis for social power, on the other at that idealization of the Self that was, with Kant, to internalize the bourgeois social command. Deleuze and Guattari, as Bogue shows, take pains to explore the historical development of ideology via an analysis of the deployment of signs and linguistic structures. They are with Zarathustra in being Yea-sayers, proclaiming that there is no 'No' in the unconscious.

In *Nietzsche and Philosophy* Deleuze focuses on Nietzsche's bold linkage of truth and value. According to Nietzsche, only the passive slave defines truth by means of the negative, for it is in the despot's interest to feed an ideology of definitions and propositions in which truths are purely transcendent and unrelated to power. The challenge of the negative is thus not even that of the Hegelian negation of negation, for truth is to be the outcome of a will to power that detects among the dynamic forces of nature whatever leads to creative enhancement. Affirmation is creative and not negating. However, a necessary distinction needs to be made which is missing in Deleuze and Guattari and in Bogue's reading: that between negation in the sense of logical contradiction and negation in the sense of rejection by a counter-affirmation of desire. A Dionysian view equates too easily the game of logic and its 'Laws of thought' with the historically oppressive use of it by those who identify logic with the prevailing power-structure. It is in the masters' interest to blur the distinction, making logic underwrite their own demands. Nietzsche engages in a different dialectic: the game of logic is to be played in the world. In this game both negation and affirmation have an essentially fictive nature.

When Deleuze considers the writings of Proust and Sacher-Masoch a similar theme emerges. Like Nietzsche they do not consider negation to be hard-and-fast. The ideal for Proust and Sacher-Masoch is not something forever fixed beyond the inadequacy of the real 'but a contestatory force of violent disequillibrium within the sensible world' (p. 54), in which the Nietzschean Will to Power manifests itself as a natural force. In *Difference and Repetition* and *The Logic of Meaning* Deleuze's target remains that residual Platonism which privileges the idea over 'the image', over the sensible world. Bogue makes clear Deleuze's central point: that the nets of repetition which language throws over experience are certainly transcendental but do not have a divine or ideal-metaphysical base. One might add, which Deleuze does not, the Nietzschean point that this would make the base a fictive one.

The manipulation of such nets of linguistic structure is for Felix Guattari a 'territorializing and deterritorializing', concepts that first appear in his early articles. Capitalism, in common with other oppressive systems, endeavours to enforce rules, concepts, and hierarchies via rigidified transcendental fantasies, yet there is always the possibility of a group employing 'transitional fantasies' (p. 86) whereby its members can articulate new modes of interaction. In *Anti-Oedipus*, Deleuze and Guattari jointly take up a doctrine of natural forces and Will to Power. They claim that the whole of the world is a process of the production of forces, desires, and transcendental structures. This process takes place on two levels, a 'molar' level of social machines and a 'molecular' level of desiring machines. The social machines are the apparatuses of the state system and the desiring machines are the wills to power in action in bodies. In *Mille plateaux* they argue that all these wills to power exist in a state of continuous variation, all exploring virtual possibilities. The desiring machines thus continually experiment, out of which experimentation non-hierachical developments are allowed to burgeon.

Their contribution is thus seen as essentially pragmatic, an anarchist philosophy of praxis, leading to the transformation of capitalism. It is perhaps something of a lacuna in Bogue's otherwise excellent exegesis that he should regard their attack upon the oedipal family and on psychoanalysis as peripheral to this praxis. It is surely such familial territorializings that have to be 'traversed', as much as the definitions of power-systems at the level of the state.

Cambridge

NORMAN BLAKE

- Roy Harris and Talbot J. Taylor, *Landmarks in Linguistic Thought: The Western Tradition from Socrates to Saussure* (London and New York: Routledge, 1989), xviii + 199 pp., £35.00 (hardback), £9.95 (paperback).

The main title of this book, *Landmarks in Linguistic Thought*, gives perhaps a better understanding of what it is about than the subtitle, *The Western Tradition from Socrates to Saussure*. It is designed as an introductory book about the history of linguistics or rather linguistic thought, in so far as so much of what was written earlier was about language in general rather than about language study in particular. It is a book of landmarks, because there is no attempt to trace the history of linguistic thought, which is why the phrase *The Western Tradition* could be misleading. The tradition is not delineated, but some of its landmarks are sketched in. Landmarks are features in the landscape which pay no attention to the intervening valleys or plains. This book focuses on one writer and selects a passage from that writer as a means of discussing some of his thought about language. There is no necessary link from one landmark to the next except that the treatment is chronological. Although some concepts overlap, these chapters do not try to highlight the links between the consecutive writers, for they stand very much as isolated entities. They are, in order of batting: Socrates, Aristotle, the Bible, Varro, Quintilian, Thomas of Erfurt, Caxton, the Port-Royal Grammar, Locke, Condillac, Horne Tooke, Humboldt, Müller and Saussure. No justification is offered for this choice of individuals, though presumably a spread among the various ages was aimed at. It is odd to find Caxton among the linguistic thinkers because he had nothing to contribute to concepts about language. Quintilian is more of a grammarian than a writer expressing linguistic thought, and the Bible itself fits somewhat awkwardly into this group for it does not discuss language as an intellectual concept, though it does have something to say on the way in which things on this earth were named. The Middle Ages is rather badly represented, even though the way in which the earliest Icelandic grammar tackled its description of a language other than Latin is not without interest. Indeed the vernacular lanaguages come out rather badly. No doubt reasons of space dictated a restriction to the western tradition and the cut-off point as Saussure, but it does make Saussure look like the end of a tradition rather than a beginning. There is nothing on the impact that non-European languages made on linguistic thought, such as the discovery of the importance of Sanskrit. Indeed the neo-grammarians and the comparative historians don't do very well in this survey. It may well be that in a short book like this too much is attempted, though the subtitle *The Western Tradition from Socrates to Saussure* does promise much.

Individual chapters take one of two forms. Mostly there is a quotation from the author in question and then this quotation is examined in detail to explain some of the ideas which a particular author had. This means that individual chapters are not designed as a comprehensive account of that individual's thought, but more as an impressionistic survey of some of the problems which concerned him. The opening chapter is entitled 'Socrates on names'. It opens with a quotation from Plato's *Cratylus*, in which some of what may have been Socrates's views on language are found, since none of his writings survive. The passage is about the correctness of names and it represents one of the earliest recorded discussions about language in the western tradition. The debate as a whole forms the central part of the chapter, and the authors elaborate on the concerns of the Greek philosophers about names. The passage is as much philosophical as linguistic, though a sharp division between the two perhaps does not need to be made at this stage. The second approach is to provide a quotation from the author under discussion, but then to set that author in a much wider educational and linguistic background. This applies to those authors whose contribution to linguistic thought was less than seminal and whose importance is therefore more as representatives of the age they lived in. This is true, for example, of Varro, whose work is of interest to some but hardly forms a landmark in the accepted meaning of that term. The chapter deals with the concept of linguistic regularity and this is discussed fairly widely since regularity had become an important topic following the expansion, and hence the consequent linguistic diversity, of the Greek world.

The book concludes with a very short bibliography. This provides the references for the quotations used and gives a few additional books which may be consulted. The bibliography is very thin and perhaps not too helpful for those interested in the history of linguistic thought and uncertain where to go next. The advantage of this book is that it gives a flavour of the linguistic problems discussed in particular ages; its weaknesses are its discontinuity and lack of coverage. Those who want a history should not choose a book of landmarks, but for those coming to the subject for the first time this book may well provide them with a taste for what linguistic controversy is and encourage them to dip further into the subject.

Sheffield University